LAND-OF-MISTS

LAND-OF-MISTS

Book III of The Navigator Kings

Garry Kilworth

ORBIT

An *Orbit* Book

First published in Great Britain by Orbit 1998

Map and illustrations by Wendy Leigh-James

A CIP catalogue record for this book
is available from the British Library.

ISBN 1 85723 559 2

Typeset in Sabon by M Rules
Printed and bound in Great Britain by
Creative Print and Design Wales

Orbit
A Division of
Little, Brown and Company (UK)
Brettenham House
Lancaster Place
London WC2E 7EN

This, the third novel in the Navigator Kings trilogy, is for the children of the two sets of adults to whom the first two books were dedicated. Coincidentally, and rather aptly, these young men are like the Oceanian hero Craig of this final novel in the series, all half-Celtic. They are:

Peter Fedden
Craig Fedden
Richard Fedden

and

Craig Chidlow

This book is also dedicated to those on the far side of the world in Oceania: the dancers, drummers, poets and others who keep the ancient traditions of Polynesia alive and well in these culture-eroding times. They are represented here by two islanders. Firstly, the then Minister of Culture for the Cook Islands. Secondly, an oral storyteller, the Speaker-for-the-Seventh-Canoe, who was kind enough to meet and talk with me on his island of Aitutaki. Others were equally giving of their time and help, even though I was weaving fragments of the Polynesian people's history, along with their myths, fables and legends, into the dubious form of a westernised fantasy. They are:

Mr Kauraka Kauraka: anthropologist

Mr Tunui Tereu (Papa Tunui): historian

Contents

Author's Note

This is a work of fantasy fiction, based on the myths and legends of the Polynesian peoples and not an attempt to faithfully recreate the magnificent migrational voyages of those peoples. Other authors have done that, will do it again, far more accurately than I am able to do. This particular set of tales, within these pages, alters a piece of known geography, while hopefully retaining the internal logic of the story; my apologies to the country of New Zealand, which has changed places with Britain. (New Zealand and the Maori are not forgotten and appeared in Book II of The Navigator Kings). The gods of the Pacific region are many and diverse, some shared between many groups of islands, others specific to one set of islands or even to a single island. Their exact roles are confused and confusing, and no writer has yet managed to classify them to absolute clarity, though Jan Knappert's book is the best. Where possible I have used the universal Polynesian deities, but on rare occasion have used a god from a specific island or group for the purposes of the story. Since the spelling of Polynesian gods and the Polynesian names for such ranks as 'priest' varies between island groups, I have had to make a choice, for example *Tangaroa* (Maori) for the god of the sea and *Kahuna* (Hawaiian) for priest. In short, for purposes of homogeneity I have taken liberties with the names of gods and with language.

For the facts behind the fiction I am indebted to the following works: *The Polynesians* by Peter Bellwood (Thames and Hudson); *Nomads of the Wind* by Peter Crawford (BBC); *Polynesian Seafaring and Navigation* by Richard Feinberg (The Kent State University Press); *Ancient Tahitian Canoes* by Commandant P. Jourdain (Société des Oceanistes Paris Dossier); *Pacific Mythology* by Jan Knappert (HarperCollins); that inspiring work, *Polynesian Seafaring* by Edward Dodd (Nautical Publishing Company Limited); *Aristocrats of the South Seas* by Alexander Russell (Robert Hale); the brilliant *Myths and Legends of the Polynesians* by Johannes C. Andersen (Harrap); and finally the two articles published back to back that sparked my imagination and began the story for me way back before I had even published my first novel, *The Isles of the Pacific* by Kenneth P. Emory, and *Wind, Wave, Star and Bird* by David Lewis (*National Geographic* Vol. 146 No. 6, December 1974).

Also: *Myths and Legends of the Celtic Race* by T. W. Rolleston (Constable); *Dictionary of Celtic Mythology* by Peter Berresford Ellis (Constable); and *Celtic Gods Celtic Goddesses* by R. J. Stewart (Blandford).

Once again, and finally, grateful thanks to Wendy Leigh-James, the design artist who provided me with a map of Oceania decorated with Polynesian symbols and motifs and the various windflowers which decorated each of the ten separate parts of each volume.

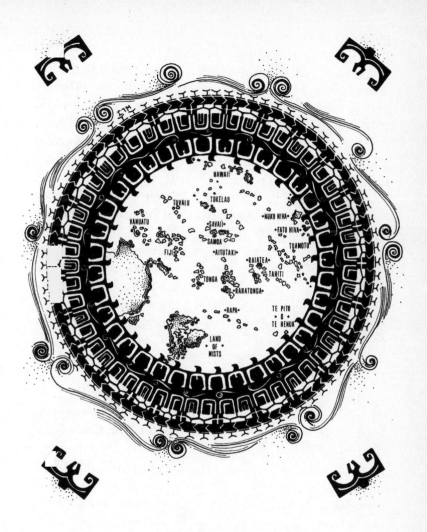

Oceania

Pantheon

Amai-te-rangi: Deity of the sky who angles for mortals on earth, pulling them up in baskets to devour them.

Ao: God of Clouds.

Apu Hau: A god of storms, God of the Fierce Squall.

Apu Matangi: A god of storms, God of the Howling Rain.

Ara Tiotio: God of the Whirlwind and Tornado.

Aremata-rorua and **Aremata-popoa:** 'Long-wave' and 'Short-wave', two demons of the sea who destroy mariners.

Atanua: Goddess of the Dawn.

Atea: God of Space.

Atua: Ancestor's spirit revered as a god.

Brighid: Celtic Goddess of smithcraft and metalwork.

Dakuwanga: Shark-God, eater of lost souls.

Dengei: Serpent-God, a judge in the Land of the Dead.

Hau Maringi: God of Mists and Fog.

Hine-keha, Hine-uri: The Moon-Goddess, wife of Marama the Moon-God, whose forms are Hina-keha (bright moon) and Hine-uri (dark moon).

Hine-nui-te-po: Goddess of the Night, of Darkness and Death. Hine is actually a universal goddess with many fuctions. She is represented with two heads, night and day. One of her functions is as patroness of arts and crafts. She loved *Tuna* the fish-man, out of whose head grew the first coconut.

Hine-te-ngaru-moana: Lady of the Ocean Waves. Hine in her fish form.

Hine-tu-whenua: Benevolent goddess of the wind who blows vessels to their destination.

Hua-hega: Mother of the trickster demi-god Maui.

Io: The Supreme Being, the 'Old One', greatest of the gods who dwells in the sky above the sky, in the highest of the twelve upper worlds.

Ira: Mother of the Stars.

Kahoali: Hawaiian God of Sorcerers.

Kukailimoku: Hawaiian God of War.

Kuku Lau: Goddess of Mirages.

Limu: Guardian of the Dead.

Lingadua: One-armed God of Drums.

Magantu: Great White Shark, a monster fish able to swallow a pahi canoe whole.

Manannan mac Lir: Celtic Sea God.

Maomao: Great Wind-God, father of the many storm-gods, including 'Howling Rainfall' and 'Fierce Squall'.

Marama: God of the Moon, husband of Hine-keha, Hine-uri.

Mareikura: Personal attendants of Io, the Old One. His 'angels'.

Marikoriko: First woman and divine ancestor, wife of Tiki. She was fashioned by the Goddess of Mirages out of the noon-day heatwaves.

Maui: Great Oceanian trickster hero and demi-god. Maui was born to Taranga, who wrapped the child in her hair and gave him to the sea-fairies. Maui is responsible for many things, including the birth of the myriad of islands in Oceania, the coconut, and the length of the day, which was once too short until Maui beat Ra with a stick and forced him to travel across the sky more slowly.

Milu: Ruler of the Underworld.

Moko: Lizard-God.

Mueu: Goddess who gave bark-beating, to make tapa cloth, to the world. The stroke of her cloth-flail is death to a mortal.

Nangananga: Goddess of Punishment, who waits at the entrance to the Land of the Dead for bachelors.

Nareau: Spider-God.

Nganga: God of Sleet.

Oenghus mac in Og: Celtic Lord of Fatal Love.

Oro: God of War and Peace, commander of the warrior hordes of the spirit world. In peacetime he is 'Oro with the spear down' but in war he is 'killer of men'. Patron of the Arioi.

Paikea: God of Sea-Monsters.

Papa: Mother Earth, first woman, wife of Rangi.

Pele: Goddess of Fire and the Volcano.

Pere: Goddess of the Waters which Surround Islands.

Punga: God of Ugly Creatures.

Ra: Tama Nui-te-ra, the Sun-god.

Rangi: God of the Upper Sky, originally coupled to his wife Papa, the Goddess of the Earth, but separated by their children, mainly Tane the God of Forests whose trees push the couple apart and provide a space between the brown earth and blue sky, to make room for creatures to walk and fly.

Rehua: Star-God, son of Rangi and Papa, ancestor of the demi-god Maui.

Ro: Demi-god, wife of the trickster demi-god Maui, who became tired of his mischief and left him to live in the netherworld.

Rongo: God of Agriculture, Fruits and Cultivated Plants. Along with Tane and Tu he forms the creative unity, the Trinity, equal in essence but each with distinctly different attributes. They are responsible for making Man, in the image of Tane, out of pieces of earth fetched by Rongo and shaped, using his spittle as mortar, by Tu the Constructor. When they breathed over him, Man came to life.

Rongo-ma-tane: God of the Sweet Potato, staple diet of Oceanians.

Rongo-mai: God of Comets and Whales.

Ro'o: Healer-God, whose curative chants were taught to men to help them drive out evil spirits which cause sickness.

Ruau-moko: Unborn God of Earthquakes, trapped in Papa's womb.

Samulayo: God of Death in Battle.

Tane: Son of Rangi the Sky God, and himself the God of artisans and boat builders. He is also the God of Light, (especially to underwater swimmers because to skin divers light is where life is), the God of Artistic Beauty, the God of the Forest, and Lord of the Fairies. As Creator in one of his minor forms he is the God of Hope.

Tangaroa: God of the Ocean, who breathes only twice in 24 hours, thus creating the tides.

Taranis: Celtic God of Thunder.

Tawhaki: God of Thunder and Lightning. Tawhaki gives birth to Uira (lightning) out of his armpits. Tawhaki is also the God of Good Health, an artisan god particularly adept at building houses and plaiting decorative mats.

Tawhiri-atea: Storm-God, leveller of forests, wave-whipper.

Te Tuna: 'Long eel', a fish-god and vegetation-god. Tuna lived in a tidal pool near the beach and one day Hine went down to the pool to bathe. Tuna made love to her while she did so and they lived for some time on the ocean bed.

Tiki: Divine ancestor of all Oceanians who led his people in their fleet to the first islands of Oceania.

Tikokura: Wave-god of monstrous size whose enormous power and quick-flaring temper are to be greatly feared.

Tini Rau: Lord of the Fishes.

Tui Delai Gau: Mountain God who lives in a tree and sends his hands fishing for him when he grows hungry.

Tui Tofua: God of all the sharks.

Ua: Rain God, whose many sons and daughters, such as 'long rains' and 'short rains' are responsible for providing the earth with water.

Uira: Lightning (See Tawhaki).

Ulupoka: Minor god of evil, decapitated in a battle amongst the gods and whose head now rolls along beaches looking for victims.

Whatu: The God of Hail.

PART ONE

In the land of firewalkers

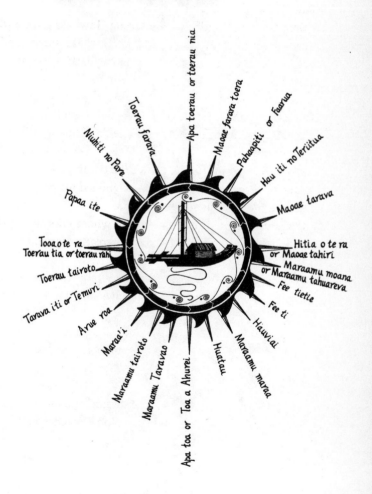

1

The Fijian war chief Nagata and his warriors were paddling up the Sigatoka River. They travelled cautiously, for the Sigatoka was the ancestral home of two particularly unpleasant gods: Dakuwanga the Shark-God and Dengei the Serpent-God. While both these deities were concerned mainly with the dead, they would quite happily destroy the living, if sufficiently annoyed to rouse themselves from their resting places.

'Use your paddles smoothly,' warned Nagata, 'in case we waken those who sleep lightly.'

The chief and his warriors were on their way to their warclub tree. Warriors all over Oceania were arming themselves and making ready for a long voyage. The great Rarotongan ariki, the noble Kieto, was massing Oceanians for a long voyage to a place called Land-of-Mists. There would be fleets from distant Hawaii, from Rapanui, Samoa, Tahiti, Aitutaki, Tonga and many, many others throughout the blue watery world of Oceania.

Along the murky river swirling with brown mud went the canoe, battling upstream against the sweeping flow of the Sigatoka, avoiding dead floating trees taken from the valley's edges. On all sides were stone-walled hill forts, for the Fijians were mighty warriors and their various clans were forever battling against one another.

Suddenly as the canoe rounded a bend it snagged a fishing line. The line went taut and halted the canoe. The hands of the fisherman on the bank were obviously very strong.

Nagata was annoyed and indignant. The paddlers had just got a good rhythm going and it was upsetting to have that brought abruptly to a dead stop. The war chief was particularly incensed as on this part of the river the current was so strong it was difficult for his warriors to build up any speed.

'Whose line is this?' cried Nagata, angrily, as the thick sennit continued to hamper the canoe's progress. He reached over and wrenched a massive pearl-shell hook from the bows. 'Whose hook and lure are these? Come out and be recognized. I shall brain the person to whom this fishing tackle belongs with my gata waka club.'

The leaves of an hibiscus tree on the bank parted in response to this shout. Two large hands appeared, one holding the line, the other forming a shaking fist. Nagata was suddenly appalled to see that no body was attached to these hands.

He knew immediately to whom the severed bodily extremities belonged.

Tui Delai Gau, God of the Mountain, was a giant who lived in a tree. He sent his hands fishing whenever he was hungry. He could also send his head up into the air, to spy on trespassers.

'I'm sorry,' said Nagata to the hands. 'I – I did not know I was speaking to you, my lord . . .'

There was, of course, no reply, for hands cannot speak. However, a head appeared over the rainforest, some distance inland, and a loud moan escaped its lips. The hands began walking down the bank on their fingers in response to this cry. They entered the water. Then they began swimming towards the canoe with funny fish-like movements. The thumbs stayed above the water, as if guiding the hands in the right direction.

One of the paddlers shouted in fear, 'I have a wife and child – it was not my fault!'

He dived over the edge of the canoe and began swimming towards the opposite bank. One by one the other men dived over the side of the canoe and did likewise, leaving Nagata to deal with Tui Delai Gau's hands on his own. The god's hands gripped the end of the canoe and pulled downwards quickly. Nagata, at the other end, was shot high into the air. His precious club went flying and he himself landed on his head and shoulders in the mud of the shallows ahead of his swimming comrades.

When they reached Nagata, they rescued him, pulling him out of the clay bottom.

In the meantime Tui Delai Gau's hands were destroying the canoe, ripping it apart. They tore the gunwales from the hull, the sennit stitching ripping like cloth. They wrenched the prow from the bows. Finally they broke the back of the canoe, sending the debris floating back down the river towards the sea.

When the hands had finished their work, they swam back to their fishing spot and pulled in the line. The awed men watched as the hook was baited with something that looked suspiciously like a man's liver and was then cast in the deep middle part of the River Sigatoka. They nodded in admiration as the bird's-feather lure was played on the current, so that it skipped and danced like a live thing on the river's ripples.

Within a few moments Tui Delai Gau had caught himself a handsome fish.

'What are we going to do now?' asked one of the men of their chief. 'We have no boat to reach the weapon-tree.'

'We must walk,' grunted Nagata. 'How else will we be able to arm ourselves with war clubs?'

So they crept through the rainforest, but this was a dangerous business in Fiji. Since they were visiting the warclub tree, they were not heavily armed. They needed to arrive empty-handed to carry the weapons home. And not only were there old clans of Fijians established in territories along the Sigatoka, but recently some Tongan clans had arrived.

These were fierce people who had been banished from their own islands for being troublemakers. The Tongans had quickly established hill forts and ring-ditch forts of their own. Once a clan was embedded in a fortification of this kind, it was almost impossible to root out and destroy. From this strong base they would raid less fortified villages and prey on passing travellers.

Within each village was the dreaded Killing Stone at which the clan would slaughter their prisoners as offerings to the gods, and afterwards cook and eat them.

At this moment the Fijian group was passing through the land of the Waiwai clan who owned just one of the hundred ring-ditch forts along the Sigatoka. They were a terrible people. Their village was surrounded not by just one moat, but three, plus a loopholed stone wall. Once you were taken prisoner and carried beyond that wall, those ditches, you were lost for ever.

'Keep close to me. Make no noise,' whispered Nagata, promising himself that next time they selected a warclub tree, it would be much closer to home.

The trouble was, one needed a young nokonoko tree for such a purpose, and the nokonoko grew in only a few locations.

Finally they were through the land of the Waiwai and they could see their sacred tree, up on the bank of the river. It was protected by magic charms – wicker sharks, dangling from its branches – and no other tribe would dare steal from a tree which was protected by the magic of a priest. Their skins would blister, their eyes would pop out completely from their heads and their tongues would swell and grow pustules.

A warclub tree is certainly a wonderful sight.

When a clan selects such a tree, it does so with a view to growing its weapons over the long term. Each branch, each bough, is trained in a particular killing shape from the time when the tree is supple enough to be bent and twisted easily. Sennit cord, stones and logs of wood are used to make the shapes around which the branches are bound. In time the nokonoko wood becomes harder and tougher than rock. From a distance one could recognize all the different varieties of club: the i wau, of which there were eighty different types, and the i ula, the lighter, more personal throwing clubs. These merely needed to be detached from the tree to become a weapon to wield.

Indeed a warclub tree, bristling with such weapons, looks like a festival tree hung with gifts for warriors.

'Quickly, cut some weapons from the tree,' said Nagata. 'We must not linger.'

He was not only worried about the other clans, there was still Tui Delai Gau to worry about. The god might send his head up high above the forest again, to see where they were. Sometimes these lesser gods brooded on things and decided at a later time that a little mayhem, destruction and murder would not go amiss. The minor gods were less secure than the greater gods, and insults festered in them.

'Quickly, quickly!'

The clubs were cut down with small flint axes, gathered in bundles, strapped to the backs of the warriors. Finally, everyone had as much as they could carry. Nagata led his men back through the rainforest along the valley towards the sea. His was a coastal clan, a people who felt themselves quite superior to those hot musty peoples living in the sweltering villages of the hinterland.

Nagata's people had fresh sea breezes to cleanse their huts, light-bright sunshine to lift their spirits, clean sand for their floors, pretty decorative shells on their hut walls, laughter, gaiety, the soft sound of the surf on the reef and the cry of the seabirds over the ocean. The tribes of the

hinterland had mud, thick dank jungle and still, stale air.
They were definitely inferior peoples to those who lived on
the coast.

But dark places breed dark thoughts, and dark thoughts
make savages of men. Thus the interior tribes were fearsome, bellicose creatures who would rather crush a skull
with a battle club than remember the birth day of a loved
one.

When Nagata and his men were creeping through a
tunnel formed by strangling fig trees and she oaks in the
land of the Waiwai, they suddenly saw a pair of hands
before them. In one of the hands was a sokilaki barbed
fighting spear. In the other, a sobesila mountain club.

'Tui Delai Gau!' cried one of Nagata's men.

But he was wrong. The hands were human and belonged
to a warrior of the Waiwai. In the darkness of the rainforest, behind him, were twenty other warriors. They had
heard the commotion on the river earlier and had found
Nagata's men's footprints in the soft sand at the river's
edge. Now they had caught the trespassers sneaking back.

'Thieves! Plunderers! Pirates!' yelled the first Waiwai
warrior, with a snarl.

Nagata felled him with a quick strike to the throat.

A brawl ensued, with several blows falling on heads and
shoulders, and many spears being exchanged. There was
much fierce yelling and scuffling, but in fact the area was
too hemmed in by trees to allow the fight to develop into
anything more than a restricted skirmish. Finally, Nagata's
men managed to fight their way through the Waiwai, with
the loss of only one warrior and two wounded. The Waiwai
were satisfied. They had their feast for that night. Nagata's
men were not pursued.

When Nagata finally reached the mouth of the Sigatoka
River, he fell on his knees and kissed the sand. Mangoes
and breadfruit were picked from the trees. Fresh coconut
water was extracted from the shells. The people rejoiced at

the safe return of their chieftain, mourned the loss of the one warrior, whose widow was instantly compensated. A necklace of shark's teeth was given her by a deputation of great woolly-headed Fijian warriors with glum round faces.

Sacrifices were made to Tui Delai Gau and hung on a lantern tree. There were many-coloured fruit doves, orange-breasted honey-eaters, black ducks and white-collared kingfishers. A cloak made of the skins of ocean geckoes and green tree skinks was draped over one of the branches. Mats with strong geometrical patterns woven by women were laid around the base of the tree covering the root area.

That night there was feasting and dancing in the village of the Naga. Drums beat healthy rhythms, scented leaves sent up heady fragrances from the fires, kava was drunk into the small hours. Warriors walked on white-hot stones to prove their manhood, for this was the land of the fire-walkers. They were seemingly careless of the heat, a trick of the mind learned over the centuries.

They had their weapons of war, with which they would follow the mighty leader of their expedition, Kieto, to the Land-of-Mists. There these weapons would be put to good use, slaying a people with red hair and white skins known as the Celts.

Later that night, when the village was asleep, tipua came to the lantern tree and stole the cooked birds and the beautiful lizard-skin cloak with its shiny green scales and small tight stitching. Giggling they went back into the forest with their treasures, knowing that the tribesmen would wake in the morning and believe the Mountain God had been appeased.

Goblins are like that: they care for no man's honour.

2

Mist drifted low over the heather, falling down the sides of deep gullies, over the lintels of rockhangs of the glen. The man who tramped resolutely through this mist, scattering these vapours with his walk, was in the fifth decade of his life. He strode on thick red legs, his feet bound with rags to keep them from the cold, along a ridge towards a needle of rock. He was a Celt, a Scot from the kingdom of Dalriada, sworn enemy of Angles, Britons, Jutes and, above all, Picts.

The Celt's hair was dark and as shaggy as the mane on a mountain steer. His neck was thick and bullish. The width and muscle of his shoulders were a testament to his great physical strength. In his right hand he held a roughly forged, wide-bladed sword with a rusting trailing edge. In his left fist was a wooden targe with the bark still gripping it.

The granite monolith which appeared to be his destination pierced the late winter sky like a black twisted tree. This rock was riven with dark magic, which was why the old crone sat at its base, the smoke from her fire curling around its tortured shape. The Celt hailed her as he reached the snowline and stamped along its edge to where the shrivelled hag was hunched.

'Old witch,' he growled, 'what have you for me?'

'Ah, Douglass Barelegs. Do ye bring me gifts? Even a woman with powers needs her wee surprises.'

He threw her a lump of something wrapped in a dirty rag. Whatever it was, it sweated grease in thick patches. She took it with a claw-like hand and sniffed it noisily, making appreciative sounds afterwards.

'Is it a dead man's heart ye bring me, laddie?'

'Whatever it is,' he replied, 'you'll eat it, so why bother with its identity. Have you news for me, woman? Someone told me you had something to tell.'

'Was it a corbie told ye so, eh, laddie?' she cackled, stirring her little fire with a stick then placing the bag of offal on a hot stone beside it. 'D'ye listen to sich creatures?'

'Don't play games with me, old hag,' he said, sweeping his sword-arm backwards as if about to take her head from her shoulders with the honed edge of the blade, 'or I'll chop your neck off at the roots.'

She screwed up her features. 'No need to get testy on me,' she snarled. 'I can keep things to myself if I wish it.'

He gripped the oakwood handle of the sword, its two halves bound with sweat-stained cord around the hilt-spike, ready to deliver the blow. She looked along the iron blade, the light dancing erratically over the hammered surface where it was pitted and flawed, and knew she was a second away from death. Her sneer turned to a look of pathetic terror.

'Don't . . .' she said. 'He's coming.'

The Celt stayed his hand, letting his arm fall down by his side. His face registered a look of mixed hope and disbelief.

'He? You mean Seumas-the-Black is finally on his way back to his homeland?'

'Aye,' she laughed, 'but whether he'll reach here is a matter for the gods.'

The Celt chose not to indulge in the same doubts as the crone. He preferred to imagine Seumas stepping from a boat while he himself waited to take his head from his shoulders. Douglass wondered whether his mother would be with the Pict. He did not dare ask the witch for this information, in case her answer was not the one he wanted.

The hag drew her ragged shawl around her thin shoulders and peered at him through the smoke of the fire.

'The man who killed yer fether has a son,' she croaked.

His head came up quickly. 'What? He and my mother, the Dark One?'

She smiled, enjoying the fact that he was shocked by this news. 'Nay, laddie – his spawn from another base union. The young whelp is a mongrel. I see his name written in the smoke. Craig, it is. The Man of the Crag. He comes too.' The witch stared into the middle distance. 'It is of great importance that ye kill him quickly, for he is a Man of Two Worlds. The prophecy says that sich a man will open the tower and destroy my kind for ever . . .'

'Damn you and yer prophecies, you old crone – who cares whether your kind is gone?'

'Ye will, Douglass Barelegs, when there's nay magic for ye to draw on and work yer schemes, yer sedition, yer betrayals. Ye dream of power, ye have great ambitions locked in yer breast, Douglass, but ye cannae get onything wi'out the likes o' me. Ye have to kill this Craig the moment ye set eyes on the man, or we'll bayth perish. We'll bayth vanish in the mist.'

The face of Douglass twisted into a mask of hatred and he raved into the wind. 'I'll kill the two of them! I'll kill them all! At last my fether's death will be avenged. I'll kill fether and son – and that wipperjinny of a mother too if she's with them. I was ten years old when she ran away with that murtherin' bastard – took off with some sea raiders from the outer islands I'm told. Gone to Yell, Fetlar or Unst, to soil his blanket with their greasy union.

'That wipperjinny ran off with her dead husband's murthurer, to fill his bed with her slattern's body. If I had not been with my grandfether on a raid, I would have killed her then. Now the bitch will die with him. My only regret, my only shame, is that they've lived so long. A whole life together. My fether had none. He was struck down in his prime by a cowardly cur . . .'

The old witch stirred the fire again, looking at him through the veil of black smoke with narrowed eyes.

'It was said that yer fether taught ye how to beat yer mither wi' a heavy stick in them far-gone days. Maybe a-tween the two of ye she couldna stay? She drudged for ye and ye rewarded her wi' nothing but hurts and bruises. I think I micht have run away ma'sel in sich circumstances.'

The sword arm came up again.

'Watch your tongue, you old bitch, or I'll cut it out and hang it from a bush.'

The witch wisely kept her counsel after that while the greybearded man raged about how he was going to stomp faces into the ground, break bones, sever heads. While he was talking he put the end of his sword in the fire, leaving it there like a poker heating itself. From down below in the glen came the blast of a horn, which echoed around the mountainsides. Douglass stopped ranting and stared down into the trees. His clan was being attacked, but it was useless to hurry down there, for it would finish before he arrived. Raids tended to be swift, merciless and all over in a short while.

Douglass picked up his sword again. The end of it was now glowing red. Without any warning he placed the hot part against the bare skin of the crone's withered arm. The spot sizzled, sending up a rank smell of burning flesh. The witch screamed in agony, jerking her arm back. She sucked the spot where the shrivelled flesh had been burned with her toothless mouth, moaning in the back of her throat as she did so.

'That's just a taste of what you'll get if I find you've lied to me, you bag of bones. Next time it'll be your eyes.'

With that he strode back along the ridge, leaving her whining against the face of the stone tor. He could not hear what she was saying but he knew it would be bad. She would be asking the demon of the stone to suck his brains through his eyesockets while he was asleep. Douglass was not afraid of threats of this kind from the witch. She was good at seeing the unseeable, but not so good at persuading the forces of evil to destroy her enemies.

'May yer heart rot in yer ribcage, Dark Douglass,' she shrieked after him. 'May yer testicles shrivel like kernels in auld nutshells! May yer . . .'

And so they went on, while he found his path down the mountainside, to the pine-scented glen below.

3

Azure skies, blue seas, white sands. It did not seem right having a funeral on such a bright day, in such a colourful place. There were multi-hued shells on Rarotonga's beach as he walked: sea combs, green turbans, scarlet tops, textile cones. Dorcha had loved the sea shells. Back in Albainn the whelk and mussel shells had been terribly dull by comparison. Dark shells out of dark seas: almost black seas on some grey stormy days.

Seumas suddenly remembered he had companions: his son, Craig, and the ageing Boy-girl.

'I was thinking how much your adopted mother loved the colour of these Oceanic isles,' said Seumas to Craig. 'She was a dark woman with a dark soul, but she liked the world around her to be colourful.'

Boy-girl, with grey swept-back hair, still walking tall and stately, with impeccable elegance, protested.

'A dark *soul*? Surely not, Seumas. She was the best of people – loving and kind.'

'I don't mean dark in that sense. I mean she was *mysterious*. I never really got to know her, deep down. There was some place she used to go inside, where I could not follow. It used to make me very jealous. I wanted *all* of her. I wanted to follow her into every little corner of herself, but I got used to being denied.'

Craig said, 'She loved you, Father. You had more love from her than any man can expect. If my own wife Linloa loves me half as much, I shall be satisfied.'

Seumas sighed. He did not want to sound ungrateful. It was true, he had felt loved. But Dorcha had been such a prize for him he could never quite believe she had been his. And perhaps every man wanted more? Perhaps the best of women always withheld some part of themselves? It ensured they were not owned by the men they loved. No one should give everything, or their partners will have nothing to strive for, nothing left to desire. We all want what we cannot have.

'Stung by a box jellyfish,' he snorted. 'You would have thought she might have fallen from a cliff in a tragic accident, or be taken by a shark while bathing. But to die of a box jellyfish sting! It does not seem right.'

'If she'd been taken by a shark, and mutilated, you'd have hated it, Seumas,' said Boy-girl. 'You'd have spent the rest of your life hunting sharks and killing them, you know you would. As it is, it's not very practical or very dignified to go on the rampage slaughtering jellyfish. And her body was whole. She looked so beautiful this morning, on her bed of flowers.'

'Boy-girl is right, Father,' said Craig.

The young man who walked beside Seumas had one leg completely tattooed. This was a badge of the highest office in the Arioi – a Painted Leg – the top rank. The young man had been one of the finest drummers Oceania had ever known. In those days he had been called Kumiki, but had taken on a Celt name to honour his father. His wife Linloa still called him Kumiki in private, to show that his mother's side of the family should not be forgotten and her ancestors were respected.

His mother was dead, however, and his father still alive, so it seemed right and proper to propitiate the living, especially since Craig had spent the first eighteen years of his life hating his father and threatening to kill him.

So half-Celt, half-Hivan, Craig was part of two worlds – the world in which he lived and the world which Kieto was going to conquer. His father, he knew, was torn in two by this expedition to the Land-of-Mists. Seumas loved his adopted people, but blood runs thick and he hated the idea that he was about to become a traitor and help lead an invasion against his ancestors, the Picts of Albainn.

Seumas was now an old man, over sixty years of age with creased muscles and hollow cheeks. He had gone back to wearing his hair in a long braid, but now it was white instead of red. It was Craig who had the red hair, but his skin tones reflected those of an Oceanian. Craig-Kumiki was truly the offspring of a union between mist and sunshine.

'What did she want that damned cross on her grave for?' grumbled Seumas, going off on another tack. 'Those silly ideas of hers.'

'Well, there I must agree with you, Father,' Craig said. 'She had some strange notions about the gods – said they were not much longer for this world – whatever that meant. She seemed to think that only Io, the Great One, had any significance whatsoever, and that he was known by many peoples under many names.'

Boy-girl said, 'We must respect her wishes though. She asked for a simple wooden cross and white flowers on her grave. That's what she wanted and that's what we had to give her. I like the idea, actually. It has taste.'

'Taste,' grumbled Seumas. 'You're always on about taste – heel, Dirk.'

The last two words were directed at a dog which had come bounding along the beach to meet them.

'Taste,' said Boy-girl, her nose in the air, 'is one of the most important things in life.'

Seumas made a non-committal noise which was meant to be a protest. He had argued too long and too often on this subject with Boy-girl, and he almost never felt he had won. Boy-girl was much too clever for him. Much too witty. Much too quick with words. Boy-girl had a dagger for a tongue, which could cut a man down to half his size in less than a moment.

Seumas turned to Craig and said in his original tongue, '*Tha mi seann duine.*'

'What, Father?' faltered Craig.

Seumas shook his head and sighed. 'Have you learned no Gaelic, since I first tried to teach you? I said, *I am an old man*. It's an easy sentence. Did you get nothing from it?'

'Nothing,' Craig replied, sadly. 'I'm afraid your lessons have been a waste, Father. I'm as ignorant now as I ever was, where your old tongue is concerned.'

The old man shook his head again in sadness at this news.

The group turned the end of the bay. The dog was gambolling around them, dashing into the water here, into the rainforest there, generally making a nuisance of himself. He was one in a long line of Dirks which stretched by into Seumas's past as a string of hounds. Seumas had never felt whole without a dog, though he knew the islanders made fun of him for it. They ate their dogs, raised purely on a diet of fruit, while he turned his meat-eating pets into hunting hounds.

As they rounded the point, they came across great activity. Industrious carpenters and priests were in the process of building thirty great tipairua canoes. Mighty trees had been felled for the twin hulls of each canoe, across which their platforms would be built. On these platforms would stand two masts, to bear twin crab-claw sails. And two huts, to store the food for the voyage to the Land-of-Mists. These were invasion craft, built to travel thousands of miles to go to war.

Kieto was supervising the building of the canoes, with his older brother, Totua. They were drawing pictures in the sand with a stick, using the marks of writing brought back by the great Hiro from his travels in the direction of Tooa o te ra on the windflower. The priests were studying the marks intently. None were used to this new form of communication and great concentration was required.

On seeing the Pict approach, Kieto said something to his brother Totua, and then left his side.

'Seumas?' said Kieto, looking up as the three approached the group of priests. 'How are you feeling today?'

'Much like any man who has lost the better part of himself,' replied Seumas.

Kieto put a hand on his shoulder in sympathy. Now that Kieto was a highly eminent ariki, second only on the island to its two kings Tangiia and Karika, he carried great mana. But Seumas was also considered to be a distinguished warrior and he too bore much mana. So the two were able to be familiar with one another, without fear of harm.

'Yes, she was a wonderful woman.'

Standing close to Kieto were twins, a boy and girl, about eighteen years of age. These were the ariki's children, Hupa the girl, and Kapu the boy. Both were carrying bows and quivers of arrows, made for them by Seumas. Both were wearing necklaces of shark's teeth as a symbol of the high rank of their father and thus of themselves as his heirs.

'We are sorry our aunt has gone,' said Hupa, who was more of a warrior than a maiden. 'We miss her.'

It was rumoured that Hupa was the head of a secret society, formed of women warriors. They called themselves the Whakatane, which literally means 'turn into a man', but in essence meant to act like a man, to do manly things. It was said that Hupa's name within the society was Wairaka. In legend Wairaka was a chief's daughter who saved a troubled voyager canoe while the men were distracted by the beauty of a foreign landscape. She was the first Whakatane and Seumas had heard that Hupa and her followers made sacrifices to Wairaka in a sacred place.

'Thank you, Hupa, I'm sure she misses you too.'

Seumas was himself a little distracted at that moment. He was thinking about the coming invasion of Land-of-Mists. It was with some despair that Seumas realized there was nothing which could stop it now.

'Your plans seem to be progressing,' he said to Kieto in a disapproving tone. 'When is the fleet to sail?'

'Before Hine-keha shows her full face.'

'Within the month. And we sail first to Raiatea?'

Kieto nodded, warily, knowing that Seumas was torn in his loyalties.

'I must make sacrifices to my atua, at Tapu-tapu atia, Most Sacred, Most Feared. Raiatea is my birthplace and where my ancestors reside. Then we shall sail to Tongatapu, where the fleets from other islands will gather prior to sailing to the land Kupe first discovered, the Land-of-Mists.'

'Kupe did not discover it first,' growled the elderly Seumas. 'There are people living there.'

'You know what I mean,' replied Kieto.

'You will not win this war, Kieto.'

Kieto sighed. 'Do not go over this again, Seumas. It is inevitable. It is unstoppable. There will be voyager canoes from Hawaii, from Rangiroa, Manahiki, the Hiva Islands, Samoa, Tonga, Tuvalu, Tokelau, Rapanui – even from Fiji. The Oceanians gather in great numbers. Never before has a flotilla of this size been assembled against a common enemy.'

'Enemy? They have done nothing to you.'

'But given time, they will. We shall invade them, before they invade us. It's as simple as that.'

Overhead there were some dark birds wheeling through the skies. These were saddlebacks, brown with orange wattles, and were considered a good omen to the priests and carpenters who were building the canoes. In legend a pair of saddlebacks had guided seafarers from Hawaiki to a safe haven. These two became the pets of a tohunga named

Ngatoro-i-rangi. It was believed that they could foretell the coming weather.

In point of fact, saddlebacks were sacred birds.

Seumas noticed the birds and a rash and unworthy idea came to him which he grasped without thinking.

'May I borrow your bow and and arrow, Kapu?' he said, reaching for the weapon.

The boy-twin handed the weapon to his 'uncle'.

Seumas fitted the arrow to the cord and drew back on the bow. Aiming into the air he released the missile. It flew straight and true, striking a saddleback through the breast. The unfortunate bird fell to the beach. Dirk, like the good hunting dog he was, ran and picked up the bird in his gentle jaws, carrying it back to his master.

The priests around Kieto let out a cry of shock and some put their faces into their hands. Even Boy-girl was appalled by what Seumas had done. Kieto stared at his friend in disbelief and then shook his head sadly.

'I know what you have tried to do, Seumas, but it will not work. The bad luck will fall on your head, not on ours. This is no way to stop the fleet sailing.'

Seumas stared into the ariki's eyes. Then he let the bow fall to the sands and walked away. Craig followed him. Now thirty years of age, Craig was a mature man, one who had travelled almost as widely as his father, but even he was shocked by what Seumas had done.

'That was not good, Father,' said Craig, catching him up. 'You must have known that such an act would not be enough to stop Kieto. *Nothing* can stop him now. Even if he were to announce tomorrow that he was not leading the invasion, another would spring up and take his place.'

Seumas shook his head grimly. 'I know – I didn't think. There is still inside me a little of the impetuosity of my days as a Pict, running through the heather of Albainn. Then we did things first and thought about them afterwards. I killed your adopted mother's first husband that way. Struck him down without a second thought, so that I could steal the sword he carried.'

He sighed. 'Dorcha was able to curb my rash acts, when she was around. I would always stop and think, would Dorcha approve? Now she's gone and see how quickly I slip back into my old ways. Well, the deed is done, the bird is dead.'

Dirk came trotting up, still carrying the saddleback carefully in his mouth. Craig took it from him and tossed it away into the rainforest.

'Stay, boy,' said Seumas, as Dirk looked confused and about ready to dash into the undergrowth to retrieve the bird. 'Leave it, Dirk.'

'Father, you must dine with Linloa and me tonight. She is cooking fish and sweet potatoes. I mentioned I might be bringing you back to our hut and she was pleased.'

Seumas knew this was untrue. Linloa was very good, but she had fed and watered Seumas over the past month, while Dorcha had been ill with the jellyfish poison. Seumas knew she would have had enough of her father-in-law for the time being, for he had not been a good guest while his wife had lain dying. Restless, complaining, and becoming irritated with his infant grandchildren, Seumas had not made Linloa's hut a happy place.

'No, I prefer to be on my own tonight, if you don't mind, son. It's good of you to ask, but there are things to think about. I'd better make some sort of sacrifice to the gods, to try to appease them for killing that innocent bird.'

He stared into the sunset. 'Why did Dorcha have to go and die now?' he said bitterly.

'We all have to die, Father.'

'Yes, but box jellyfish do not normally kill adults, not even elderly ones. Your mother died on purpose, I'm sure of that – she went because she wanted to go. She could have held on, recovered, but she left me anyway.'

Craig did not disagree with his father.

'Perhaps – perhaps she had experienced the best of her life and felt she had to go? You know she often said to me, "Craig, if I die tomorrow I will have had a good life, one with more happiness than a woman has a right to expect." It is a great compliment to you, Seumas, that she felt that way.'

Craig did not know how to deal with his father when he was in this kind of mood. Seumas was still an alien to him in many ways. The Pict had once told his son that his head was still full of strange white winters. Craig was not able to understand this, not able to comprehend what he had never known. There was a desperate need in Craig to really understand his father, to know him deeply, but all Craig's efforts at this ended in failure. He realized after a while that he would never be able to get inside Seumas. His father was a great mystery to him and this fact made the young man very unhappy.

'She did it on purpose, to upset me,' Seumas growled. 'She always wanted her revenge. She never really forgave me for killing her first husband, you know.'

'She loved you to distraction, you silly old man,' cried Boy-girl, who had come up behind them quietly. 'I've never heard such nonsense. Dorcha punish you after all this time? – oh yes – she was prepared to die in pain to do it, was she? Go home and drink some kava, Seumas. If you're not careful I shall be consoling you so much, you'll be inviting me to share your bed, and then you'll have something to complain about.'

'You'll never get into my bed, you old witch,' growled Seumas. 'You keep away from me.'

'I'd rather sleep with Dirk, these days,' she sniffed, smiling. 'He snarls less than you do.'

The goddesses and gods of Oceania held a gathering somewhere within the Twelve Worlds on earth, under the sea, or in the heavens. Only Io did not attend. This was because the Old One never left his dwelling in the Twelfth World. His pleasure or displeasure could be felt in the lower levels, when it was necessary for him to make his mood known, so there was no need for him to leave his place of residence. In respect of this gathering, the subject of which he knew in advance, his messengers let it be known that he would not give an opinion and that his state was too lofty to join any campaign.

It was noted by the other gods that some of Io's celestial Mareikura, his personal messengers and attendants in the Twelfth World, were hovering quietly within sight and sound.

When Oceania itself was in turmoil, the gods were also in a state of agitation. There was no separate earth, for mankind, gods or ancestor spirits: all dwelt in the same place and felt the same effects of any upheaval. They were either for the invasion, or against it. No god or atua could be impartial, except perhaps Io, who had the right to reserve judgment until such time as he felt it necessary to give it.

'We all know what is happening amongst the men and women of Oceania,' said Tawhaki, the God of Thunder, whose armpits gave birth to Uira, the Goddess of Lightning. 'There is to be a war, but such a war as Oceania has never known before. Our peoples – those who live on the islands of our blue waters – are going on a long voyage to a strange land. There to do battle with an alien people who worship gods not of our ilk. What I ask is, do we let them go alone?'

Papa, Goddess of the Earth, nodded sagely. 'You are saying we should go with them?'

'He is saying,' said Tane, God of the Forests and Lord of the Fairies, 'that the enemy will have an unfair advantage. They will have their gods to assist them, while our people will be without supernatural guidance.'

Hine, that powerful goddess with many forms and faces,

including death, was surprisingly not in favour of going to war, even to assist Oceanians against an unknown foe.

'You know I have many shapes and colours,' she told the other gods, 'from the Indigo Lady to Lady of the Early Gentle Floating shadows. I can be useful to you in war, in several ways, and will go if there is general agreement that we should, but I fear this conflict will end in disaster for us all.'

Ira, Mother of the Stars, spoke quietly in favour of supporting the Oceanians in their endeavours.

'We may find these new people need new gods and goddesses, and here we are to fulfil that need.'

Next, Rangi, the Great Sky-God, spoke, evoking a response from Tangaroa, the Great Sea-God.

'What say you, Prince of the Ocean? Do we travel with the fleet and battle against these strange gods of these alien people – the gods of the Celts and the Angles? Do we fight in those dark skies above the Land-of-Mists? Do we battle with them in their dark ocean? Shall Tane go to war in the gloomy forests where only one kind of tree seems to grow? Will Rongo trample their ugly vegetation underfoot?'

Tangaroa deliberated long and hard before answering. 'As to whether we go or stay, I do not think we have a choice. I feel an attraction for this island which is impossible to resist. You feel it too, all of you, or we would not be here today. But are we all capable of fighting? You, Rangi, are not the warring kind. Nor Papa. Myself, Tawhaki, Whatu, Maomao, Pele – we have weapons of thunderbolts, hail, wind and fire. Others, such as Oro, are ready armed for war. But many of you will be struggling without weapons, with just your own strength, your own will.'

'No matter,' said Ra, interrupting, 'it is clear we must all go. If Rangi must fight it will be with their Sky-God and the struggle will be equal, in so much as Rangi and the Other will both have the same weapons. It must be on these terms, that each will fight his matching equal. Tawhaki will fight their God of Thunder, I shall fight their Sun-God.'

'And all of us must go?' asked Nareau, the God of Spiders. 'Even those of us regarded as lesser gods? Moko, the God of Lizards? Dakuwanga, the Shark God?'

'All,' said Ra, 'with only one exception – the Old One, Io, will remain to watch over our domains. If you have no counterpart with whom to fight in single combat, then you will serve those of us who have. You may act as weapon-bearers, you may stoke the forges of the weapon-makers, whatever is necessary. So, are we in agreement – the gods of Oceania will go to war?'

'We will,' came back the consenting chorus.

Ra replied, 'Then let us gather with the fleet at Tongatapu and follow them into the Unknown Region.'

Craig left his father and wandered back to the hut he shared with his wife and three children. Despite his savage appearance – the three bars tattooed across the bridge of his nose and over his cheeks – he was no more ready than his father to go to war. Consequently he was in a contemplative mood. The Hivan warrior in him urged him to take his well-built frame and expend his energy on the battlefield, winning honours and glory. The father and husband in him however, which was rapidly becoming the more dominant part, told him to stay at home.

Entering his hut, he rubbed noses with the small, round-limbed Linloa, whose cooking was only second to her good nature. Craig loved his wife in that comfortable way which some successful men manage to acquire. Celebrities such as himself, the greatest drummer the world had known, could have had many affairs, several wives.

Craig was one of those men who had known dazzling achievements at a time in his life when they could have caused great conceit, but he managed to remain levelheaded and faithful to one woman, because that was his nature. So long as his marriage and his home life was stable, Craig was capable of the most outstanding accomplishments. Take that rock base away from him and he became insecure and uncertain.

'And how is the greatest Beauty that Rarotonga has ever known?' he said, kissing Linloa's lips on entering.

She placed a fresh ei on his head, made of frangipani and flame tree blossoms.

'Ever? I think the Princess Kula might have something to say about that – or perhaps some of those virgins, the crew of Ru's *Princely Flower*? Beauty? I think not.'

'In my eyes you are unequalled,' he said, smiling.

'Now that's different. In the eyes of a short-sighted man. Yes, I can accept that.'

'I'm not short-sighted!'

'You must be if you think I'm beautiful.'

She turned away from him but he could see that she was happy.

'I'm – I'm *pleasant* to look at, I'll grant you that, husband. If that satisfies you, then I'm a contented woman.' Then she turned back to look at him, her face intent, and added fiercely, 'But if you ask who on Rarotonga has the most *love* in her heart for her man, why then you may compliment me, husband.'

He laughed and kissed her gently, 'You are a funny mixture of passion and homeliness, Linloa. I suppose I must be the luckiest of men – I *know* I am. Where are my children? I must see them before they fall asleep.'

'I'm afraid you're too late,' she answered, now stirring the sauce for the fish, 'they exhausted themselves running around the boatbuilders today. They're already asleep on their mats. You can give them a goodnight kiss if you like.'

He went to the back of the hut, where the delicious smells of his wife's cooking were hovering in the air and driving the house spirits crazy, to find three little curled bundles on a mat of woven pandanus leaves.

The youngest and the eldest looked so sweet and magical,

with their brows clear and their skin so bright. The middle child, the gods watch over her, was unfortunately extremely ugly. This did not matter to Craig of course, and Linloa, like any mother, would refute it hotly. She saw only beauty in *all* her children. But it was a fact, the middle child was as ugly as a baby hog and perhaps would suffer a little for it, though she had a quiet, placid nature and was a sunny child in all other aspects.

There was a god who was responsible for and watched over such children as the middle-child. The god's name was Punga, who first gave the world bugs and beetles, and reptiles of a repulsive nature, and grotesque fish like the stone fish, the sting ray, the sunfish, the blowfish. Punga was the God of Ugly Creatures, and as such, his creations were special to him. The homely, the hideous, even the ghastly, were cherished by him. This middle-child was one of Punga's charges. Punga loved dearly all the world's ugly creatures and protected them against unjustified mockery and vindictive bullying. Punga would not let the infant suffer too much under the taunts of others.

'Sleep well, my little ones,' whispered Craig. 'May your dreams bring you spiritual riches.'

After the meal was eaten, Linloa enquired guardedly after Seumas.

'I invited him back for the meal,' said Craig, 'but he wouldn't come.'

'Why not?'

'He thought he had imposed enough. He thinks he's becoming a cranky old man.'

'He is,' said Linloa, 'but we love him just the same. Still, I'm glad he did not come with you. We have not been together alone for many days now. It is pleasant just to sit here with you in Ra's dying rays and listen to your voice.'

Craig sat with his back against the wall of the hut and watched the sun swoop down below the horizon, like a hawk stooping on a rat. He too was glad his father had not joined them, though he felt guilty for being selfish. There would not be many evenings left to spend with his wife, before he went away to war. Craig needed such evenings to remember, to sustain him, for the voyage itself would be hard and lonely.

And at the end of that journey, why nothing but a bloody war with an unknown enemy!

Yes indeed, he would need such memories to keep him from the darkness, in the time ahead.

Punga, the God of Ugly Creatures, felt a great tenderness towards the mortal Craig. It was not often that mortals prayed directly to the gods themselves. They usually went through intermediaries – through their atua ancestors – but Craig seemed especially indebted to Punga because of his protection of Craig's child. Thus the god was wont to protect the father of the child also, because of that man's strict devotion.

Punga was also going to this war in the Land-of-Mists and while he was there he resolved to watch out for his charge, the young Craig, to keep him as safe as was godly possible. The beautiful-ugly child needed such a father and Punga would try to make sure he returned to her unharmed.

There was a bond between man and god which both cherished.

PART TWO

Lioumere's iron teeth

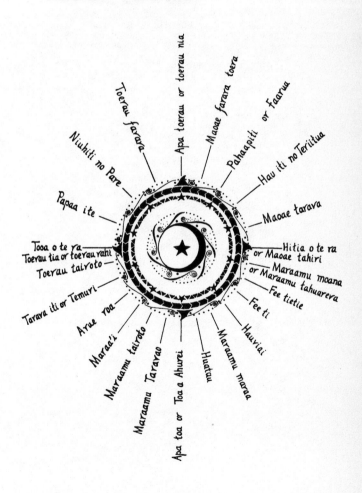

Toerau farara
Apa toerau or toerau nia
Maoae farara toera
Pahaapiti or Faarua
Niuhiti no Pare
Hau iti no Teriitua
Papaa ite
Maoae tarava
Tooa o te ra
Toerau tia or toerau rahi
Toerau tairoto
Hitia o te ra
or Maoae tahiri
Maraamu moana
or Maraamu tahuarera
Fee tietie
Tarava iti or Temuri
Fee ti
Arue roa
Hauviai
Maraa'i
Maraamu maraa
Maraamu tairoto
Huatau
Maraamu Taravao
Apa toa or Toa a Ahurei

1

The fleet set sail at the end of Breadfruit season, when the winds were favourable and the currents set true. There was a brisk sea and the tipairua canoes were running dogs carrying logs of foam in their mouths. The crew were kept busy taking in and letting out sail, seeking the maximum thrust from the wind. As always the bailers were occupied with their half-coconuts and severed gourds, shovelling out the excess sea water. Lines were run out behind, in the hope of coming across a shoal of bonito or barracuda. All the signs were favourable for a good voyage to Raiatea, once the home of Chief Kieto.

Seumas, who was travelling in the second canoe, behind the chief's, was shocked to learn his captain was Polahiki, the Hivan fisherman who wove his way in and out of the Pict's life like a rusty old needle drawing a filthy thread.

'How did you get here?' he asked Polahiki. 'The last time I saw you was off Aitutaki, when we returned with Prince Ru from Rapanui.'

'Came in on the evening tide three days ago,' said Polahiki, picking a scab and wiping the deposit on the tiller oar. 'Kieto was short of captains for his thirty tipairua, so he asked me. I am a good navigator, you know.'

It was true; Polahiki might have been the dirtiest sailor on the high seas, but he knew the ocean and he was familiar with voyager canoes.

'You better get us to where we're going, or I'll strangle you with my bare hands,' growled Seumas. 'And stay downwind of me.'

Polahiki sniffed. 'I'm captain of this craft – I go where I please. If you want to get off, be my guest. I see your manners haven't improved any. You're still a bad-tempered goblin. The only difference is, you're an *old* goblin now, which is worse.'

Seumas saw that he was going to have to put up with Polahiki, at least until they reached Raiatea. Over the first few days he kept out of the captain's way, but curiosity got the better of him in the end. There were still some holes in Polahiki's history which had never satisfactorily been explained to Seumas. The fisherman had been left behind with the Maori, when Kieto, Seumas and Dorcha, with Boy-girl and Kikamana, had fled from the Land of the Long White Cloud.

One evening, after Polahiki had taken some readings of the kaveinga, the natural star paths, Seumas spoke with him on the matter of his missing days in the land of the beautiful pohutukawa tree, with its magnificent scarlet blossoms.

'What happened to you, after we left with the old Maori man – where did you go?'

'I went to live in the cave once owned by Kurangai-tuku, the ogress who held you prisoner.'

'This much I know,' said Seumas, sitting on the edge of the platform in the bows, so that the cool hissing spray bathed his feet. There was starlight on the water ahead, picking out the green wavelets in the darkness. Kieto's canoe was up in front and a little to the starboard of Polahiki's craft. 'But you mentioned that you were involved in some fighting.'

'Not exactly fighting,' Polahiki replied. 'You would not believe what happened to me. I was the sole survivor of a massacre . . .'

'You usually are,' grunted Seumas, knowing Polahiki's ability to survive was his main skill. 'But go on.'

'Perhaps after I tell you my story, you will consider me worthy enough to share the food in your basket? Well, I was sitting outside my cave one day, when I was approached by a young chieftain of one of the Maori clans that lived locally. He told me to fetch my war club and join him in an expedition to a distant pa, where a sorcerer named Paka had taken a young maiden by force. Her name was Rona.

'When we were close to the place where Paka had the girl, an evil spirit told the young chieftain a lie, saying Rona had now been taken to Puke-tapu, near Manukau. So we went to this new place, but when we came near I realized how dangerous it was. There were skeletons of warriors scattered over the countryside, and rotting corpses, and freshly dead men. We soon found out how and why these men had been killed.

'There were two sorcerers living in the pa at Puke-tapu, by the names of Puarata and Tautohito. On the walls of the pa they had erected this massive wooden head, in the skull of which gathered hundreds of powerful atua. When a force such as ours approached the pa, the head would shout in so loud a voice that it stopped the heart of any man who heard it.'

'If it shouted at your army, why are you here?' asked Seumas. 'Why aren't you lying dead with the Maori?'

Polahiki adjusted the tiller just a fraction, according to his sense of the direction of the swell, and then continued his story.

'I was coming to that. Obviously I didn't die, because I'm here – though even death is not always an end to things, as I'll explain to you in a minute. Anyway, as we approached the pa this terrible wooden head, taller than five men, began to bellow in the most frightening tones. Its thick wooden lips below the nose that ran from brow to mouth, did not move, but wisps of something like mist came flying from them.'

'Atua,' muttered Seumas. 'Powerful spirits.'

'Precisely. Looking around me I saw that my companions had stopped in their tracks, their eyes bulging, their hearts pounding. Greenstone weapons fell to the earth, some point-first, sticking there. I could see the rib cages around me and it was as if the warriors had dwarves inside their chests, punching in fury to get out. Then by ones and twos their hearts burst and they fell dead on the ground.'

'Still . . .' Seumas said, but Polahiki held up his free hand for silence.

'I survived. Yes, for my ears were so full of wax I could hardly hear the great head shouting.' He grinned with a mouthful of rotten teeth. 'Sometimes it pays to be a dirty old fisherman who never washes his lugholes. I felt the shaking of things around me – the tree roots and the meadows beneath my feet – but as for the voice itself, it was like distant thunder, or the sound of a waterfall deep in a forest.

'I can tell you, I ran from that place, intending to go all the way back to my cave. On the way there I met another force, with a great Maori chief called Hakawau at its head. I told him what had happened. He said we had been tricked, that the maiden Rona was still with the tohunga Paka at Rangitoto. He forced me to join them and once again I went into battle with the Maori.

'This time, however, Hakawau was victorious, since he had brought with him his own potent atua. Hakawau had great mana and easily defeated Paka and rescued the girl. We then went on to fight Puarata and Tautohito at Puketapu. Before we got there Hakawau told his men to give me a good bath because he said he could not stand the stink. The bastards washed out my ears and made me vulnerable to the raving of the head.'

'But you survived yet *again*?' asked Seumas.

'Naturally. I am one of life's great survivors, for this time Hakawau's atua swept away the evil spirits from their nest inside the terrible wooden head. All the head could do was wail pitifully – sort of a thin whining sound made by the wind that blew across its mouth – and Hakawau's men stormed the pa. Hakawau went into the house of the two sorcerers, but did not kill them there and then. He refused their gifts of meat and kava, and when he left he struck the threshold of their house with the heel of his hand.

'When I went into the house a little while later, everyone inside was dead.'

Seumas nodded. 'That's some story, if it's true.'

'If it's true?' cried Polahiki, his hand jerking the tiller. 'Of course it's true – ask anyone.'

'Well, there's no one to ask, is there?' said the sixty-year-old Pict. 'We're a little short of Maori witnesses in this part of the world.'

'It is true, every word. What's more, my troubles weren't over. When I finally got back to my cave, I found it occupied. There was a man named Te Atarahi living there, if *living* is the right word to use.'

'You mentioned something about that before.'

'Yes, I did, didn't I? Well, if you saw this fellow Te Atarahi you wouldn't complain about how bad *I* smell. He stank so much the stench offended even me. His head was quite normal, except there was no hair on it, but the rest of him was just bones with skin dripping from them. He was a corpse, I tell you, but with a normal head – which looked huge on a skeleton.

'He was perched in front of my cave like a hunched bird on a stone, drinking the dew from the flax blooms. When I went near him he flapped his bony arms in a threatening manner and I was alarmed enough to run off.

'I went down to the village and told them what I'd seen and they told me the man's name. They said they'd buried him a year previously, dead as a post. Now here he was, come back from the dead, to steal my cave from me.

'Some of the villagers came back with me and we managed to chase the creature off into the wilderness. I threw stones at him that time but he kept coming back again, to haunt me. I noticed after a time that flesh began to gather on his bones like bird lime on a bare branch and one day when he came back he seemed quite normal. "Where did you live?" I asked him. "Did you have a house?" He told me that his house had been on the edge of the village. "Well, go back there and live in it," I told him angrily. "Stop pestering me for my cave."

'And he did, and that was the last I ever saw of him.'

Seumas shook his head, wonderingly. Some strange things had happened to him in his time, in the land of the Maori as well as on enchanted islands, and he knew that all things were possible. Polahiki had come out of the Land of the Long White Cloud reluctantly, so there was no reason for him to lie.

The Pict had to admit that Polahiki's adventures were interesting, but he did not want the man for a basket-sharer, and said so quite brusquely.

'Suit yourself,' sniffed the captain. 'You and that son of yours think you're better than other people . . .'

Seumas did not want to listen to this and moved aft to sleep.

He was woken roughly in the early morning. Craig was standing over him. Behind Craig was Hupa, the girl-twin of Kieto. Her brother was with their father, but she had elected to travel on the second canoe. There were occasions when she and her brother quarrelled violently and both thought it best they were not cooped up together on the same canoe.

Seumas sat up and rubbed his eyes. He was dripping with salt-spray, but that was not unusual. Most sailors spent half the voyage wet and cold, which was why they had to be so hardy. They developed a layer of fat which protected them from the rigours of their journeys.

'What is it?' he asked. 'Why am I woken?'

He was an old man now, not required for watch duties.

Then he realized why. Around the craft Seumas could make out mountainous waves building in the darkness: waves with huge white crests. They were in a vast trough, but none of the other vessels in the fleet could be seen. White spray blinded him, whipping into his face from the dipping bows. It stung his eyes and cheeks. He sat up, coughing and spluttering, wondering how he had stayed asleep until now.

'We're having a visit from the god Apu Hau,' said Craig. 'Polahiki needs all hands, Father.'

'I can see that,' Seumas replied.

He climbed to his feet just as the canoe hit the wall of a wave and tipped at a steep angle. Craig, who already had a hand-hold, gripped his arm. Stores wrapped in pandanus leaves bound with sennit cord went sliding off the edge of the deck into the water. A dugout canoe, used to reach shore in shallow harbours, strained at its lashings but thankfully remained tied. A man on the port side went overboard, quickly lost in the spindrift flying off the hull.

'A line,' cried Craig, immediately leaping overboard with one end of a rope.

Seumas quickly snatched at the other end and tied it to the mast. He saw his son disappear into the black maw of the ocean, swallowed instantly by the heaving darkness. Then his head appeared a few moments later, awash with foam, like a coconut husk being swept backwards as the canoe surged into a new wave that seemed to lift itself from as far down as the sea bed.

'Back there,' shouted a mariner, pointing to a form which had bobbed out of the water. 'Two lengths to your left!'

Craig, who now had the line tied around his middle,

struck out for the drowning sailor. Reaching him he kicked sideways, to get behind the man. Wisely he did not want to be pulled down to a watery grave with a panicking man. Finally, he had him in a head lock as Seumas and the others began to haul in.

While this rescue was in progress one of the masts suddenly let out a tremendous *crack* and snapped in two. Its sail flew away like a flapping ghost, out over high ranges of waves with flecked and twisted tops. The broken spar crashed to the deck, narrowly missing Polahiki and the man with him, as the pair of them struggled at the steering oar. Ropes whipped through the air, lashing at men's bodies. One sailor screamed as the flail cut into his bare back.

Now the voyager canoe was in a funnel of water, with two great waves on either side, running down a valley with its one good sail. There was respite from the furious gusts down in this trough, but it was a dangerous business. If one or both of those waves folded over it would swamp the tipairua and possibly take it down so far that it would not rise again.

The night above was swirling madness, and even the stars appeared to be spinning, as the wind sucked up the ocean and whipped it to froth. Polahiki was clearly trying to follow the kaveinga called Kau Panonga Roroa – the Long Group – but was continually being swept off his course. The extent of leeway drift was lost in the tipairua's wake and the captain would have few of the more reliable natural navigational aids to assist him in his direction. Only the bright, stable Sacred Timber constellation flashed in and out of view, but this was of little help when the other stars churned in the night's whirlpool.

Polahiki yelled to his helpers, asking them to watch the ocean depths for signs of any te lapa, those underwater streaks of light which are visible at night.

No such reports came back to his ears. One more navigational aid was absent.

The tipairua broke out of the end of the wide tube of water just as Seumas and the other mariners hauled the struggling pair back on to the platform. But rescuer and rescued man were exhausted by their ordeal and simply lay there like fish dragged from the depths and left to gasp out their last. Seumas too was weary from the hauling. He was no longer a young man who could go from one task to another without stopping for breath.

'We nearly lost you there, Craig,' he said, stroking his son's wet hair. 'But it was a brave thing to do.'

'I didn't think,' wheezed Craig. 'I went without thinking too much.'

'It's the only way,' said a mariner. 'If you stop to think, you don't do it, and a man drowns.'

'It might have been two,' muttered Seumas, 'but never mind that . . .'

The storm raged for a long time, until finally it faded away with the coming of the dawn. The tipairua slid out into calmer seas in an area of the ocean unfamiliar to Polahiki or any of the other navigators on board. Apu Hau had carried the canoe into strange waters and the Farseeing-virgin Kikamana, ancient and wizened, believed it might be for a purpose.

'The gods are with us on this voyage,' she told Seumas, 'so why would Apu Hau or any of the storm gods try to wreck our canoe? It must be that we have been carried here for some reason to our advantage.'

'More likely that fool Polahiki failed to avoid the storm like the other captains,' grumbled Seumas.

'I'm sorry, Father,' replied Craig. 'You're wrong this time. Polahiki stood no chance of avoiding it. I was standing on deck when a squall swept into the fleet from starboard – it carried us out of line and scattered the other canoes. There was nothing Polahiki could do.'

The captain was at that moment sleeping off his night's ordeal, having spent all of it at the steering oar himself.

Seumas had to concede that the fisherman, as old and cranky as himself, was a good sailor. Apu Hau was God of the Fierce Squall. No doubt his son was right.

Atanua, Goddess of the Dawn, rose now that the sky had been cleared of darkness by Atea the God of Space. She wore her rosy garments and her face was flushed with pink beauty. Some akiaki, fairy terns, were seen flying in the direction of Niuhiti no pare on the windflower. This was the direction in which the damaged craft, like a wounded butterfly on a breeze-swept pool, was being carried.

'Let us go with the wind,' said Kikamana, 'and see where we fetch up.'

'So long as we don't fetch up in Manu's Armpit,' grunted Seumas, referring to a constellation of stars.

The Oceanians, his son included, stared at him in such a puzzled way he suddenly realized that once again he had forgotten how different were their separate cultures. He had meant of course that they might find themselves dead and up amongst the stars. However, Oceanians would not expect their spirits to go higher than the trees after death – where the atua was known to cluster – and most would anticipate going under the waves rather than up into the sky.

'Never mind,' he sighed. 'Forget I said it.'

They were in a windless calm, the air sweltering and thick. Men and women swooned in the midday heat, giddy with the oppressive atmosphere. Sluggish waters drooled from the mouths of rips, past which the canoe moved at a maddeningly slow pace, as if drifting through a dream. In the distance an island came into view, a hogback ridge running across its dark form, the main peak a plateau, like a cloven hoof against the skyline. At the back of a beach scattered with white driftwood resembling the bones of monsters was a thick jungle of cabbage trees.

'Dead-pig island,' said Craig. 'I passed this once in my travels, when searching for my father.'

'You know its name?' asked Hupa, standing with him by the deck hut inside which most of the crew and passengers were finding shade to sleep. 'You've been on it?'

'No, it frightened me so much I didn't stop – I gave it the nickname. It looks like a pig lying on its back, don't you think? A slaughtered pig.'

'Is this where Apu Hau wants us to go? I can't think what would be here for us, can you?'

Craig at first inclined to the same opinion. He wiped away the irritating bodies of insects which had stuck to the sweat on his face. Looking at the island he could see a high column of cloud resting on its shoulders. To his father clouds were a source of darkness, but to an Oceanian clouds were associated with light. Ao, God of Clouds, was not a dark deity. The fact that the island had a tall white cloud as a headdress indicated that the place was not entirely forbidding.

'We must search this island,' he said. 'Will you come with me? I'll need someone at my back.'

Hupa took up her bow and quiver of arrows.

'I am ready for any adventure,' she said. 'Shall I wake my companions?'

She meant the three other maidens who were constantly in her company. They too were armed like warriors, much to the disapproval of the men on board. Craig believed they were part of her secret society, the Whakatane.

'I think it best if we go alone. If too many of us stumble around in a drugged state, on an island with unknown qualities, we're liable to lose someone. You and I seem to be the only clear-headed ones at the moment. I think we should go alone and see what we can find first.'

'I agree,' she replied, eagerly.

Hupa was a small, slim but athletic-looking maiden, whose lithe movements had attracted many a suitor. She had however discouraged any lover from entering her life. Her face had a fresh, round, open appearance, set with a small nose and clear brown eyes. Her hair was cut unusually short for a woman, though her pretty – some said boyish – features made up for what some men regarded as a strong defect. However, their prejudices might have had something to do with the fact that when competing with these men, that which she lacked in physical strength she made up for in sheer determination and skill.

Craig found her company pleasant, as he would any young person eager for experience in the world. She displayed no real traits of bad temper, except with herself when she failed in some physical feat, like not hitting the target with her arrows, or being beaten in a running race by a youth. Then she would chastise herself verbally in front of an audience, careless of those who heard her call herself a 'stupid vahine'.

Once they had moored the craft with a lump of coral for an anchor the pair took the dugout canoe and paddled towards the shore. Craig kept a wary lookout for signs of the Ponaturi, those savage sea fairies who would tear someone to pieces as quickly as would barracuda in the water. He remembered being told of his father's experience with those creatures, in just such a place as this.

'Why are you looking like that?' asked Hupa.

'No reason,' said Craig, not wishing to frighten her.

'You're wondering if there are sea fairies here, aren't you?' she muttered. 'I considered that too. But I think they would have been on us by now, if they were around.'

Craig allowed himself a smile. He was underestimating this female warrior. She knew exactly what the world was all about and needed no protection from him.

After passing over a lagoon where the dead coral lay broken and grey like old bones on the shallow bottom, they reached the beach behind which stood the army of cabbage trees. These proved to be very dense, so the pair walked along the weed-covered sands until they found an opening. Just before going through the gap in the ti, Hupa gave a shout and called Craig's attention to a footprint in the sand.

'Look at this!' she cried, excitedly. 'It's huge!'

Craig stared down at the massive spoor of what was surely a monster of some kind. The print was deep, which meant the creature was heavy as well as large. On first glance it might have been the footprint of a large man or woman, possibly a giant. The bridge between the pad and heel was narrow, revealing a high instep. But it was the toes that showed this creature was not entirely human. They were long and thin, more like fingers than toes, and there were only four of them. There was no 'big' toe. The gaps between were wide which made the footprint spread like a banana tree leaf.

'I had a feeling something nasty like this lived here,' muttered Craig. 'This is not an ordinary island.'

'How do you know the creature is malicious?' asked Hupa. 'It might be friendly. Could be one of Apu Hau's children – perhaps that's why he led us here?'

'I'd like that to be true.'

The couple then went through the gap in the ti. A short way into the trees they came to a wooden wall. This took the form of a palisade fashioned from massive tree trunks with sharpened tops. It was the tallest fence either of them had ever seen. It reached to the top of the rainforest canopy. In one or two places there were narrow tunnels in the sand going under the palisade. It was as if Oceanian rats as big as men had burrowed underneath the enormous posts.

Walking this way and that, the pair failed to find any gates or door, so eventually they scrambled down one of the tunnels, to come up in a village on the other side.

It seemed deserted at first, except that there were fresh smells around: the aroma of cooking, coconut oil, fermenting breadfruit mash. And the animal dung was fresh and ripe, with hundreds of flies buzzing around it. Here and there half-eaten fruit lay, the juices still oozing from the flesh.

Yet the huts and houses in the village were all in a state of disrepair. There were holes in the roofs. Thatch walls were hanging loose from posts. Totems had fallen to the ground and were lying face-down in the mud. Pigs were roaming loose amongst the chickens. Dogs had fouled the pathways and lay scratching in run-down vegetable gardens.

'Someone doesn't care how they live,' said Hupa. 'Look at the state the village is in.'

Almost the moment she spoke, a figure poked a shy head around a doorway. Some whispers passed between hidden bodies. Finally many villagers began to emerge. Unlike their houses the people looked to be in good condition. Their hair was glossy, their bodies plump and clean, their eyes bright with health. Only their melancholy looks gave any indication that things were not well on this small island.

'Greetings,' said Craig. 'I am Son-of-Seumas, a Hivan by birth. My red hair and blue eyes are natural and come from my father's people, so you need not worry about them. This is Hupa Ariki, daughter of the great chieftain, Kieto.'

'Hail, strangers,' said a fat man who appeared to be the chief, for he was wearing a headdress. 'Welcome to the larder of Lioumere-the-Ogress.'

Hupa looked askance at the man. 'Larder? That is a joke, I hope.'

The chief grinned and made a sign to his warriors, who immediately surrounded Hupa and Craig.

Craig reached to his waistband for his club. Hupa managed to string an arrow. But the villagers were on them before they could use their weapons. The luckless pair were soon disarmed and forced to kneel before the fat chief. This personage grinned at them in a friendly way and then shook his head.

'It is very sad. You have such nice names. You introduced

yourselves so politely. Now we have to offer you as sacrifices to Lioumere. I am sorry our hospitality cannot offer anything better than this, but we have no alternative.'

The chief spread his hands and gave them another friendly smile.

Craig glared at the fat man and shook his head. 'The gods will punish you and your people if any harm comes to us. We are part of the great fleet which has been sent to conquer the Land-of-Mists. Out beyond your coral reef lie thirty tipairua canoes, each carrying a hundred warriors. These will be joined by hundreds more, from all over Oceania. You shall be hanged by your thumbs from a beam and your skin flayed from your bones if you touch one hair on this maiden's head. She is the daughter of the ariki leading our vast flotilla!'

'And this warrior, Craig, has great mana. All those who touch him will die in agony,' cried Hupa.

'Alas,' sighed the chief, 'none of this matters, for you see this island is ruled by the ogress, not by us. There are four more villages like this scattered around the island. Each month she takes one person from one village, moving around the other villages in rotation. So you see, we will gain ten months respite while we have you two to offer as sacrifices. Should any more of your people come, they too will become meat for our patroness, the large and very ugly Lioumere.'

Hupa paled, saying, 'You mean she eats people?'

'It is her preferred source of food. She will have fish when we can catch it for her – whole whale-sharks disappear down her gullet in a week – and sometimes dogs or pigs. But she maintains that human bones are nourishing. She will not do without them.'

'Bones?' repeated Hupa

'She loves them.'

'Why not let her starve to death?' snapped Craig. 'Why feed her at all?'

'We have these defences, it is true,' replied the chief in a patient tone, indicating the palisade, 'but they are only strong enough to keep her out while she is in a reasonable frame of mind. However, if she were starving, frenzied, driven mad with hunger, even this palisade would not prevent her from entering. She would smash her way in with great boulders from her mountain, or use a stalactite from her cavern to batter down the walls.

'Then it would be a slaughter, like a wild dog in a chicken coop, like a hawk among a nest of rats. Our bodies would be scattered over the rainforest floor.

'At least in this way we are able to survive as a tribe, albeit we have to let two or three people go during the course of a year. There are some three hundred of us in this village – it does not seem too high a price to pay to be left alone.'

'Except for the families of those you sacrifice,' Hupa said. 'What of them?'

The chief shook his head. 'They do not exist. A young woman is given, an old man, a child. Once they have gone they were never born. No one ever speaks of them again. It is as if they were never here. A man may lose his bride on his wedding night, or a mother her youthful son on his reaching his manhood. They never existed. We continue. We live on. We may not flourish in great numbers, but we still generate.'

'You seem such a strong and fit people. Why not go out and attack her? Finish her. Rid the island of this monster who treats your tribe as livestock.'

The chief shook his head. 'We are too afraid. It was tried once or twice. She threw boulders into our midst. She smashed our skulls with her stone stalactite club. We were slaughtered. Lioumere feasted on the bodies and that kept her wrath in check long enough for our treachery to fade from her thoughts. She does not have a long memory. Her brain is very weak. In fact you could say she is a moron.'

'So, you are cowards,' cried Hupa. 'Strong, fit and able warriors like you!'

'It is because of Lioumere that we are so healthy and sound of limb and body. Those who are given first are the ill and ailing, the crippled, the mad. All our sick people, anyone who is not perfect, is a prime sacrifice. Of course, occasionally we have to sacrifice a healthy person, but for the most part there is usually someone who is not well.'

'Nice people,' muttered Craig to Hupa. 'Throw the sick and helpless to the slaughterer.'

'Put them in the bamboo hut,' said the chief. 'Lioumere will be here in the morning.'

2

Hupa and Craig spent an uncomfortable night in what was clearly a prison hut. The door was made of hardwood set in stone-hard mud walls as thick as the length of a man's arm. There were strong bamboo bars at the small narrow window. The floor too had been pounded until it was as solid as rock. They tried in various ways to escape, but even the roof proved to be made of stout bamboo poles. Guards sat outside the hut all night long and kept peering in at them.

'Look at this,' said Craig, when the dawn came and they could see their surroundings more clearly. 'I don't think many of these people went to their deaths willingly.'

There were pictures scratched into the mud walls, of weeping men and women, of children, of graves and burial mounds.

All morning they were retained in their prison. Water and food was brought to them. No one spoke to them or looked them in the eye. It was as if they were pigs ready for the slaughter. Craig put on a show of being unafraid, but he found it unnecessary, for the plucky girl was quite pragmatic herself. She did not cry out once, nor weep, nor reveal the terror which she undoubtedly felt. Instead she spent her time scowling at the guards and calling them names.

Round about noon the door was opened and two men came in and grasped Craig by the arms.

'No!' yelled Hupa, kicking at one of them. 'Leave him alone.'

But they ignored her. The door was barred against her, after they had hauled Craig outside. They dragged the struggling man near to one of the holes under the wall, which the people used as entrances and exits to the village. There they waited while drummers pounded out rhythms on their hollow-log drums, and flautists played strange tunes on their flutes. Craig felt it was ironic that he should be led to the slaughter to the sound of drums, since they were his instrument. He nodded to one of the drummers who obviously felt he was quite good at his art.

'I could drum you into the ground, my friend,' he said in a dry tone.

The drummer blinked and raised his eyebrows at the man pounding away on the log next to him.

'No, I really could,' said Craig. 'You see this?' He put his tattooed leg forward through the front slit in his tapa bark kilt. 'I'm a Painted Leg. I was once the pride of the Arioi. My instrument was the drum. You have never heard the drums played as I played them. I would like to be modest but I am no liar.'

The chief on hearing this stopped pretending that Craig was not there. He came scurrying across the village with an eager look on his face.

When he reached Craig, still being held tightly by the two guards, he said, 'You were with the Arioi?'

'I was their leader, a king, almost a god.'

'I have heard of the Arioi. It is said they had many canoes with yellow sails. Are there not poets and singers, dancers who do the exotic hura dance? Do they not have storytellers and wrestlers? Do they not put on plays of great renown on stages which are longer than a village is wide?'

'All this is true,' said Craig.

'Prove it,' the chief said. 'Show us how you play the drums.'

One of the men already drumming began to protest, saying that he was playing the rhythm which would bring Lioumere to the village for her meal. The chief waved this protest away impatiently, ordering that Craig should be released.

'You pick up the same rhythm,' he ordered Craig. 'If you're so good that won't be difficult. Perhaps we may allow you to live after all.'

Craig went and stood behind the drums. He was not sure how all these delaying tactics were going to help him in the long run. It seemed logical, however, that if he impressed these people, he might work himself into a position where he had an opportunity to escape. The problem was he knew he could not leave Hupa behind, for by the time he returned with help, she would probably be ogre meat. If he left it would have to be with her at his side.

He picked up the sunbleached, worn drumsticks.

'Behold,' he cried, 'the drumming of a Painted Leg.'

Then his practised hands became a blur to the watchers as he hammered on the hollow logs with sticks the thickness of a man's wrist. The sound of his immaculate and intricate drum rolls, his brilliant interpretation on a rhythmic theme, went out over the rainforest, into the hollows of the distant mountain. He saw the villagers' eyes open wide with disbelief at the speed with which he played. They had never heard anything like it before in their lives. They were mesmerized.

Craig played for quite a time and had almost forgotten about the predicament he was in, when suddenly there was a very loud scream from outside the walls. He stopped drumming and felt the blood drain from his face. The sound had been horrible. Its maker was clearly not human. Then it came again as an earpiercing shriek, that had the parrots in the trees squawking and screeching themselves.

Villagers put their hands over their ears as the cry pene-trated their skulls. Then a monstrous hairy hand and part of an arm appeared, up through one of the holes under the wooden wall. Long fingers with broken, dirty nails began to feel around, as if expecting to find something within reach. Coarser tufted bristles on the knuckles of the fingers stirred the dust as the fingers scrabbled in the dirt, feeling, feeling.

The chief cried, 'Fetch the girl – we must keep this one for his drumming. Fetch the girl!'

But Craig now had weapons in his hands, the two drum-sticks, almost as thick as logs. He leapt in front of the warriors and began beating them back with his clubs, keep-ing them away from the door of the prison hut. Not only was he a drummer, but a great athlete, who could leap and somersault from drum to drum. From outside the village walls, the sound of the shrieking started to become hyster-ical.

Foul stinking breath came through the cracks between the barricade's posts. Then green spittle oozed through, where Lioumere's saliva dribbled onto the outside of the wall. It too had the nasty odour of rotting meat.

Another high-pitched shriek followed, which might have come from the lips of one insane.

Clearly the ogress was not happy at being kept waiting. The hand on the end of the scrawny, muscled arm began snatching at thin air. Villagers already out of reach scram-bled back in panic, away from the clawing hand.

'Get him,' yelled the chief. 'It must be him then. She's becoming impatient. Quickly, quickly – give her the food.'

Once more Craig had become a *thing* rather than a person.

Still his truncheons thudded on the heads and shoulders of warriors who tried to reach him. Finally, one young man got through and tried to wrench the drumsticks from his hands. Craig let one of the sticks go and grasped the youth by the throat, flinging him away with all the force he could muster.

The young man, who was not more than nineteen years of age, lost his footing and went rolling in the dust. Unfortunately for him the momentum of his fall took him within reach of Lioumere's hand. The hairs on the fingers were brushed by his body and, like a rat's whiskers, they told the owner that something was there to be grasped.

Lioumere's fingers scuttled this way and that, found her victim and clutched wildly at him. She caught him by his long hair at first, making him shout in pain. Then she had his legs. She began to pull him towards the hole, making chortling sounds on the other side of the wall.

'NO!' screamed the youth in panic.

The whole yard now halted in its efforts to get hold of Craig and turned to stare in horror at the boy.

His arms reached out for something to grasp, something to prevent himself behind dragged down the hole.

'My son!' cried the chief. 'Save my son.'

The boy managed to grip a wooden post used to tether pigs. He wrapped his strong limbs around this anchor, whimpering in terror as Lioumere got a better hold on him. Finding that her prey would not move she gave a quick wrench. The boy's eyes bugged as his arms were torn from the post. He cried out once more to his father, his arms wide in supplication. Then he was drawn through the hole by his legs and was gone.

'My son,' shrieked a woman, who must have been the chief's wife. 'She's got my son!'

There was a slobbering chuckle from behind the wall, then the sound of undergrowth being trampled.

Lioumere was satisfied with her catch and was on her way back to her cave.

The woman fell on the floor in a heap, sobbing hysterically, beating the ground with her fists. The chief began pulling out his own hair in bunches, leaving bloody marks on his scalp. Other villagers were wailing and crying. One of their favourites had become Lioumere's supper. Soon his bones would be splinters and powder in her jaws and his flesh washed down with several gallons of swamp water.

The chief came over to Craig. 'You have murdered my son,' he hissed in hatred. 'You fiend. I wish we had never laid eyes on you.'

'Better him than me,' said Craig. 'It is all your fault in any case, for putting up with this situation for so long. If it were up to me, I should have killed that ogress long ago, cut off her head and thrown it to the sharks.'

'That's easy for you to say,' yelled the head man in his grief. 'You're not the one who has to go out and do it.'

Craig saw his chance of escape now.

'If you give me back my club and restore my companion's weapon, we will kill this monster for you. Perhaps we may even be in time to save your son?'

At this, the whole village went quiet. Even the missing youth's mother stopped sobbing. They stared first at Craig and then at the chief.

'It's been tried before,' replied the chief. 'She has bitten off the heads of those who went after her. Her teeth are like splinters of rock and harder than flint or greenstone. Magical teeth. Why do you think you will succeed where others have failed?'

'We can only try. Tell me, has she any weakness – any weakness at all?'

'Only her instep. She has a tender instep. They say when she was born she was ripped from her mother's womb by her father, who used his teeth.'

Craig decided this would have to be enough. He secured Hupa's release and told her what he intended to do.

'I shall go after this ogress and attempt to kill her – but you need not come with me. You can return to the tipairua if you wish and wait for me there. I have no right to ask you to come with me.'

Hupa, who had got her bow and quiver of arrows back, shook her head fiercely.

'I go with you.'

Craig sighed. 'If anything happens to you your father will burn me at the stake.'

'If anything happens to me, it will surely happen to you as well. We'll both be ogress's dung. There'll be no need to concern yourself after that. The two of us will be fertilizing the wild hibiscus trees.'

Craig smiled ruefully. 'You have such a delicate way of putting things, Hupa, being a maiden.'

She laughed in her hearty sportswoman's way and slapped him on the shoulder.

The chief said to them both before they left, 'How do I know you won't just run away, back to your canoe?'

'You don't,' replied Hupa, 'you have to have something which is hard to find in yourself.'

'What's that?'

'Trust. After what you have done to us we would be within our rights to leave your son to die. However, we are honourable people. We have made a promise and we'll honour it.'

The chief could do no more than accept this, which he did with uncertain feelings.

That night they left the compound, going up into the rainforest by the light of Hine-keha's face. Quite rightly, the chief was worried that they might run away, back to their canoe, for there was no one to stop them now. But both had given their word and they were anxious to try and save the youth if they could, despite what the tribe had intended for them. Their fate was to have been the same as his and he would not have cried for them when their bones were powder.

They followed the fresh footprints away from the walls of the village, up into the foothills to the mountain. The spoor followed a stream which eventually led to the sad-looking mouth of a cave up on a grassy rise, below a rock shelf. Here they watched and waited for the sun to rise.

When the Hine-nui-te-po had fled the scene in her cloak of black feathers, Ra the Sun God appeared behind them and crept up into the hills.

Once the sun was up there was movement in the cave. Craig and Hupa watched carefully as a horrible figure stumbled out into the day, stretched and yawned. Despite the fact that they were anticipating a strange creature, they were both shocked by what they beheld.

'What a monster,' whispered Hupa.

It was a naked female ogre but of monstrous proportions. Her head was half as large as her torso, which in itself was as long as the height of three ordinary women standing on one another's shoulders. No neck was visible below this huge ugly head, the hair of which hung lank and grey to the creature's waist, as coarse-looking as frayed rope ends. Two lidless eyes stared out from a face with no prominent nose, only twin cavernous nostrils with wrinkled edges. The same rough grey head-hair came out of these caverns, and out of thick brown ears resembling enormous figs. It was as if they were sprouting hoary bracken.

Craig murmured, 'She could bite off the head of a wild boar with that mouth.'

Her massive scallop-shaped breasts, her navel and the area between and around her legs also grew coarse grizzled hair. Her thighs were thick and muscled, as were her forearms. Her feet were long and prehensile, with cracked and broken nails. There were lumps and boils on her body, calluses and corns on her elbows and feet.

The pair watched as she picked up a log of hardwood and began crunching it in her jaws. Within a very short time the log was a pile of kindling. This Lioumere put to one side, presumably to use as firestarters at a later time.

She obviously liked chewing things, for the next thing she popped into her mouth was a fist-sized piece of rock. This she noisily ground to gravel, which she spat out on occasion, showering the leaves of the forest trees. Her mouth worked methodically, reducing some of the gravel to powder, which she blew down her nostrils like smoke.

After another yawn and stretch, she cleared her throat and hawked and spat a wad of powder-sludge mixed with mucus into the rainforest.

The phlegm landed high above the spot where Hupa was hiding, and it hung there elongating itself, bending a sapling with the weight of a gobbet of thick swamp slime.

'Charming!' muttered Hupa, getting out of the way in anticipation of the fall.

Those fig-shaped ears were not for decorative purposes only though, for the huge head came up at this single word and the ogress stared into the forest. Lioumere's mouth dropped wide open and the watching pair got another shock. The orifice, which stretched almost from ear to ear, was full of comparatively small jagged red teeth as even and sharp as a shark's, stacked in ever-decreasing crescent rows from the front of her palate to the back of her throat. There must have been over a thousand teeth in that ugly opening.

In the next moment the figure was running at great speed towards the clump of foliage behind which the ogling pair sat to view their enemy.

'Quickly!' cried Craig, fear freezing his heart. 'Run! Run!'

Hupa needed no second telling. She was on her feet and racing back down the slopes to the thicker rainforest below. Craig was right behind her. He did not look back. All he could hear were those terrible feet crashing in the under-growth behind him. There was a fast-flowing torrent at the bottom of the slope. Hupa turned on the bank and fitted an arrow to her bow, firing almost in one movement.

Craig turned as the arrow struck the instep of the ogress in the act of lifting her foot.

Lioumere screamed in agony and dropped like a felled giant kahikatea tree with a mighty thump which reverberated through the forest.

She sat up and plucked the arrow from her foot, still screaming at the top of her voice.

Without waiting any longer the two Rarotongans leapt into the fast-flowing water and allowed themselves to be swept swiftly away downstream towards the sea.

Once they had dragged themselves out of the torrent, they assessed their chances of killing Lioumere.

'It's not going to be simple,' said Craig. 'She's obviously been attacked in the normal manner before and knows how to respond quickly. We have to think of a plan to put her off her guard.'

'That's your side of things,' Hupa said, quickly. 'I'm more of a straightforward person. I'm not much good at thinking sideways. You have the right hair on your head for that sort of brainwork.'

'What's that supposed to mean?' asked Craig, indignantly.

'Well, you have red hair,' replied the artless Hupa. 'It must be a strange soil which grows such hair, with strange thoughts buried in it. I'm just a normal person.'

'Oh,' he growled, much as his father would, 'so I'm the offspring of some sort of weird goblin, am I?'

'Exactly,' answered Hupa. 'That's exactly it.'

He could detect no maliciousness or insult in her tone and concluded she was simply speaking her mind. Hupa was a guileless young woman who spoke without inferences of any kind. She said as she found. Instead of fuelling his anger it made him want to laugh. It was the kind of thing an ingenuous Oceanian might say to Seumas. He found he was pleased to be compared with his father by this innocent maiden.

'Well,' he said, after some thought, 'it just so happens I do have a plan in mind. It's a very dangerous one and a little too reliant on the ogress herself, but it may work. I can think of no other . . .'

He outlined his scheme to Hupa, whose brown eyes went big and round as the explanation came forth.

'It'll never work,' she said, flatly. 'She'll crush you under her heel the moment you approach her. And anyway, how do you know she understands human language?'

'I don't, but language is something other than just sounds – there are gestures too, which aid communication. I used to watch my father and adopted mother speaking in that tongue they called *Gaelic*. I found I knew what they were talking about, even though I did not understand the words, simply by the way they used their hands and positioned their bodies.'

'And you've seen the tree?'

'Yes, my father described it to me after his visit to the Land of the Long White Cloud. It produces a gum which the Maori chew to heighten their senses and enhance their appetite. We must collect enough to make a mouthful for Lioumere as well as myself.'

In the end Hupa agreed to the plan, though she still had grave reservations. The pair then hunted through the rainforest, collecting gum from the trees which Craig identified, until they had a huge wad of it. Craig took a piece of the gum and put it in his mouth, chewing it tentatively. Hupa did the same. She nodded thoughtfully after a while.

'The Maori are right, it does substantially increase one's feeling of well-being, as well as sharpening the taste buds.'

They spat out the chewing gum, almost simultaneously.

'Good,' said Craig. 'Let's hope they are right about the rest of it.'

So, with the gum in a hastily fashioned wicker knapsack, he went back up the slopes towards the cavern of Lioumere, with Hupa following some way behind.

Craig found the ogress sitting cross-legged outside her cave tending a fire. Lying beside her, trussed to a peeled greenwood spit, was a terrified-looking, blubbering youth. Craig was relieved to see that the boy was still alive. However, if he were not quick the young man would soon be roasted, as Lioumere was at that moment fitting two forked branches into the earth on either side of the fire, across which she presumably intended to lay the spit.

'Good day to you,' cried Craig, emerging from the undergrowth. 'How are you, Lioumere?'

The ogress's head shot up at these words and she stared in astonishment as Craig approached the fire she was poking.

The youth too was looking amazed as Craig sat down by the flames, smiled and rubbed his hands.

'Nice cooking fire you have here, eh? No earth-ovens for the great Lioumere. An open fire, with roasting hot flames! Very good. I'll bet you're looking forward to your meal.'

Craig nodded pleasantly at the trembling youth, who could not take his eyes off him.

Lioumere made a whining noise in the back of her throat and her eyes narrowed. Craig knew that she was a hair away from reaching across the fire and snapping his neck. He could see a bruise on her instep, no doubt caused by Hupa's arrow. This was going to be a very delicate operation.

'I bring you gifts, Lioumere,' he said, in a soft and friendly tone. 'Here, look, in this basket on my back.'

Craig undid the crude wicker basket they had quickly woven that morning. She looked on, curiously now. He reached inside and lifted out the wad of gum. Breaking a piece from it like dough, he put it in his mouth. Then he began chewing with a play-acted enjoyment, rubbing his stomach at the same time.

'Good,' he murmured. 'Good appetite.'

Lioumere continued to stare into his features. Craig spat a gob of juice on the ground. He nodded.

'Very, very good,' he murmured in a contented way.

He held out the remainder of the wad. Craig was counting on the guess that Lioumere could not resist anything to do with food and drink. She loved her stomach, would pander to her greed even if it meant it was her last act. She was a self-indulgent glutton.

She looked at the chewing gum for a moment, sniffed the air above it with those ugly pits she used for a nose. Then she snatched the wad from his palm, painfully scoring his skin with her sharp nails as she did so. The wound was nasty but Craig kept a smile on his face as Lioumere held up the piece of gum, studying it carefully, breathing its aroma.

Finally, to his utter relief, she popped it in her mouth. The pair of them squatted on opposite sides of the fire, chewing away stolidly for a few minutes. Gradually the muscles on Lioumere's face relaxed, the lines became less evident. Her eyes took on a slightly softer look as she masticated on the gum with her many rows of russet teeth. Finally, she revealed a benign side to her nature as the drug took effect.

'Good, eh?' said Craig. He pointed to the youth, still strapped to the peeled log. 'Make him taste better. Yes? Give you stronger appetite for cooked flesh!'

'Ahhhh,' moaned the boy, hanging his head. 'You are a traitor to your kind.'

'Not necessarily,' replied Craig, but still smiling at Lioumere when he said it. 'Watch this.'

He then made a great show of swallowing the gum and belching hard. He rolled his eyes in appreciation and patted his abdomen. 'Mmmmmm,' Craig murmured. 'So good.'

With pattering heart he watched as Lioumere kept chewing her gum, but then, just when he thought he might get to his feet and make a run for it again, she swallowed.

Craig sat there, watching hard, praying the poison would work quickly. The gum had its own toxins, which would not harm a man so long as he just chewed on it. However, once swallowed, the stomach juices attacked the gum, which subsequently released a poison deadly enough to kill a human being. His own piece of gum was lodged under his tongue on one side of his mouth.

The Maori warriors were aware of the lethal properties of the gum, but they chewed it anyway, possibly to affirm their manhood and courage. Or perhaps they enjoyed the effects so much they were willing to take the risk? Whatever, the gum was virulent, fatal to a man, once in his gut.

Lioumere stared at Craig for a long time, her eyes revealing nothing. Then suddenly they opened wide and she lurched to her feet with a loud yell. Staggering forward she stepped directly into the fire, scattering sparking logs and embers.

'Hupa, quickly!' cried Craig, as the ogress lunged for him. 'Help me!'

He spat out his own wad of gum and jumped backwards out of her reach.

Clearly Lioumere's sight was affected, for she took great swipes at the air around and above Craig's head. The Rarotongan picked up a large stone with both hands and hurled it at Lioumere's head. It struck her temple and glanced off without felling her. Hupa came running up then and loosed an arrow into the ogress's face. The missile struck an eye, which made the monster scream, before plucking it out.

'She's going,' Hupa cried, stringing another arrow. 'Look, she knows she's in trouble.'

Lioumere was not interested in attack now, she was concerned about survival. She started to run down the slope, escaping on those thick legs of hers. Her movements were giddy and weaving, like that of a drunken creature. Down the incline, away from the cave she reeled. Into the rainforest, her body crashing through lower branches and undergrowth, careless of any injuries she might receive. It

was clear she knew she was in trouble and wanted somewhere hidden to work off the sickness which had come
upon her so suddenly.

'Quickly, follow her,' cried Hupa.

The pair ran down after the ogress, leaving the youth
protesting, asking to be set free. The boy obviously wanted
to get away while Lioumere was gone, thinking that once
she recovered he would still be her prey. Craig and Hupa's
priorities were different though. They felt it was essential to
kill her while she was being attacked by the poison.

The youth need not have worried, nor indeed the pur-
suers of the ogress.

When they had traversed the winding trampled path to
its end, following crushed bushes and broken trees, she
was lying dead on her face. The poisons had at last reached
her vital organs. Her monstrous head was half buried in the
soft moss. One arm was hanging limply over a rotten log.
The other was flung forwards, grasping a protruding rock.
Already an army of ants was marching across her back,
indignant to find their pathway blocked by this hairy
mound of flesh.

'Are you sure she's dead?' whispered Hupa. 'Shall we
crush her skull with rocks?'

'No,' murmured Craig.

The son of Seumas was now feeling some remorse for
having destroyed this wonder of supernature. It was true
that Lioumere had preyed on the people of the island,
cooked and eaten them for goodness knew how many
years, but that was because she was an ogress. That was
how her kind survived. In her ignorant state people were
considered pigs, chickens or dogs. Human beings were livestock and quite properly slaughtered for the purpose of
ensuring one had food in the larder.

'Help me turn her over,' said Craig. 'Then I must make a
pair of pincers out of some hardwood sticks and coconut
fibre.'

When both tasks had been carried out, Craig then began to extract the Lioumere's teeth. He found some pitcher plants and began to fill them with the teeth. It was his guess they were hard stone of some kind, though they felt heavier than any rock he had come across. When he had finished there were ten pitchers of teeth. He strung them together in two fives on a piece of vine and slung the whole lot around his shoulders. The load was immensely heavy.

'I'll go back and let the boy go,' Hupa said. 'Your club is back there under the hill. I suggest you cut off her head and carry it back to the village. Otherwise we won't be believed and it'll take an age to get away.'

'Right,' answered Craig, not relishing the idea of hacking off Lioumere's head, even though his paddle club was rimmed with shark's teeth and was probably as sharp as any axe. 'Come and find me once you've released the youth.'

He did as she suggested, however, once he had his paddle club in his hands, and chopped the ugly head from the shoulders of the fallen monster. Hupa then returned and the pair of them dragged the head through the rainforest by its coarse grey hair. When they passed a forest pool a singing log called out in an eerie whistling voice, asking if it was the head of Lioumere. The pair replied that it was. The log, which was probably a taniwha in disguise, then demanded they throw it in the pool.

'It belongs here, hidden in the forest,' sang the log. 'You must leave it here, not deposit it in a village of fools and cowards, so that they might make a trophy of it.'

Craig saw what the log meant. It was not right that the tribe should use the skull to brag of their prowess, when they had done nothing but submit to Lioumere's rule for many years, allowing their children to be taken away and eaten. That chief would put it on a pole and puff about his bravery.

'How will we prove she is dead?' asked Hupa of the singing log, 'if we relinquish her to you?'

'You have her teeth,' whistled the log. 'How would you get her teeth without her head?'

'That's true,' said Craig. 'Throw the head into the pool – it's getting too burdensome anyway.'

The couple dragged the head to the pool's edge, then let it roll into the waters. It went down like a stone to the bottom, where they could see it looking up through the lidless eyes, the toothless mouth half open. The hair floated like fronds, forming a cushion of follicles around the log.

Soon the fishes began to nibble at the lips and ears. Within a few days there would be nothing but a gigantic skull greening on the bottom of the pond. The grey hair would remain and no doubt grow to fill the shady hollow.

'Those are magic teeth,' called the log after them, as they went on their way. 'Use them wisely.'

3

Having restored the youth to his father and mother, Craig and Hupa took their leave of the village. The locals would come nowhere near them anyway, even to look at Lioumere's teeth. They believed the couple must have so much tapu they were highly dangerous to normal people. Even as the pair were leaving, the villagers were fencing off the places where they had sat, so that no one might come to harm by touching those spots. Once the tapu had worn off, then the fences would be removed.

Hupa and Craig paddled back to the tipairua, anchored just outside the reef. When they arrived an anxious-looking Seumas was pacing the deck. Others were awake now and seemed refreshed after their sleep. Hine-tu-whenua was blowing a fine brisk breeze, away from the island and in the direction of Raiatea. Tai-moana, the voyaging canoe's drum known as Threnody-of-the-seas, was being sounded. Tiki, in his pride of place before the mast, looked woodenly solemn and intent of purpose.

As soon as they were on board and the dugout secured, Polahiki ordered the sails to be raised.

They were on their way again.

'Where have you been?' demanded Seumas. 'We've been worried since yesterday about you both.'

'No you haven't,' replied Hupa with her usual candour. 'You were all drugged with sleep when we left. It was only after we completed the task for which Apu Hau must have brought us here that you woke and started biting your nails.'

A wry smile appeared on Seumas's hoary face.

'Trust you to pierce my pomp,' he said to her. 'You're right. It's not long since we woke. But finding you missing, both of you, we began to panic. Polahiki was convinced the sea-fairies had got you and had dismembered you both. So, tell me about your adventures! What is this about the God of the Fierce Squall and his purpose?'

They sat on the deck in the shade of the pandanus-leaf hut eating taro and telling Seumas the story of Lioumere. While the story was in progress Seumas kept stealing a glance at the pods of teeth on the vine which Craig had unslung from around his neck. When they had finished Seumas asked, 'Can I see these magic teeth?'

Craig opened one of the pitcher plant pods and revealed the heavy russet teeth. Seumas picked one out and held it up, studying it in the light. His expression changed so alarmingly that Craig asked his father if anything was the matter.

'What? Oh, no, no. Everything is fine. Are these really magic? What could one do with them?'

Hupa said, 'If they harbour magic, then one could do almost anything. It is obvious though that they have something to do with the coming war. We must keep them well preserved, ready for the time when we need to use them.'

'For what?' snapped Seumas.

'Father?' said Craig, surprised. 'Why are you angry at Hupa?'

Seumas seemed to bring himself under control with great difficulty.

'Ah , I'm sorry. I'm getting to be a testy old man. I didn't mean anything by it. Could you – could you let me have one of those bags of teeth?'

'For what purpose, Father?'

'I – er – for an experiment. I'll return them to you later. I would be very grateful.'

Craig looked at Hupa who shrugged and nodded.

'No need to return them, Father – you may keep them.'

Thanking them both, Seumas took the bag of teeth and secured them to his waistband.

Craig and Hupa now went off to get some sleep. They were exhausted after their labours on the island. Around them the mariners were busy at work. Shark callers were beating the water behind the canoe, using their chants to attract the sharks into the nooses they trailed in the water. Some were casting coloured stones into the wake in a further effort to get the creatures into their clutches. Everyone was looking forward to shark steaks for supper that evening.

Seumas went to a quiet spot to study Lioumere's teeth. He knew exactly what they were made of – *iron*. The Oceanians at last had some iron in their clutches, but they did not know it. Arrowheads could be made from Lioumere's teeth, which would penetrate the shields of the Celts. A thousand arrows with metal points would help to even the imbalance between the metal swords and spears of the Celts and the wooden and stone weapons of the Oceanians.

Seumas was not interested in creating balances between the two potential warring factions. He needed the teeth for another purpose, a selfish purpose. He required them for their magical properties only. If he told his son the teeth were made of iron, then Craig might demand their return, for they were precious metal. Seumas hoped the magic in the teeth was strong enough to do what he required of it.

'What have you there?' asked a voice behind him. 'They look like chips of redwood.'

Seumas clutched the pod of teeth closely to his chest.

'Nothing, Polahiki,' he blustered. 'They're mine.'

Polahiki looked surprised. 'I didn't say they weren't,' muttered the fisher-captain. 'I was simply making conversation, but never mind. I have my navigation to attend to.'

'Yes, go away and adore your fleas.'

'Huh!' muttered Polahiki. 'No need to get nasty.'

Seumas realized he was being unreasonable but could not help himself. He knew there were those on board who were saying he had become haggard since his wife's death. His face had grown leaner and had adopted a haunted expression. They probably knew the grief was working at his soul, gnawing on his spirit, reducing him to a wretch of a man. When he had last looked at himself in a basin of water, he himself had been shocked by what he saw – shadowy gaunt cheeks, grey pallor, grizzled chin. There were deep furrows in his bony brow and red rims around the hollow eyes. It was the face of a man condemned. He looked like a wasted man, a man of sticks and straw.

'But I have the magic now,' he told himself, in that quiet voice that men going mad are wont to use. 'I can do what must be done . . .'

Prince Daggan stared from the main window of his house built high on the slopes behind the beach at Raiatea. It was a magnificent house, better even than the house of his father, the king. Made of hardwood, with a roof of woven leaves, the floor space was ten times that of a normal dwelling. There was latticework in the walls to allow the cool breezes which blew up from the ocean to penetrate the room. The window itself, hanging from thongs, could be closed against storms. Now it was propped open with a short pole, to permit viewing.

And a fine viewing platform it was too, positioned up there above the bay. Prince Daggan watched as the fleet from Rarotonga sailed into the lagoon. He could see his rival, Kieto, standing at the mast of the leading tipairua. It grieved Daggan that a man who had begun life as a commoner, should now be considered worthy enough to lead a whole nation into battle. It should not be so. Was royal blood worth nothing in these times?

'It should be *me*,' muttered Prince Daggan. 'I should be the war chief, not that crass labourer.'

But Daggan had not even been considered for the position. People had only ever spoken of Kieto, simply because as a boy of seven Kieto had sailed with Kupe to the Land-of-Mists.

So what? Daggan had thought. The whole expedition had been an accident. To follow an octopus and discover an unknown island! And certainly Kieto's presence on board that craft had been a matter of pure chance. It could not have been Daggan, of course, who had not been alive at the time, but did that give the new ariki Kieto a precedence over those of higher rank?

'I am a prince – born a *prince* – while this man began life as a fisherman's son. It is not right he should lead us. *I* should lead. And perhaps listen to advice from such people as him – but not necessarily take it. I have been trained in the arts of war, as befits a king's son. My grandfather was King Tutapu, a mighty warrior who was brought down only by the trickery of his so-called wily brother Tangiia.'

'Your grandfather was one of the most feared kings in the history of Rarotonga,' said Daggan's wife Siko, sitting on a mat in the corner of the room. 'You should be proud you have his blood.'

She was preparing some breadfruit mash with taro and roasted rat meat.

'Of course I am proud,' replied Daggan, unable to turn away from the window as the fawning populace of Raiatea were paddling out into the lagoon in their thousands to greet a long-lost son of their soil. 'Look, there goes my father – damn him. It's a sickening sight when a king gets dressed in his dogskin coat and feathered helmet to greet the whelp of a lowly fisherman and his bitch wife. Is he not afraid his tapu will strike the commoner dead? Is he not afraid his mana will overwhelm the tutua, the low-born Kieto?'

'I heard your father say that Kieto was a natural noble, rather than one born or bred.'

'A *natural* noble,' spat Daggan. 'What is that? Do the gods confer nobility on toads? Do they fill the worms with grandeur? Better than *this* I would think.'

Daggan's wife, tall and sleek and smelling of fresh coconut oil, came and placed a long-fingered hand on his bare shoulder. Her sharp nails rested lightly against his skin. There were times when those nails inflicted pain on him – a pain which he enjoyed – but at that moment there was enough ache in his heart to sustain his masochistic tendencies.

'We must think of a way to rid ourselves of this Kieto, so that you, my husband, will be able to step forward and offer your valuable services as leader of the invasion fleet. Already I have plans in progress to make this possible. We need but a little more time.'

Before marrying her half-brother, Siko had been a sorceress of some renown. She still practised the black arts, without the knowledge of her father-in-law, to whom she had made a promise to give up her former ways. Now her husband was in need of her skills and she was happy to come to his assistance.

'Can you do that?' asked the prince, turning and looking eager. 'Is it possible?'

'Of course it is possible,' she replied, 'but we need to be very careful. Should any hint of a plot reach your father's ears, both of us will be banished. He dotes on that Kieto too much, while his own dear son . . . but never mind. We will make that good. I just need a little time to fashion a scheme.'

'Well, be quick,' cried the prince, a little too aggressively for her taste. 'Be quick.'

She let the sharpness of her husband's words pass her by. She was used to his impatience. Instead she revealed what she had already found out.

'We may have an ally soon, in our endeavours,' she said, standing in the speckled shadowy-lights of the latticework. 'I have consulted my atua and they send me favourable messages concerning the goblin.'

The prince's head came up swiftly. 'Seumas? What of him?'

'He has need of me and my magic, while bringing a little magic of his own.'

'This doesn't involve the screaming of his dead pig?' said the prince, turning pale. 'Not the bladder and bamboo pipes with which he professes to produce music? I couldn't stand that. The last time I heard them I almost wet myself . . .'

'No, nothing like that. He wants me to weave a spell for him. Raise someone from the dead. I shall soon have him in the palm of my hand. We can use him for our own purposes, my husband.'

Daggan moved closer to his wife. She was beginning to excite him with her words.

'How do you know all this?' he asked, huskily.

She laughed. 'Am I not the queen of sorcerers? How should I not know? Spiders come to me in the night and whisper hallowed secrets. Bats fly in at my window with messages from afar. Goblins, fairies and dwarves stop me in the forest and pour their poisonous schemes in my ears.'

His eyes opened wide at these words and he began to tremble a little.

'Stop,' he said. 'I don't want to hear these things. They trouble me. But if we can do it, sister! If we can do it, my lovely wife! To rid ourselves of this Kieto? Why that would be worth almost anything.'

His hands were running over her breasts now, dropping down to feel the hidden crevice between her legs. There were beads of sweat in the corners of his eyes. His breath had a strong musty smell to it

She undid her tapa bark skirt and let it fall to the floor.

'Make love to me, brother-husband,' she said, her nostrils flaring. 'I must have you, *now*.'

They clutched each other and fell on the floor. There was a short struggle, she reaching and trying to untangle his clothes much like a fisherman will grapple with a fish caught in his nets. Finally she had freed the fish and it slipped quickly into her grotto. Too soon though, it left that narrow cleft for open waters again. She would have preferred that it visited for a longer period, but she knew her own husband's strengths and weaknesses.

'So when shall we make our move?' asked Daggan as they dressed themselves again. 'Can I leave things to you?'

'Of course,' replied the unsatisfied Siko, wondering if that tall male servant was still pulping the breadfruit just inside the forest pale. 'I shall go now and make preparations this instant. You rest your weary body, my husband, for you have served me well today.'

'Yes, I have, haven't I?'

PART THREE

The Indigo lady

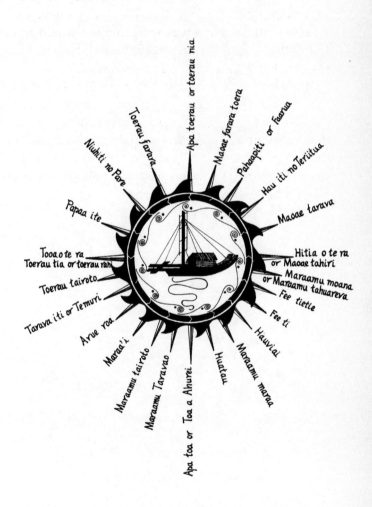

3

When he arrived in Raiatea, Kieto was still one tipairua missing: the one with his daughter and Seumas on board. Kieto was beginning to wonder whether he had been right in appointing Polahiki as the vessel's captain. The Hivan fisherman was probably not up to handling a great voyager, despite the fact that he was an excellent navigator.

Two other tipairua had gone missing in the storm which Apu Hau had forced upon them, but these two quickly caught up and rejoined the main fleet after the storm had blown itself out. Where was Polahiki's craft? Had it gone down with all passengers and mariners? It would be a tragedy if it had, but Kieto was not yet willing to accept such a terrible scenario.

He told his son Kapu, 'I cannot go to Most Sacred, Most Feared. I will speak to King Rangari and tell him the ceremony must wait until I am satisfied the craft is not lost.'

'Yes, Father,' said Kapu, who was as anxious as Kieto about the missing tipairua. His twin sister was on board and while they fought a great deal, he still loved her as a brother should and wanted her to be safe.

Seven days later a sail was sighted on the horizon. To Kieto's relief it was Polahiki's craft which came scudding over the reef into the lagoon. There was much joy on the island at the news. People streamed down to the beaches in their hundreds, forsaking their chores for a glimpse of Seumas-the-Pict and his famous son Craig, whom they knew as Kumiki the Painted Leg – next to Lingadua, the greatest drummer who ever existed.

They were not disappointed. Craig had always liked the adulation of his followers. Seumas was less enthusiastic about the praise which poured forth, as garlands of frangipani were hung around his neck and a ring of blossoms placed on his head. Nevertheless he accepted it with a smile and good grace, sending a priest-messenger to thank King Rangari for taking the trouble to leave his house to greet him and the others with a wave.

The great king did not of course go too close, for his tapu was so strong his shadow might have destroyed those on whom it fell. There were those who professed they could feel the presence of his mana too, from a great way off. Instead the king remained partly up the hill, where he could be seen by all, but could not inflict unintentional harm. He was surrounded by his priests, who, being his half-brothers and cousins, were virtually immune, though even they did not go so far as to actually touch his person.

His son and heir was by his side too, but left him to come down to the beach to extend the king's welcome to Kumiki-the-Drummer and Seumas-the-Pict.

'Greetings, Seumas,' cried the nobleman, 'you remember me, Prince Daggan?'

'Yes indeed,' murmured Seumas. 'How are you?'

'I am well,' smiled Daggan. 'I was sorry to hear about your wife Dorcha. I remember she was a special favourite of my grandfather Tutapu. We all grieved at the news.'

'Thank you,' replied Seumas.

'May I then invite you to a private gathering, Seumas? Just myself and my wife. We would like to share in your sorrow – not openly of course – just the three of us sharing a basket. You have been the basket-sharer of a prince before, so my rank should not hold any special fears for you. We might talk of old times, of mistakes made, of glories not yet forgotten.'

'I seem to remember your family and mine were on opposite sides of the conflict,' said Seumas, soberly.

'All history now,' smiled Daggan. 'Today we are all friends – let there be no more strife amongst Raiateans or Rarotongans.'

'Then I should be honoured,' murmured Seumas, remembering now that Daggan's wife Siko was a sorceress of some note.

'It is the time of Hine-uri, so bring a torch in order that you might see your way up the mountain path. That is my house up there on the slopes. We shall expect you this evening.'

'Hine-uri,' nodded Seumas. 'The Indigo Lady. The lady of the occult. They say the dark arts are practised during her rule of the moon.'

'Do they? I suppose they do. Well, then? Tonight.'

With that the prince turned on his heel and made his way back up to where his father sat on a high wooden chair, waving a scarlet feather at the tutua below.

Seumas returned to where Kieto and Polahiki were talking with Craig.

'You did the best you could,' Kieto was saying to Polahiki. 'If Apu Hau wanted to take you to that island, there was not a great deal you could do about it. And these teeth you took from the ogress, Craig – you have them with you? Let me see them.'

The teeth were fetched, all except the one set which was now in Seumas's possession.

Kieto studied them, weighing the pods in his hands.

'They're very heavy. I have never felt stones as heavy as these before. What sort of magic do you think they are good for?'

Craig shrugged. 'I am no tohunga or kahuna. We had best ask someone like Kikamana, the Farseeing-virgin, that sort of question.'

'Kikamana is still resting after the voyage. She's quite frail these days. When she emerges from the temple I will ask her,' said Kieto. 'In the meantime you had better leave these in my keeping. They may be valuable. On this island we have enemies as well as friends, eh, Seumas?'

This remark was clearly intended to draw out from Seumas the reason why he had been engaged in conversation so long with Prince Daggan, a sworn foe of Kieto, but the elderly Pict merely shrugged.

'We have had our enemies here in the past, it is true, but I think we should put those days behind us.'

Kieto stared at his old friend for a long time, but then, it seemed, overcame his fears.

'You're probably right, Seumas,' said Kieto. 'Let's forget local enemies and look to the common foe – the Celts and Angles. Perhaps we could go over some stratagems while sharing a basket this evening at my campfire? You should be there too, Craig – and one or two others I shall inform.'

Seumas uttered a sharp 'No' without meaning it to sound so abrupt.

'What?' asked Kieto, looking affronted.

'I mean, I'm sorry, Kieto – like Kikamana I am very tired after the voyage. I need to rest and clear my head of salt-spray and too much sun. Please forgive me when I say I am *unable* to attend – but you go ahead, with your chiefs.'

Kieto's brow cleared instantly of its dark look and he put a placatory hand on his friend's shoulder.

'No, *I'm* sorry, Seumas. You have been the energetic warrior for so long now I keep forgetting that you are past being a young man. A *fit* man, I hope, but needing more rest these days. It is I who should beg your forgiveness. I am thoughtless of the needs of others in my single-minded endeavours for a successful expedition, and my manners are not what they should be.'

They parted then on good terms, Seumas going to the hut of an old friend to get out of the blazing sun. He felt guilty that he had not told Kieto the truth, but he knew the younger man would not understand. Seumas did not want to be persuaded out of his present course of action, and so intended that it should remain clandestine, as befitted its dark nature.

When he took off his waistband, a short time later, there were two leather pouches hanging from it. One contained the teeth of Lioumere. The other, his wife's ashes.

That evening, after dark, Seumas took a lighted brand and made his way up a winding path to the house he could see lit by lamps above on the slopes. There was a delicate darkness that had settled softly on the island. Overhead a puff of cloud hid the stars directly above the island, but around the edges of this limited vaporous veil the sparkling chips of light clustered. Had there been no cloud it would have been bright enough to see the path simply by their light alone.

It was one of those nights on which any man at peace with himself might have expected to encounter wonderful fairies, or tree dwarves or even mountain goblins. But Seumas's mind was not on such ethereal creatures. He was thinking of Dorcha. A tipairu, lipsipsip or tipua could have leapt out in front of him and shouted 'Boo!' and Seumas would have brushed it aside in annoyance and continued on his way.

When he reached the house he looked back down the path, to see the sea glinting below, the white surf thundering along the reef visible in the starlight.

'Who's there?' called a female voice, causing a flutter in his heart for a second. 'Make yourself known!'

'Seumas-the-Pict,' he answered. 'Known in my own country as Seumas-the-Black, of the Blackwater clan.'

A moment later the beautiful Siko appeared in the doorway, holding a lantern in her hand. It was peculiar because she had sounded just like Dorcha, though of course he could see it was not his beloved wife. A strange coincidence, but he put it down to the fact that he had been dreaming and praying so hard it would not have been surprising had she materialized before him.

'Is that your full name?' Siko asked, curiously. 'Seumas-the-Black. I never knew it before.'

'Oh,' said Seumas, a little distractedly. 'Yes, yes it is. Why do you ask?'

'Names are sources of power to a witch. You should not be so free with your name, Seumas. Come in.'

He stepped into the magnificent house, saying, 'Those who may wish to do me harm may have it so far as I'm concerned.'

'Oh,' she said, the light from the lamp giving her face deep shadows, 'that sounds like the voice of despair.'

'I am not the same man since my wife died. She was everything to me. Now I am not only old and a dried husk of what I once was, but I am lonely. Very, very lonely. There does not seem to be much to live for now, except my son and his wife, and my grandchildren. My son is with me but I doubt I shall see the others again. I have a strong feeling I shall not return from this war. My bones will lie in Pictland, in Albainn, before the winter hammers that land to hardness.'

'Is that why you carry your wife's ashes on your belt? So that you can be in the Land-of-Mists together? You want your resting places to be one? Doesn't her other husband lie there too? Won't you be taking her back to him as well?'

Seumas's hand went to the pouch which contained the fired remains of Dorcha.

'How did you know?' he asked, quietly. 'How did you know what was in the pouch? And about Dorcha's other man?'

She smiled. 'The one you killed for his weapon? I am a sorceress after all. Come through and see my husband. He awaits with the feast we have had cooked for you. Pork, dog, rat and fowl, as well as parrot fish and manta ray wings. Taro, arrowroot, banana . . .'

'I don't eat dog meat,' he said, following her. 'I never have.'

Prince Daggan rose as Seumas entered, in the way that even nobility rises when a distinguished elderly man enters the room. Once again Seumas was reminded that he was now in the evening of his lifetime. He was given due deference, but he was not important any more. Discussions went on around him rather than through or with him. His words were listened to politely but a marked tolerance showed on the faces of those who harkened. Regard to his age and affection for him as a person ruled over interest in what he had to say.

'Good evening, Prince Daggan.'

'Good evening. I understand we must congratulate your son on defeating an ogress? That was some exploit.'

'He had help – the young Hupa Ariki was with him.'

'She is but a maiden. I doubt she influenced the outcome of the battle too much.'

'No, no, I understand from my son that she took an equal part in the giant's slaying. Young women these days are very skilful with weapons. Hupa in fact is unmatched in the use of the bow and arrow.'

'Really,' smiled Siko. 'We do not altogether approve of such things on Raiatea, but perhaps it is different on a new Faraway Heaven such as Rarotonga? You probably need female warriors to supplement your numbers? Anyway, enough chatter, please eat – I shall leave you alone.'

Seumas remembered that in the main, women on Raiatea did not eat with the men, especially when there was pork on the table.

'Can your wife not share our basket this evening, Prince

Daggan?' asked Seumas. 'I especially wanted to ask her something – something about her profession.'

The prince nodded gravely and motioned for his wife to sit with them on the mat, with the feast spread out within the trianglar shape they made.

They began to eat the food set before them, though Seumas only picked lightly at this and that, still distracted by his reason for being in this house. Delicacies laid out on pandanus and banana leaves, soaked in coconut sauce, or garnished with wild honeycombs, or marinated in mango juice, were all there to be had, but none of them excited his taste buds in the least. Finally he blurted out his reason for being there.

'Siko, madam, in your capacity as a magician are you familiar with the art of *kapuku*?'

'That of reviving the dead? Of course.'

'Could you raise someone for me? Given the right conditions of course. I have payment.' He touched the other pouch on his belt.

Siko waved aside the mention of the payment.

'I must know some things about the dead person. How long have they been interred? Is the body still whole? What is the reason for the raising . . .'

'Love,' said Seumas, quickly. 'The reason is love.'

'And the answers to the other questions?'

'The death has been recent, within two months. There is no body. Only ashes.'

'Ah,' murmured Daggan. 'You speak of your wife, Seumas. It is she who hangs on your belt you wish to revive?' He turned to Siko. 'Can you work with ashes, my dear? Is it possible to bring back the person whole after fire has wasted the body?'

Siko shook her head, sadly. 'Nothing can bring back the whole person, but we can call the sau, bring it back in its human form, though that form will not be substantial. Her presence will be there, but you may not touch her, Seumas.

She will be here as mist, though you will be able to see her as she once was, speak with her, listen to her words. Is that enough?'

Seumas felt his jaw go rigid and he was silent for a long time. Finally he answered, 'It will have to be.'

The atmosphere in the room had become quite sultry by this time. The burning lamps were giving off some kind of thick, cloying perfume. Seumas began to wonder what kind of oil was being used in those lamps, but he was too single-minded about his needs to complain about his discomfort.

Siko said, 'You realize what you ask? We would be breaking the king's law here. If we were discovered raising the dead, we would probably be put to death ourselves. People have a great fear of breathing life back into those who have gone.'

'I know.'

'And we shall have to appeal to Kahoali, the God of Sorcerers.'

Seumas said, 'Is that so terrible?'

'It can be. We need to make suitable offerings in order to obtain his assistance. One of the essential ingredients is the eyeballs of a freshly murdered man floating in a cup of kava. Does that trouble you?'

Seumas looked at Prince Daggan, who turned his head to avoid their eyes meeting.

'Where would we get such things?' asked Seumas, turning back to Siko again.

Siko gave him a tight smile. 'We already have them.'

He knew what she meant and he realized with a sinking feeling that he was slipping deeper and deeper into the horrors of dark magic. In the past Seumas had always felt men and women should be free to follow their own gods, whoever those gods might be. But there were some deities who required offerings no honourable or law-keeping man could or should consider.

If they had not actually done it themselves he knew that

Siko and Daggan had ordered the murder of a man in order to obtain his eyes. Through her dark arts Siko had foreseen the coming of Seumas and his request for her aid. The preparations for that aid had already been carried out.

Seumas found himself mumbling, as he unhooked Lioumere's teeth from his belt.

'These are from the jaws of an ogress called Lioumere. They are said to be magic. You may take them in payment for your services.'

Siko smiled, accepting the pouch of iron teeth.

'This is only part payment,' Daggan reminded his wife. 'Seumas needs to provide us with a service too.'

'I'll do anything,' replied Seumas, sinking even further into the morass of crime, 'if you will give me back my Dorcha, even if it be for only a night.'

The atmosphere in the room was stifling now. Seumas wanted to gag and throw up his meal on the floor. He forced it back down his throat with difficulty. His skull ached and a fierce pain throbbed behind his eyes. He felt as if he were drowning in some pool of viscous fluid. His movements were sluggish and heavy as he buried his face in his hands.

Siko said softly, 'You will warn us when the Rarotongan Kieto is on his way to Tapu-tapu atia, to pray to his ancestors for a successful voyage and campaign. You will do so from Fisherman's Rock, down on the beach. If it is day you will signal to us here with a wave of a piece of indigo cloth. If it is night you will use a lamp to send an occulting signal . . .'

'Why? Why must you have this information?' croaked Seumas, knowing in his heart that they meant to do some harm to his friend. Kieto would be at his most vulnerable when he went to Most Sacred, Most Feared, for he had to commune with his atua alone, unarmed and most probably in the darkness. 'You will not assassinate him?'

'That is not for you to know. Do you want to see your

wife here, this evening? Do you want to have her with you? She will be your slave. You will be able to summon her whenever you wish it. Do you want that?'

'Yes, yes, anything,' groaned Seumas. 'It doesn't matter. I only want to see her one last time. The last thing she heard from me was angry words. I had no time to say I loved her. No time to say I was sorry. No time to say good-bye. How could I know that such a wound would kill her. I was angry with her for swimming in the lagoon when there was a swarm of box jellyfish about. She died with my shouts in her ears.'

Daggan, now that he had what he wanted, reassured his guest concerning his fears. He told Seumas not to worry, that it would not be necessary to harm Kieto. That all they wanted to do was ensure that he did not take the fleet to Land-of-Mists.

'Other atua will replace those he intends to speak with,' said Daggan, 'and these others will persuade him that the gods do not wish him to lead our warriors into battle. No real physical harm will come to him.'

Seumas allowed himself to be consoled, knowing deep down that he was a fool for doing so.

'Give me the dust,' said Siko. 'Hand me your wife.'

Siko took the ashes of Dorcha from Seumas and told the Pict to follow her. Leaving Prince Daggan behind she went off into the night without a lamp. Seumas stumbled after her wondering how she could see in the dark when he had to cling on to her garment in order to keep to the path. Eventually, after weaving their way up a narrow trail, they reached a remote place in the high hinterland where there was a large cave. A musty smell came from the interior.

Inside the ceiling rustled with bats and long fat cave worms crawled over the dung-covered floor.

'We must begin the ceremony in a state of iniquity,' she told him. 'Lust and carnal desire are part of Kahoali's requirements. You must take me here on the floor, amongst the worms. I must have your seed inside me before we begin the rituals. Take me savagely and with loathing.'

She let her skirt fall to the ground and then lay on top of it with her legs open.

'Forgive me, Dorcha,' groaned Seumas, as he went down on her body. 'It's for you . . .'

While they were fornicating, Seumas forced his mind to the time when he and Dorcha had first witnessed the release of the coral-egg bundles in the Rarotongan lagoon. The female corals prepared their eggs in advance of the release, while the male corals developed the sperm. Some corals were both male and female, needing only themselves. A few days after the fourth full moon in the year the corals released their bundles of sperm and eggs simultaneously all over the reef, so that fertilization could take place.

Seumas and Dorcha had seen this event several times now and never ceased to be amazed at the spectacle. Pinks, blues, oranges, reds: a huge variety of coloured bundles released by the polyps floated to the surface of the water to mate mindlessly in the gentle ripples of the lagoon. A delicate coming-together of the sexes: the tranquil sea their copulating agent.

Not like this violent struggle between two bodies in the bat shit on the floor of a witch's cave.

'I've finished,' he said with relief, thinking his orgasm would never come. 'It's over.'

She rose and unlike him chose to remain naked.

Further in the cave she lit a lamp which let out a foul-smelling stench. There were ti'i all around the cavern, standing on ledges. Ugly effigies with leering mouths and lolling tongues. Siko, with her hair wild and stained skin, began to intone karakia, while setting up various objects to do with her spell. Cave spiders and rats came out of their holes to witness this ritual occult magic, their small eyes gleaming in the light of the single lamp. Seumas felt uncomfortable.

'Do I have to wait in here? Can I go outside.'

'As you wish,' murmured Siko, hardly paying him attention.

Seumas left the cave and sat amongst the trees within hearing distance. He was wondering what would happen if Siko was pregnant from his ravishment of her body. It was a thought he did not allow to develop, the consequences of it being too awful to contemplate. He picked some wild flowers in the light of the stars while he waited: a bouquet to hand to his beloved when they met once again.

While he sat and waited Seumas fell into a doze, from which he was awoken by the sound of grating high-pitched voices coming from within the cave. It seemed that Siko was arguing with someone inside that inner blackness. Neither of them was the voice of Dorcha. He imagined that Siko was now conversing with atua, or even the God of Sorcerers himself. He was glad he was outside. It was not something he wished to witness. There were enough nightmares in his head without adding to them.

Later, there was silence. Seumas rose, wondering whether he ought to go in now that the noises had ceased. He did not relish the thought of witnessing some ugly exhibition, however, so still remained hovering on the threshold. A few moments later Siko came hurrying out of the cave. She looked ghastly, as if she had come into contact with all the demons of the underworld and had only just escaped unscathed.

'It is done,' she murmured, then hurried off down the path into the rainforest, without another word.

Seumas remained at the cave entrance in trepidation, not daring to enter. All at once a terrible fear had gripped him. An apparition was beginning to form out of the inner darknesses of the cave. He knew by the unnatural cold wind which blew from within that this would not be *his* Dorcha, but a Dorcha now reluctantly released by the keepers of the dead. This was her mindless soul coming to him, not her real temporal character, the person he had loved while she had been on earth.

He shivered violently in the unhealthy atmosphere.

Dorcha then came out to see him. There was a smile on her face, but it was not one which warmed his heart. It was the fixed smile of the dead. He recognized only the fragrance she had carried on her body when she was alive. This and only this told him he was in the presence of Dorcha. She spoke to him in a soft wasted voice, her body drifting apart in places and then re-forming like smoke from an unseen fire.

'Seumas, you have asked for me and I came.'

Seumas swallowed hard, wondering what he had done, remembering what he had promised in order to have it done.

'Is that you, my darling?' he whispered, hoarsely. 'Is that really you?'

'It is I, Seumas, my love, my life.'

He reached out to touch her, their relationship having always been strongly tactile, then remembered she was but a shade from another world.

'Did they force you to come, or did you come willingly?' he asked. 'I would not have you do something you did not desire, Dorcha. Will you chastise me now for my actions? I betrayed Kieto in order to get you to return. I wanted to say I was sorry – sorry for being so furious with you. But you went and died in my arms before I could recant.'

'I do not remember you being angry and I care nothing for Kieto,' she replied, coldly, her eyes melting and resetting in a disturbing way. 'I care nothing for the living, except for you of course. I only care that you love me enough to want me here, even though this world is a frightening place to me, full of the energy of the quick.

'I come from a place where there is a slow movement into a dark void called eternity, where time does not exist, where flowers and other objects bearing worldly contours are regarded as the shapes from which insanity is formed.'

He let the posy fall from his grasp to the forest floor.

'I – I thought you would disapprove of my actions.'

'How can I disapprove of things I do not understand? When I was alive I must have comprehended these things, but now they are so foreign to my way of discerning they mean nothing to me. It is good to hear your voice, Seumas. I might have forgotten you too, but you are an essential part of my spirit, the essence which is *me*. In life we became one, so part of me is still alive in you and part of you died with me.'

He sobbed, his voice full of anguish. 'I knew it was so, Dorcha. I knew that was how it must be. We were one person, you and I. I want us to be whole again. I want us to know ourselves as we were. I am not myself any more. I am this shadow of a man, not fit for anything except carrying an obsessive dream.'

'It is not possible, Seumas. We cannot be as we were. But we can accept how we are now.'

He nodded, the misery in him more than he could bear. He had thought he would be overjoyed at seeing her again, hearing her voice, but it was as if he had raised the worst part of that darkness which had always resided within his spirit. This was not good. He did not feel well again. He felt as if he had swallowed grave earth and the clay was creeping through his veins with the cold and ugly purpose of destroying his spirit.

'Shall we talk?' he said, in despair. 'Shall we talk of old times? I shall remind you of our life together. You will see how happy we were once . . .' and without waiting for her answer he began the story of their love as if it were a litany, letting it come from his lips in a monotone.

Even before the dawn came she had begun to disappear, the terrible boredom of his presence, his tale of two people in love, overwhelming the forces which had demanded she

be there. She evaporated gradually, while Seumas was still
caught in the agony of his narrative, trotting out the words
which now meant nothing at all to one of the subjects of
the tale. The tedium, the dullness of his account was driving
her mad and she had to leave or turn into one of those
insane spirits that haunted the woods and hills of
Rarotonga never knowing the peace of death.

'Don't go,' he cried, the tears streaming down his cheeks.
'The price to call you forth was treachery. I have not yet
had the value of that tarnished coin . . .'

'Goodbye,' she whispered from the mist which now
drifted over the grasses revealed by the dawn. 'Goodbye,
my grand Pict – we will be together soon.'

He was left alone on the hillside with nothing but the
sound of the wind – and a lingering fragrance.

2

Seumas followed the path down the slopes. His mind was whirling with thoughts. He had promised to betray his friend, Kieto, and payment for that promise had been delivered. Dorcha had appeared and might have stayed with him, had he wanted it. The dead are different from the living, however, as Seumas had found to his cost. The Dorcha who had returned was not the Dorcha who had left. They were too strange to one another and could not remain in each other's company.

'Where have you been?'

Seumas looked up quickly, the guilt flooding through him.

'Nowhere. What's it to you?'

It was Boy-girl who had asked the question. Her long hair decorated with sea-shells and ribbons was wet through. She had obviously been for an early swim in the lagoon. She looked thoroughly taken aback by his abruptness and bad manners, and raised her eyebrows in that arch way she used on occasion.

'Sorry I spoke to you at all,' she said. 'You'd better let everyone know you're in a bad mood, or we'll all get our heads bitten off.'

'I – I'm sorry, Boy-girl,' said Seumas. 'I was thinking of something else. I'm tired.'

'You look tired. Have you been for a dawn walk?'

'Yes, that's it. I went up into the mountain. I can think more clearly up there. I had bad dreams and wanted to wipe them from my head. You know.'

She nodded, now mollified by his tone.

'I do know, yes. I have bad dreams all the time. It comes with age I suppose. No – that's not true, I used to have nightmares as a child. We're coming full circle, that's what it is, Seumas. We're slipping back to childhood.'

'Oh, if that were true,' he said, wistfully. 'I would love to be a boy again.'

Seumas left Boy-girl and went back to his hut. Dirk was with Craig and so there was no one to greet him. The place seemed very empty. Feeling both exhausted and miserable he lay on his mat and fell fast asleep.

Much later he was awoken by a sound and sensed a foreign presence in the room. Sitting up quickly, he saw two silhouettes in the light of the doorway.

'Who is it?' he murmured.

'Rian and Ti-ti,' came the answer.

Instantly Seumas was on his feet, a club in his hand. These were two brothers who had been married at one time to Dorcha. Rian had been trying to kill him ever since she had left them. Both brothers had accused him of enticing her away, despite the fact that Dorcha herself had told them she had a mind of her own and could make her own choices in the matter.

'It's all right,' said Rian, stepping forward and making a placatory gesture. 'We're not here to harm you.'

'Why are you here then?' he asked, reasonably.

It was Ti-ti who answered this. 'We – we wanted to hear how she died.'

'Dorcha? You think I killed her I suppose?'

'No,' replied Ti-ti, 'for we know you loved her as much as we did. We were here and you were there. We could not even come to her funeral. We thought you might tell us how it went and whether she ever spoke of us, when you both went to live in Rarotonga.'

Outside the hut the sun was going down quickly, leaving a red flush in the sky. It seemed he had slept through the whole day. He motioned for the two men to sit down on a mat. He noticed now that they were both grey-haired and Rian was quite thin, his muscle tone having gone. Once upon a time he had hated these two, but now they looked like harmless old men. They nodded at him as he gave them something to drink in a half-coconut shell.

'You want to know how she died?' he said. 'She was in pain at first, but then her body began to go numb. A jellyfish sting. Can you believe that? Our Dorcha taken by something as silly as a jellyfish sting? She spoke of you before she died, of course. She told me to tell you both she had been happy with you, while you were all together.'

Ti-ti let fall some tears at this news and even the tough Rian's eyes looked misty.

'She said that?'

'Yes,' lied Seumas, who had made the whole thing up, 'I was going to come and see you, but the voyage has made me weary. I'm not the man I once was.'

'None of us are,' said Rian, standing. 'We thank you for your time, Seumas. Death brings men together. We'll leave you now. The funeral was a good one?'

'As grand as they come. She went out in fine style. The flutes were playing, the drums were pounding. There were a thousand blossoms for her shroud and palms for her path. People wailed and pulled at their hair. Others cut themselves with sharp shells. One man gave me a carved canoe, sacred and cherished, to serve as her coffin when she was cremated. She was greatly loved and admired.'

'You had her body burned?' said Ti-ti.

'She wanted me to bring her ashes here, to scatter them on the island she loved.'

'It was done?' asked Rian.

'Just as she wished, up there on the slopes.'

Satisfied, the two brothers now left, going out into the darkness of the evening. Seumas went out to one of the fires and brought back a brand to light his lamp. This he placed on the window ledge of his hut, so that its light shone within and without. He remembered miserably that he had a task to do. He had not told Prince Daggan and Siko, but he had already known that this night was the time when Kieto would be going to the temple.

Some time later, as Seumas sat outside the door of his hut, Kieto came past.

'You are going to commune with your atua?' asked Seumas, dully. 'Is that where you're going?'

Kieto looked down at his old friend. 'Why, of course it is. You know that, Seumas. I shall come and talk with you afterwards. We have one or two things to discuss. Perhaps you could ask Boy-girl and Craig to join us?'

Seumas said that he would. Kieto went on his way, towards that part of the island where Most Sacred, Most Feared was situated, deep in the rainforest, under the shadow of a rock hang. There were the island gods, images planted in the ever-damp moss around the terrible Investiture Stone.

Seumas's spirit was in agony as he watched Kieto go into the rainforest. The Pict stared up at the house on the hill, knowing he was being watched for a sign. If he was going to keep his promise to the sorceress, it would have to be now. But how could he do that? How could he betray his friend? Why had he agreed to such treachery? His selfishness, his obsession with his dead wife, had led him along an ignoble path.

Standing now, he paced up and down in front of his hut, wondering what he should do. Now that it came to the point, he could not betray Kieto. That much was impossible. The right thing to do was to go up to Prince Daggan's house and tell him and Siko that he could not carry out his side of the bargain. They would probably murder him, but he deserved as much.

He looked up again at the house. The lamps had been extinguished rather abruptly. That was puzzling. Had the pair gone out somewhere? Surely they would be watching for the signal from Seumas, desperate as they were to know when Kieto would be at Tapu-tapu atia. It was almost as if they had already received the sign they wanted from him.

Suddenly, Seumas looked at his own lamp. It was situated on the ledge in the window, at about chest height. He had been walking up and down in front of it. *An occulting light.* Seumas realized in horror that he had inadvertently given the signal by pacing backwards and forwards blocking and unblocking its beams from the sight of those above. To the couple on the hill it would have been an occulting light.

Seumas began running towards a clutch of visitors' huts that were some distance apart from where Seumas dwelt.

'Craig, Craig, come quickly! Kieto's in trouble. I think he's about to be abducted.'

Craig appeared almost at once. Hupa and Kapu came from another hut. Soon there was a party of them running towards the path which led to Most Sacred, Most Feared. Seumas was trying to explain on the run.

'It's my fault,' he told Craig, 'I betrayed him to Prince Daggan and his wife Siko.'

'That witch?' muttered Craig, with Dirk at his heels. 'What are you talking about, Father? Keep silent until we have dealt with the matter.'

Seumas, anxious to confess his guilt, nevertheless bit his tongue.

When the party was halfway there, a deep-throated and bloodcurdling howl went up somewhere in the rainforest. The tone sent shivers down Seumas's spine. It sounded like a large wolf, which was impossible in an Oceanian land. There were no wolves. Therefore it must have been a dog, but Seumas had never heard one of the local dogs howl like that. It sounded as if the creature was out on a hunt, out to kill.

Dirk's hackles went up and an ugly growl formed in his throat.

'What is it?' cried Hupa. 'What made that sound?'

Kapu, her brother, turned pale and stopped running. 'I'll get help,' he said, turning back to the village along the path.

When the others reached the clearing of Tapu-tapu atia they saw Kieto standing with his back against the tall Investiture Stone. He was holding his left arm. Facing him, with its back to the group, was a fearsome creature out of a nightmare. Its naked body was that of a muscled, hairy man. Its head was that of a huge dog. The monster was making ready to rush Kieto.

Seumas quickly grabbed the snarling Dirk by the fur on the back of his neck, to keep him from hurling himself to almost certain death.

'Father!' shrieked Hupa. 'Don't move!'

She quickly fitted an arrow to her bow. Just as the fiend was making its run she fired. The arrow struck the beast in the nape of the neck. The shock of the wound stopped it in its tracks but failed to bring the brute to its knees. Instead, it turned, with fury on its face, to regard the intruders. The eyes in the great head burned with anger, the slavering jaws opened to reveal bloodied fangs.

'Get my daughter away from there!' cried Kieto. 'This Kopuwai will kill you all.'

Craig seemed not to have heard this order. He moved forward with the agile grace of a drummer turned warrior. Planted in the ground halfway between him and the beast was the stone image of Paikea, God of Sea-Monsters. Craig wrenched this totem from the ground. It was shaped much like a large war club with a spike at the bottom and a rounded head with a face on the top. Craig began swinging the weapon back and forth as if daring the Kopuwai to attack him.

A second arrow loosed from Hupa's bow struck the man-animal in the chest and it was distracted from Craig's gaze. It let out one of those mind-splitting howls. Then it rushed forward, intent on getting to Hupa. Craig braced himself, planting his feet at shoulder-width apart. He swung the stone club at the creature's rib cage as it tried to run past him.

The club smashed into the side of the Kopuwai's breast and the watchers heard the crunch of bone.

This caused the Kopuwai to turn its attention back on Craig. It reached out with strong arms to grab him, its savage jaws snapping with a ferocious and ugly sound. Standing over a head taller than Seumas's son, it almost got a grip on his shoulders. But Craig was already swinging for the second blow. This time the club came down on the monster's skull, crushing it like a breadfruit. Human hands came up to protect the canine head against further injury. The creature howled in fear and agony. Its tongue lolled from its mouth.

A third blow from the stone club was delivered to the creature's left shoulder.

Still the beast did not die, but ran off into the rainforest, its feet crashing through the undergrowth.

Seumas let go of Dirk's ruff and ran to Kieto, to find him holding a stump where his left hand should be.

'Severed at the wrist,' growled Kieto, obviously in pain. 'Take me to a fire.'

Craig replaced Paikea where he had found him, the stone god being somewhat bloodstained. Paikea was the son of Papa, Goddess of the Earth, and Craig would make reparations to her later. In the meantime there were other things that were of more importance.

They hurried Kieto through the rainforest back to the village. There the wound was cauterized with a blazing

torch. Kieto's face registered his agony. Once the flame
had been applied he passed out and was carried to his
hut. Craig went to speak with Seumas, now standing
quietly by.

'Well, Father, what was this about a betrayal?'

'They said no physical hurt would come to him,' Seumas
whispered hoarsely. 'They promised he would be
unharmed.'

'You are talking about Prince Daggan and Siko? What
did they say to you? Why are you involved, Father?'

Seumas hung his head. 'I wanted to see Dorcha one last
time. I *had* to see her – you *must* understand that. I wanted
to say goodbye, to explain things . . .'

'Father, we all want to do that. But unfortunately our
loved ones do not die when everything is perfect. There
are always some things left unsaid, things left undone.
Death is not something to be wrapped up neatly like breadfruit in pandanus leaves, the sennit knot tied, the ends of
the cord clipped.'

'I had to see her.'

'You keep saying that, but we all feel that way. We all
want that last conversation. We all want to be forgiven for
our transgressions. We all want to reaffirm our love. But
death doesn't usually wait for such occasions. Sometimes,
yes, we are lucky and manage to shed our guilt, but more
often than not all the loose ends are left untied, all the
wounds open.'

Seumas hung his head, finding his son wiser than himself, which given their respective ages he felt should not be.

'I'm sorry. In return for the sorceress Siko letting me
have one last time with your mother's ghost, I promised to
give Daggan a signal when Kieto went to the Investiture
Stone. I was promised no harm would come to him. I
thought they meant to kidnap him until after the fleet sailed
with Daggan at its head. I will go to the king and speak
against his son.'

'You will do nothing of the kind, Father. They'll certainly execute you too, if they find the pair guilty. Treason is regarded as just as heinous a crime as attempted murder. We are virtually at war. At such times punishment is always meted out with more severity than in times of peace. Even your friendship with Kieto might not save you.

'It's best you remain silent over this. I hope no one overheard you when we were running to Kieto's assistance. If asked why you thought something was wrong, you had better say you heard an earlier howl, which none of us did.'

'I don't care what happens to me,' said Seumas. 'I deserve all I get.'

'You might not care at the moment. Your wife has just died and you feel empty and wasted. You probably don't care whether you live or die. But *I* care. You are my father. I have just lost the only mother I have ever known. I do not wish to lose a father in the same year. Stop being a selfish old man. Think of others. You have your grandchildren to consider, as well as me. You were never a pathetic man before. Stop feeling so sorry for yourself, Father – pull yourself together.'

'That's easy for you to say.'

'No it isn't – it's very difficult. I hate being disrespectful to my father. But if I let you alone you'll follow this path of self-destruction. What else did you give to Siko in payment for producing Dorcha's phantom?'

'Lioumere's teeth.'

'Well, she'll probably use the magic they can produce to cause some political strife on the island. At least we won't be here to witness it. Is that all?'

'Yes, I suppose so,' said Seumas, finding it a new experience to be chastised by his son. 'By the way, the ogress's teeth are made of iron. I have told you about iron. We can use the rest of them to make arrowheads.'

'Iron? That rock you call *metal*?'

'It isn't rock, it's something you get from rock, by melting it down. The essence of rock, the soul of stone. It will pierce the strongest shield, the thickest hide. There's enough teeth to make a thousand arrowheads.'

Craig put an arm around his father's shoulders and gave him a tight smile.

'We'll give them all to Hupa – that woman is a marvel with the bow and arrow. Did you see that shot she made? In half-darkness too. Smack on target.'

Seumas nodded. 'She's a good archer. I don't think I've seen better. But there will be enough to fill her quiver and those of many others. It won't help us a great deal against swords, but it's a start I suppose.'

'Come, Father, you're determined to be the pessimist, aren't you? Let's go and eat with Boy-girl. She always brings you out of yourself. You usually end up arguing with her over some point or another, but at least it takes you away from morbid thoughts. Drink a *little* kava, but not too much, or you'll get maudlin . . .'

Oh you gods, thought Seumas as he followed his steady and confident son, is this old age, when the young treat you like a child? Let me get to the Land-of-Mists and into battle, where there's swords and horses. I'll show this laddie who's the father and who's the son then. He'll know then who has knowledge of real battle and who does not.

PART FOUR

King of the
fair-haired Fairies

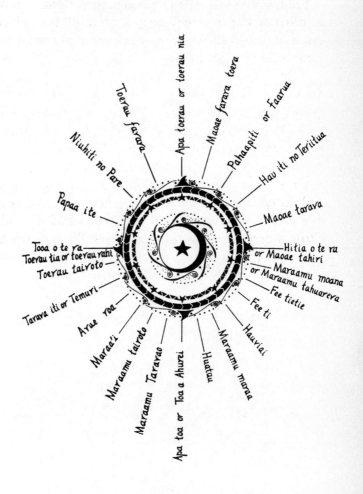

Toerau farara
Apa toerau or toerau nia
Maoae farara toera
Pahaapiti or faarua
Niuhiti no Pare
Hau iti no Teriitua
Papaa ite
Maoae tarava
Tooa o te ra
Hitia o te ra
Toerau tia or toerau rahi
or Maoae tahiri
Toerau tairoto
Maraamu moana
or Maraamu tahuareva
Tarava iti or Temuri
Fee tietie
Arue roa
Fee ti
Maraa'i
Hauviai
Maraamu tairoto
Maraamu maraa
Maraamu Taravao
Huatau
Apa toa or Toa a Ahurei

1

Later Seumas was called to Kieto's sick bed, where that man lay recovering from the loss of his left hand. After the cauterization the wound had been smeared with a balm and bound with healing leaves. Kieto kept slipping in and out of a fever at this point, but he was anxious to know the answers to a few questions.

Seumas was asked by Kieto why he had known the ariki had been in trouble. The Pict told him that he had been visited in a dream by Dorcha. Though Seumas did not say so outright, he implied that Dorcha had warned him that Kieto was being attacked. Kieto accepted this explanation, dreams being one of the main ways spirits of the dead communicated with the living. Hupa was not altogether satisfied though and asked why Seumas had called out that Kieto was being abducted.

'The warning was rather vague,' said Seumas. 'I understood it to mean he was being carried off.'

Kieto would hear no more criticism of his friend Seumas.

'What does it matter how he knew?' said the ariki. 'He saved my life. Seumas is a true friend and always has been, ever since I was a small boy. I love him as I would love my father or my brother. He is a man among men, a great warrior, and mana is gathered in him like stars are clustered in the roof of voyaging.'

Seumas suffered this embarrassing praise in silence, fortunately taken by others for modesty, under the hawk eyes of his son. The two did not mention the matter to each other again. There were other people who knew his secret of course – the prince and his sorceress wife – but they had good reason to keep silent. Craig paid them a short hostile visit.

'When the gods made the first people,' Craig told the prince and his wife quietly, 'they ran out of human blood and had in some instances to use the blood of animals . . .'

'I am familiar with the story,' said the prince, coldly.

'Then you know that in certain cases people take on the traits of particular animals. A person with traces of rat's blood in them will most likely turn out to be a thief. Someone with the blood of a parrot will be a loud-talking braggart. Those bearing the blood of ants will be busy, energetic people . . .'

'Get to the point,' snarled the prince. 'You wish to tell me I have the blood of some foul beast in my veins?'

'No,' said Craig, looking him straight in the eyes, 'I'm here to tell you about me. I have the blood of the shark in me. I kill coldly and without mercy. Once I have targeted my prey, nothing short of death will stop me from tearing him to pieces. Do you understand me?'

Despite the protection of his rank and arrogance, a visible quiver of fear went through Prince Daggan on looking into the fathomless blue eyes of this young man.

'I am tapu,' he told Craig, haughtily. 'I am a prince.'

'And I,' replied Craig, 'am a hammerhead.'

Craig left the prince smouldering with rage at being spoken to as if he were a tutua by a half-Hivan, low-born son of a goblin.

'I'll roast his eyes,' snarled the prince to his wife as he crashed around the house in a blind rage destroying objects whether he loved them or not. 'I'll have his liver on a spit.'

Siko, who was never one to worry about lost causes or those which held no profit, brushed his anger aside.

'You waste your fury and energy on nothing,' she said. 'He is the one who is suffering, or why would he come up here to front a prince in that way? He is the one who desires revenge. We failed in our objective, that worries me more than some boy whose soul is seething with shame for his father's actions. Forget him and his father. Had he come here because of some malicious intent, I would have said yes, have him put to death. But he is suffering – let him continue to suffer.'

Prince Daggan calmed down immediately. 'How well you put things, my dear,' he said. 'How inadequate I am.'

Yes, she thought, but said nothing.

In the village below there were problems with the Kopuwai. The creature had not died and was still on the loose. It had gone back to a secret cave in the rainforest and returned with a pack of vicious two-headed dogs, which it set on the village. The dogs slaughtered chickens and livestock until the Rarotongans managed to kill most of them. The remaining two or three were driven back into the rainforest.

A band of warriors under the leadership of Kikamana then found the cave where Kopuwai lived. They tried to smoke him out by lighting fires at the entrance to the cave. When he failed to appear they went inside and found he had crawled into a narrow passage in the ceiling of the cave to escape the smoke and had become stuck and suffocated to death.

They took his body, severed the dog's head from it, and gave the two parts a ritual burial at either ends of the island.

'I feel sorry for the creature,' said Hupa. 'He and his fiendish hounds were created by some warped sorcerer. It was no fault of the Kopuwai that he was a monster. It might have been kinder to have captured him and set him free on some uninhabited isle where he could do no harm.'

'Then some poor unsuspecting castaway might end up on the island and be eaten for breakfast,' replied her brother Kapu. 'In any case, he was so ferocious it would take an army to get him into a cage alive. I wouldn't want to be one of those who tried it.'

Hupa shrugged. 'I just felt sorry for him,' she repeated.

Attention was then taken up by the arrival of the Hawaiian fleet under one of the sons of Nana-Ula, King of Hawaii. On board, much to the delight of ex-Arioi members like Craig, was the famous Oceanian bard and astrologer, Kama-Hau-Lele. This old man had recited epic poems on the voyages and exploits of ancestor heroes, during Nana-Ula's passage from his original homeland in Tahiti to the island of Hawaii.

'Kama-Hau-Lele is one of our greatest people,' Craig told his father. 'And I am going to meet him.'

Seumas said sourly, '*Your* people.'

'And yours,' replied Craig. 'You have been here longer than you were ever in your birthland. You are an Oceanian now, Father, whether you like it or not. Your Picts would not recognize you as one of themselves now.'

The Hawaiian war fleet was one of the most magnificent sights Craig had ever seen. Though the canoes were necessarily voyagers they had flying war pennants of yellow, red and black streaming from the prows. High, curving staves came out of the prows, elaborately carved, with Tikis standing on their tops facing the occupants of the canoes, rather than the open sea to the front. Warrior platforms had been built fore and aft and were now full of chiefs in splendid yellow and red cloaks and capes falling from their shoulders. On their heads they wore tall glossy helmets, which gleamed in the bright sunlight, their colours reflected in the shimmering lagoon waters.

Hupa, standing with Craig, professed to have lost her breath in the wonder of the sight. Seumas and Boy-girl were quietly admiring the scene. Kieto was now up and on his feet, almost his old self, and was off somewhere else, greeting the son of Nana-Ulu.

'I hear the Hawaiians fight in a crescent-shaped formation, like that of a quarter moon,' said Hupa. 'Their warriors are greatly feared for they seem invincible in battle.'

Craig, who no longer wore his hair in the Hivan style of two horns jutting from his head, felt bland and dull beside these men and women who imitated the birds in their appearance. He had seen such splendour before, amongst the Tahitians, but not to this degree. The Hawaiians seemed to him to be a higher form of life, a magnificent people, each one of them a prince.

The Hawaiians began to come ashore accompanied by the music of drums and flutes and other woodwind instruments. One of the drummers glanced at Craig as he passed, seemingly noticing his three bar tattoos. The man then looked back with a puzzled expression, to inspect Craig's legs. His eyes opened wide when he saw the painted one. Finally he looked up at Craig's hair, as his companions began to wonder what was the matter with him, since they were trying to keep time to his drum.

'Red hair!' cried the Hawaiian, excitedly. 'Painted Leg!'

All the musicians stopped and the chiefs and lesser individuals marching up from the shallows on to the shore with much pomp and circumstance stared disapprovingly at this little knot of young Hawaiians failing in their duty.

Now one of the flautists took up the shout. 'It is the famed Kumiki, the drummer of the Arioi! He is here! He is here!'

They rushed forward excitedly to crowd around the embarrassed Craig. They showered him with questions, telling him they had heard of his marvellous drumming, and wished he would give them a performance. Hawaiian chiefs then came and stood with the group, catching some of the excitement, realizing who it was that had caused the fuss. Finally the crowd parted for an old man with a crooked stave, who came up slowly and stood before Craig.

'I am Kama-Hau-Lele,' he said, staring into Craig's flushed features. 'You are the Painted Leg, Kumiki?'

Craig looked into the kindly face of the old man, covered with wisdom lines.

'Yes,' whispered Craig, finding himself confronted by one of his heroes. 'I am Kumiki.'

'Will you play for us, young man? Tonight, at the feasting? I have been told your performances are unequalled in the skill of their rendering.'

'And I, yours,' said Craig, growing bolder. 'Perhaps you would favour us with one of your stories, if I take to the drums this evening?'

The old man smiled. 'It will be fair exchange.'

The young man who had first noticed Craig was busy collecting shells from the hands of his friends and, after the crowd had broken up, Craig asked him what it was about.

'Why, I won my wager,' said the Hawaiian drummer. 'I whispered to the others that you would play for us – they bet against it. We Hawaiians love to gamble, on anything, anything at all,' he laughed. 'You seem puzzled.'

'We do not know this sport,' said Craig. 'Father, have you heard of "gambling"?'

'Oh, I've heard of it all right,' said the crusty Seumas. 'It's a fool's game. You can lose all you have in a single evening. I once knew a man who lost his wife and children to another, simply because he thought his beetle could win a race against a frog over twenty paces. Another man bet a companion that he could gather fifty eggs in one morning, from tall sheer cliffs in a high wind. He failed and lost the croft which had taken him six months to build.'

Craig grinned. 'That egg man was you, wasn't it, Father?'

'It could have been,' said Seumas, 'and if it was, you can be sure I'll never gamble on anything again.'

The Hawaiian youth laughed at these exchanges, saying, 'I love to gamble. Nothing would stop me. If I had a kingdom I would gamble it for another.'

'Then there's no help for you, young man,' Seumas said. 'You are lost to the world.'

'What about archery,' Hupa said. 'Do you wager on the outcome of archery?'

The boy noticed her bow and quiver of arrows.

'It is one of the major events on which we gamble.'

'Would you like to gamble on me hitting something now?' she asked, stringing an arrow.

Craig put his hand on her arm. 'Not now. Later, when you have some competition, Hupa.'

'A young maiden?' said the youth. 'I'd bet against you anytime – our archers are brilliant.'

Hupa nodded, putting away her arrow.

Craig said, 'All right, you get your best archer and then we'll have a little competition.'

'Excellent!' cried the youth.

That night at the feasting, Craig played his drums for the Hawaiians, who listened enraptured. Seumas could not help but feel immensely proud of his son. One or two Hivans present claimed him as their own, as did the Rarotongans. When a hero emerges from the crowd he is divided up amongst his fellows.

Afterwards, true to his word, Kama-Hau-Lele told the story of how the demi-god Maui and his father pushed the sky further up so that people below it had more room.

'Rangi the Sky-God and Papa the Earth-Goddess had already been forced apart by Tane's children, the trees,' intoned the old man, 'but at that time trees were themselves bent double by the weight of the sky and people had to crawl around on their hands and knees, trying to get their work done – their fishing and hunting, their growing of crops, their building of low squat houses – while in this crouched position.

'Even the sun was upset with the situation, since it could not travel very far over this low region, which meant men spent most of their time in darkness.

'Finally, Maui decided he had had enough of working under a low sky made of blue rock against which everyone cracked their heads and knocked their noses on sharp and blunt projections. He asked for his father, who was a minor god called Irawhaki, and suggested that the two of them lift the sky up higher. His father agreed that it was a poor state of affairs when men could not do their work for fear of breaking their skulls.

'The pair of them put their shoulders under the sky and gradually forced it higher and higher. When they had it almost head-high they started to push with their hands, but even when it was above their heads it was still not high enough. Maui's father, being a god, made himself and his youngest son grow tall while still pushing up against the sky. Eventually the blue rock was way above the heads of people, above the tops of the trees, and even higher than the tallest mountain.

'Maui's father then told his son he had worked enough and went back to his favourite Underground world, which was not the world of the dead, but some other place where a different kind of people lived. The same world in fact which Maui discovered when he lifted a house post and looked down through the hole to see people moving about below the earth.

'Still the sky did not look quite right to Maui, who was more artistically inclined than was Irawhaki. The trickster hero did not like the rough bits, sticking out all over the place, and he climbed up onto the sky and with a stone hammer knocked off all the knobs and sharp projections. Then he smoothed out the bumps. Finally the sky was as you see it today, a beautiful flat blue dome of rock.'

Craig was spellbound by the deep, resonant timbre of the orator, and nodded enthusiastically when the story was finished.

'I like that,' Seumas said, 'father and son doing things together. But one thing I've never understood. Why is everyone so keen on him, this Maui.'

'It's because he's one of five brothers,' replied Craig, 'and is in fact the youngest. Our culture is full of stories of younger brothers, their ranking in the family being very low, using their ingenuity and cunning to raise their status.'

The following morning there was an archery competition. Since people had been talking about it at the feast the night before the whole affair had expanded. Many youths and some maidens – Craig suspected they were all from Hupa's secret society, the Whakatane – gathered to test their skills against one another.

Before the contest started the Hawaiian and Raiatean youths were scoffing at the young women, asking them why they were pretending to be good at manly sports. Their taunts died on their lips, however, when the maidens began to put arrows in the targets. Finally it came down to a match between one of the Whakatane and a Hawaiian youth. By this time many of the gamblers in the crowd were quietly backing the maiden.

They lost their bets, but only by a very narrow margin. It was clear to the men that the women were just as good as they were with the bow and arrow and that only good fortune had allowed one of their number to triumph in the end. A second contest might have easily had a female winner. The men went away quietly and soberly, a little wiser than before the competition had begun.

'Well done, Hupa,' said Craig. 'Pity about that last arrow.'

Hupa had been knocked out of the competition earlier than her skills really deserved, but she expressed satisfaction that the men had not run away with the contest.

'I think we women showed them that they had better keep their mouths shut the next time they see one of us with a weapon in our hands.'

'I believe you've given them more than enough to think about – the Hawaiians lost a lot of their wagers in the beginning, when they were betting on their boys.'

Hupa nudged him and gave him a little satisfied smile.

'Good,' she said.

The combined fleets of Rarotonga, Raiatea and Hawaii set sail for Tongatapu, where they would rendezvous with the Samoan, Hivan, Tongan, Fijian, Tahitian and many, many other fleets to form one mighty armada for the invasion of Land-of-Mists. Coloured banners flowed in the breezes, crab-claw sails filled their chests with wind, steering oars cut the surf.

On board the tipairua and other craft, navigators conferred with navigators, comparing shell charts and talking of points of the windflower. Captains called to captains, wishing each other the fortune of the gods, especially Tangoroa, the Great Sea-God, on whose back they would be scudding. Crew called to crew and warriors to warriors. A great excitement was in the air as Ra crossed the blue roof of voyaging and smiled down upon the brave Oceanians about to dare the unknown. Sacrifices were made to Ira, Mother of the Stars, under whose guidance the vessels would remain for the next several months.

Kahuna and tohunga were busy with rituals amongst the voyagers and in the temples on the island. Ancestors were being petitioned, asked to act as mediators between the people and the gods. Fires were burning offerings and ahu were smothered with fruit and meat, awaiting unseen hands to bear them away. Religion and magic were humming through the trees, whistling through the rigging of the canoes, crackling through the hair of the seafarers.

They received a tumultuous send-off as Raiateans, and even people who had canoed all the way from Borabora, massed on the beaches to wave them away. Drums pounded on sea and shore. Blossoms were tossed into the ocean to float on the waves. Tiki in his many images set his face to Te muri on the windflower.

Once out on the ocean the fleets did not attempt to keep in constant touch with one another. There was no sense in clustering so many craft together over such a long distance. In certain circumstances – a squall or a fierce wind – it might even be dangerous. They might be driven into one another. In any case, some were faster and went ahead, others preferred a different use of the wind, a slightly different course. After the first few days they fragmented, spread over the face of the sea, yet most in sight of at least one other craft.

The crews and passengers fell into their usual routine of dividing the day up into three parts, so that one watch was always awake, always on the alert. On Polahiki's craft that unwashed but reliable sailor allowed the main fleet to sail close to the wind, while he took a course which he knew would lead him into faster currents that would eventually assist his voyager in overtaking the other canoes.

Inevitably he eventually found himself alone. Sighting a green glow on a distant cloudbase, he knew there was an island with a reflecting lagoon beneath. They were beginning to run short of supplies on board, having lost a batch of coconuts to a freak wave. He decided to stop at this unknown island and stock up on whatever the place had to offer.

It was dawn as Hine-tu-whenua gently assisted the canoe into a rather pretty and tranquil lagoon with colourful corals, which seemed to be teeming with fish, crabs, eels and shellfish. There was no smoke coming from the island, no signs of it being inhabited. It seemed they had stumbled accidentally on a Faraway Heaven. Seumas, Hupa, Craig and the Boy-girl were standing on deck as the tipairua cruised into the turquoise inner waters and bumped gently against the coral sands of the shallows.

'Right,' cried Polahiki, 'water and coconuts, and anything else we can find. Let's get to it. Come on, move yourselves. I want to be away from here before darkness falls. I don't trust these lonely islands stuck out in the middle of nowhere.'

'What a forceful captain we seem to have chosen for ourselves,' murmured Boy-girl. 'Well, I for one am going to see what lies beyond the shoreline trees.'

'Is that wise?' asked Seumas. 'You know we've got into trouble that way before. What if this island is a magical island? Perhaps there's a fierce taniwha just waiting to devour some poor wayward sailor . . .'

'I haven't seen a taniwha yet,' said the excited Hupa. 'Perhaps we should go to look for one?'

'I'm too old for that sort of thing,' replied Seumas. 'It's true, however, that all the magical islands I've visited so far have not been attractive at first sight. They're usually hot and sultry, with dead coral lagoons and ugly mangroves that come right up the waterline. This island looks as if it's just been modelled in the hands of some happy god.'

'Well, I'm not too old,' Boy-girl said, 'not quite yet. I think this place is absolutely charming. There are not even any flies or unpleasant insects in the air. And listen to the birds singing! What about you, young Craig? Will you come with us? Let's go and explore the hinterland, just for a short way.'

'I'd better go to make sure you don't get into any trouble,' Craig answered.

Hupa did not like this reply and told him so. She said she was quite capable of taking care of herself. Craig apologized, saying he knew how competent she was, '. . . But you need more than youthful courage, Hupa – you need experience too. I have been to many strange islands in my time. So has Boy-girl. You've only just left Rarotonga.'

So the three of them went inshore, leaving Seumas to supervise the gathering of the stores with Polahiki.

2

Once the three explorers had got past the initial tree line, they came upon hilly grasslands beyond. It was an amazing place. Craig told Hupa that it was somewhat similar to the landscape Seumas had described to him when speaking of Land-of-Mists. One or two trees studded the scene, but for the most part it was like a green swell out on the ocean, dipping and rising in a smooth feminine way, with valleys which dropped into clefts through which streams tumbled and rushed, banks of wild flowers on either side.

The three companions strolled across a meadow dripping with small plants whose tiny blooms caused their stalks to curve over gracefully in miniature arches. Insects like small bright stones hummed and buzzed above the plants. Birds dropped down into the tangled grasses, to rise again with something in their beaks: a piece of dried hay; a fluffy windblown seed; a fragment of food. Pockets of herbs here and there exuded wonderful fragrances.

'How delightful,' said Boy-girl. 'Have you ever seen anything more entrancing?'

A lethargy began to creep through Hupa. She watched as the others sighed and stretched out on the grass. Craig was settled a bit further away. Boy-girl allowed her elegant length to decorate a hillock nearby. The three of them rested there in the warm sunshine, each pair of eyes gradually closing as the balmy breezes caressed their lashes. Finally, they all dropped off to sleep within a short time of each other.

When Hupa awoke there was a cool breeze blowing up the hillside which chilled her. Boy-girl was snoring softly, still in the same spot where she had fallen asleep. Craig was nowhere to be seen, an impression in the grass where his body had lain.

Hupa sat up and stared all around. The scene had not changed except for the shadows of the clouds which now swept across it. What a stupid thing it had been to fall off to sleep in a place of which they knew nothing! The three of them could have been slaughtered while they dozed, by some tribe of people, or perhaps a taniwha. And where was Craig now? Surely he would not have gone off without waking her and Boy-girl.

'Boy-girl, wake up!' cried Hupa. 'Craig's gone.'

Boy-girl stirred, sat up and rubbed her eyes, the ornaments in her hair and on her clothes rattling.

'What? What is it? Did I drop off for a moment?'

'We've all been deeply asleep for ages,' answered Hupa, striding about. 'And now Craig's missing. He wouldn't have gone off and just left us, would he?'

Boy-girl suddenly came to her senses. 'No, he would not.' She felt her head. 'Some of my shells are gone,' she said, 'and one or two ribbons. Who would have stolen them? Who *could* have, without waking me. Look, there are tiny handprints on my tapa skirt. Can you see anything? Any tracks?'

'I'm just looking,' replied Hupa, peering at the ground. Then she came across a tiny track where the grass had been flattened. Near to this were footprints, made by some person. They had to be Craig's imprints. Here and there was a crushed flower, a squashed fungus. Whoever or whatever had taken Craig, it seemed he had gone by persuasion rather than force, since the prints were indicative of a casual stroll.

And why would they take just one of the three, leaving the other two? It did not make sense. Had Craig been walking in his sleep? Why hadn't he shouted an alarm?

'I'm going to follow these tracks,' said Hupa. 'You go back to the beach and tell Polahiki what has happened.'

'Shouldn't we both go back to the canoe?' asked the elderly Boy-girl. 'I mean, it might be dangerous for you.'

'I'm well armed,' replied Hupa. 'Would you argue with me if I was Craig and it had been *me* who had been abducted.'

'No,' said Boy-girl, truthfully, 'but you are the daughter of our war chief. I – I feel somehow responsible for you. I'm not sure it's right for me to let you go.'

'There's no right or wrong about it,' snapped Hupa. 'I'm going and that's flat. You either come with me or you go back and get some help. One or the other.'

'Since you put it like that, then I haven't got a great deal of choice, have I? Be careful, Hupa. As Craig said, you have the ability, but not yet the experience. Take things very slowly, weigh up situations . . .'

'Yes, yes,' replied Hupa, now walking down the other side of the meadow. 'Tell the others.'

The impetuous young maiden was soon striding out, following a plain trail across the meadow. Through brook and vale she went, past woodland copse and over downy slopes. Now the clouds were racing her on the roof of voyaging above, like canoes anxious to get back to haven before the night fell. Their boating shadows rippled over the hills ahead, disappearing into the mountains beyond. The island was larger than Hupa had first imagined, having a high range of crescent peaks.

To keep her spirits up Hupa began to quote poetry, often turning it into tune with her high clear singing voice.

She felt it was pointless to remain quiet. Whoever had stolen her companion away knew she was there in any case. On and on she went, following the clear track until she suddenly realized she was not alone, that there were creatures around her, walking along and keeping pace with her.

She glanced about her in surprise to see fair-haired women and men no larger than children half her height. They were not looking at her, but simply strolling along beside her and behind her. Dressed in a gauze material which billowed gently in the wind and revealed their perfectly beautiful naked forms beneath, they seemed quite undisturbed by the fact that she had discovered them. In their hair and about their bodies they had the swollen blooms of multi-hued flowers, dozens of them. The perfume from these was overwhelming. On their arms and legs were strange shimmering tattoos, but none on their torsos or their faces.

Hupa knew at once she was in the presence of fairies.

She stopped and asked one of them, a male, 'Are you the Peerless Ones, the Tipairu of the hills and forests?'

'No,' the fairy replied, his voice sounding like the rustling of crisp dry leaves. 'We are a different race of fairies – the Turehu of Rarohenga.'

'Rarohenga?' she said, alarmed. 'I have heard from our storytellers that Rarohenga is a land below the earth.'

'This is true,' replied a female fairy, her long, light, tawny hair lifting in the breeze, 'but here in this land we may come up for one month of the year.'

'Can you tell me where my companion is?' she asked the fairy, fearfully. 'He is a man with red hair.'

'Yes,' said another fairy as they crowded around her, touching her legs and waist with their tiny delicate fingers, 'the beautiful man whose hair is the colour of the evening sun is with the King of the Fairies, Uetonga. There are plans to marry him to Princess Niwareka. There is to be dancing. It will make the flowers burst forth on the hillside.

There is to be music. It will make the blossoms spring to the branches of the trees.'

'Who is Princess Niwareka?'

'Why, she is the daughter of the king, of course,' came back the answer, accompanied by tinkling laughter. 'She is a fairy of incomparable beauty, whose lovely form makes the trees sigh with contentment. She is much prettier than *you*. Niwareka is virtue itself. She is purity itself. Niwareka is as chaste as spindrift on the waters of the ocean. Not like some we could mention, if we felt like being rude to strangers.'

The fairy looked pointedly at Hupa and its companions tittered nastily.

Hupa was taken aback by this reply, but only for a moment. She realized that the fairies believed her to be Craig's lover and expected her to be jealous. They were expounding the virtues of their princess because they believed Hupa wished to win Craig back from this creature.

'I'll have you know I'm a virgin too,' said Hupa, assertively, 'and I have no desire to have a lover at the moment. In any case, the man you have in captivity is already married and is the father of children. Would you steal a man away from the wife he loves for your own selfish requirements?'

'Yes,' replied the fairy, simply. 'We are selfish creatures, don't you know?'

The Turehu led Hupa to a village surrounded by a natural briar hedge covered in finger-long thorns. One of the fairies trilled a strange language. A spiked gate swung open and the small creatures bustled Hupa through it. Inside the rolling hedge of thorns there were small huts with carved portals and one large meeting house in the centre of the village.

Around the meeting house were clustered a thousand more fairies, with one rather petulant-looking, slightly corpulent male sitting on a throne carved out of a living pohutukawa tree in full bloom. He was cushioned on red blossoms that seemed to curl lovingly around his compact form.

Hupa guessed this must be King Uetonga. As she looked into his eyes, she could see they were purple with tawny flecks. They were not the eyes of a human. They looked as if they belonged in some exotic animal, some fabulous creature from another world. His bountiful sandy hair billowed long and soft around his small body, making his head appear twice as large as that of anyone else. Like the other fairies he was wearing some sort of wispy material which was wafted by the slightest of breezes.

'Who is this who comes here?' cried the king. 'Another person from the outside? Have you brought me presents? A fine cloak? A leather carving?'

'I have come for my friend,' said Hupa, boldly. 'The other member of our tribe who you hold here.'

'The man I enthralled? He must stay. He is to marry my daughter. If you have no gifts for the King of Fairies, for the Lord of the Turehu, then you must go quickly, before we trick the eyes from your head, or the toes from your feet.'

But Hupa was determined not to leave without Craig, who would be lost forever if she did not get him out from under the fairies' spell quite soon. Once the small creatures returned to Rarohenga, below the earth, Craig would never be able to find his way back, even if he wanted to leave them. And they were very good at making mortals believe they *wanted* to stay.

She strolled away from the main knot of fairies and stood at the back when Craig came forth, his eyes vacant-looking and a silly smile on his face. By his side was a fairy with tawny hair so long it trailed after her in the dust. Her face was as pretty as a white shell. She had a sweet smile on her lovely features and kept looking up at the stupefied Craig, as if he were the most handsome creature in the whole of Oceania.

'You see!' cried the king, for Hupa's benefit, 'he does not want to leave. He loves my daughter, the fairy princess. And she dotes on him – adores him. You have lost him.'

Hupa ignored this and remained in the village until nightfall. The fairies did not seem to go to bed at all, but danced the night away, and looked just as refreshed in the morning. Their music kept Hupa awake most of the night, though she managed to get some rest. Fairies came up to her in the morning, their faces flushed with the excitement of the dances, to place garlands of flowers around her neck.

Craig looked worn out, but still there was more dancing as the dawn turned to a full light.

'I want to take this man away with me,' she said, confronting the fairy king once again. 'What must I do to make you let him go?'

The king looked her directly in the eyes and her mind began to spin in giddy circles.

'Can you play a flute so sweetly that we will be beguiled by your talent and be forced to let him go?' asked the king.

'No,' admitted Hupa, 'I have no musical skills.'

'Can you recite poetry so beautiful it robs one of breath to hear it?'

'No, I have written no poems or songs.'

'Can you sing in a voice that will charm the scarlet pohutukawa blossoms from the trees?'

'I cannot play, I cannot recite, I cannot sing.'

'Then what can you do?'

In a flash she fitted an arrow to her bow and aimed it directly at the king.

'I can split your tiny heart in two from a hundred paces,' she said, 'with one eye closed.'

There was a gasp from the fairies, who stopped dancing immediately. They stared in horror at this mortal maiden who was threatening their king with her weapon. Princess Niwareka let out a high-pitched cry.

The king gave Hupa a faint smile.

'What, would you kill a fairy king with flint and wood? Don't you know it is stone and tree from which we fairies spring?'

'This haft has an arrowhead made of iron, from the teeth of Lioumere the ogress! These are magic arrows. They never miss their target. Look into my eyes if you doubt the truth of this statement, for I'm sure a fairy king can separate truth from lies from the mouth of a mortal.'

The fairies gasped in shock yet again.

'Iron?' said the fairy king, weakly. 'What is *iron*?'

Hupa repeated what she had been told by Seumas.

'Iron is metal. Metal is the essence, the very soul of stone. It will bring kings low. It will level armies. Iron will pierce the toughest wooden or hide shield, the strongest turtleshell breastplate. And – more important to one such as yourself, a fairy king – this iron is magical!'

Hupa turned and loosed her arrow at a palm. It struck the soft trunk like a neck of flesh and pierced it through. The sharp iron arrowhead split the slim trunk in two halves, which fell away from each other on each side. It was as if someone had cleft a piece of kindling with an axe. And this deed had been performed by a slim young maiden!

The fairy king stood up, now impressed by this maiden and the use of her weapon.

'You have more of these arrows with the magical iron points?'

Hupa spoke slowly, quietly and precisely, for fairies' ears are sensitive and fairy language is more formal than that normally used by ordinary people.

'I have three such arrows and this magnificent bow, which was made for me by the Pict, Seumas-from-the-Blackwater. He is a mountain goblin from a strange place, called Land-of-Mists. The man you have captive, Craig with the red hair, is the son of Seumas-the-Black. I ask you to release him or I will surely kill you, King Uetonga.'

There was another gasp from the watching fairies,

obviously appalled that this human was threatening their king, even though they knew him to be immortal. They moved back, expecting Uetonga to shrivel her with a look. Instead the wise royal creature cocked his head to one side and smiled.

'You are in love with this man, or you would not dare menace a fairy king in his own land.'

Hupa blushed to the roots of her hair.

'I thought so,' said Uetonga. 'My daughter was told never to take a man who was beloved by his own kind, but to be sure he was free and loose, like a log drifting on the ocean.' He turned to Niwareka. 'What, daughter? Did you think to steal another maiden's lover? I am of the feeling he must go back.'

Princess Niwareka stepped forward, her pale face turning pink with passion.

'NO!' she cried.

'Quiet, daughter,' replied the king.

Uetonga stood up and stepped down from his throne to stand in front of Hupa. The top of his billowing hair, like a dandelion in seed, only came up to Hupa's waist. Yet she could sense a tremendous power in this little being. There was the feeling that if he wished he could leave her charred to a crisp with a mere click of his fingers.

Yet the Turehu were known to be honest fairies, who struck bargains more often than they stole. The king took another of the arrows from the quiver at Hupa's waist and examined the point carefully.

'It's very sharp,' he said, 'smooth and heavy.'

'There is nothing like it in all Oceania.'

'Show me to how to shoot your bow.'

Hupa instructed the king, who seemed to pick up the technique remarkable quickly. Soon a second arrow thudded into a palm tree, which then split in twain as before. The king kept hold of the bow after he had shot the arrow. He reached across and took the third arrow with the iron tip from Hupa's quiver. He fitted the arrow to the cord and aimed it at Hupa's heart. She lifted her chin and stood without a tremble. The fairies waited with bated breath for the release of the arrow, but finally the king eased the tension on the bow.

'Take your bow and arrows,' he said, handing them to her. 'Now let us hear from the redhair. I think I might release him, if I have a mind to.'

With that he snapped his fingers and Craig shook his head as if coming out of a trance. Princess Niwareka screamed shrilly enough to burst the eardrums of a hog. She clung to Craig, who was now looking bewildered.

'I found him,' she shrieked, hurting Hupa's ears. 'I found him asleep on the cold hillside. I beguiled him with sweet honey dew delivered from my very own lips. I kissed him awake, I kissed him entranced, I made sweet love to him. I *want* him. I *want* him. He's mine. You can't let him go. I *want* him, I tell you! I will keep him.'

She stamped her foot and several patches of flowers nearby withered and died. She spat fury at the ring of fairies closing around her and a tree shrivelled down to its roots. She blew hot air down her sweet little nose and a stream dried up leaving its fish to gasp and choke in the air.

'What's happening?' Craig asked, looking as if he thought he were still caught in a nightmare. 'Where am I?'

'You were on your way to Rarohenga, courtesy of King Uetonga, grandson of Ruau-Moko, God of Earthquakes,' replied Hupa. 'You have been captured by fairies, but the gracious and generous king is about to set you free.'

'Perhaps,' replied Uetonga, his expression entirely enigmatic. 'Perhaps.'

'And who is this?' asked Craig, trying to shake off the wailing princess, who nonetheless clung to him like a ramora sticks to a shark. 'What have I done to her?'

'Nothing,' smiled Hupa. 'She wants you to love her.'

The normally pretty princess's face was now screwed up

into something quite ugly. Craig stared at her in pity. One
or two fairies wrenched the princess from him, prising her
little fingers open to get her to let go. She bit the hands of
several of her companions with her tiny white teeth, leaving a perfect crescent of marks on their skin. She scratched
at their faces. They seemed used to her tantrums and
laughed.

'Niwareka needs a constant supply of young mortal
males to woo,' said the king. 'There are twelve unhappy
bridegrooms already in Rarohenga, discards of my fickle
daughter. They are all deeply in love with her. They pine for
her company, they sigh and weep, but she pays them no
attention. Once she has had a pretty human for a short
time, she grows tired of him. This may be your fate too,
young man, unless you impress me.'

'If I can't have *him*,' said Niwareka, her tear-stained
face coming up out of her hands for a moment, 'I want
some presents. Give me some beautiful whalebone carv-
ings: some scrimshaws fashioned by a seafaring man. Give
me some precious shells: a wentletrap, a glory-of-the-seas,
a sun shell. Give me some scarlet feathers from the kula
bird. I want tapa bark cloth with nice brown patterns.
I want pretty pearls from the ocean bed. I want – I want –
I want . . .'

'You shall be quiet, daughter, and show some gracious-
ness in your defeat.'

The king spoke sternly to Niwareka, but Hupa could tell
he was distressed by her behaviour. Uetonga obviously
loved his daughter to distraction. There was some indication in the king's tone that it was by no means certain that
Craig would go free at the end of it all.

Hupa desperately searched her mind for some way of
showing King Uetonga that Craig was unique. Her eyes
fell upon his painted leg. Of course, the *drums*, what else?
Fairies loved exciting rhythms almost as much as dancing.

'Perhaps your daughter would like the young man to

play the drum for her – he has been favoured by Lingadua, One-armed God of the Drums,' said Hupa. 'Craig, show us how you create your rhythms. Give us a display of your talent.'

Uetonga seemed very interested and nodded. 'Yes, young man – if you please me, you will buy your freedom.'

A small drum was brought, the largest the fairies owned, a sharkskin over the end of a hollowed log.

Hupa said, 'Play, Craig.'

Craig did not bother with sticks, but used the tips of his fingers and the palms of his hands to create a wonderful rhythm which had the fairies hopping and skipping. They jigged up and down, whirled each other around, did triple somersaults through the air. King Uetonga looked on, a slow smile gathering about the corners of his mouth and eyes. Clearly here was a man who had magic in his hands, beloved of the god Lingadua.

When Craig had finished the fairies crowded round him, catching their breath.

'May we go now?' asked Hupa, quietly.

'Leave us,' said the king, nodding. 'Be on your way.'

Niwareka let out another of her shrieks. This one split a third trunk in two halves, as perfectly as one of Hupa's arrows.

'Will she be all right?' asked Hupa, anxiously. 'She sounds as if she's unhappy.'

'My daughter,' said the magenta-eyed king, 'will never be all right.' He then turned to Craig again. 'Before you go young man, you may wish for some gift from us, to compensate for your distress. We have troubled you without your permission, so now you may ask something of us. Anything, name it – it shall be yours.'

At this point Hupa realized Craig could ask for riches – scarlet feathers, money cowries, livestock, many canoes – or fame – to be raised high in rank, to have some ambition for status fulfilled. He could have asked for long life, for everlasting health, for undying love. *Anything*, the fairy king had said.

Craig glanced first at Hupa, then stared at Uetonga, as if hesitating, as if what he was about to request was impossible, too much, even for a fairy king.

'I wish to understand my father,' said Craig, quietly.

The fairy king replied, 'It is done.'

Hupa took Craig's hand and led him from the fairy place, through the gateway of thorns, away from the village where the lovely Niwareka was stretched full length on the green turf, her sobbing face buried in the grasses. Craig seemed to come reluctantly.

'Hadn't we better make sure she's all right?' he said.

Hupa pulled him away with her. 'You're still besotted with her, Craig. It's not real love. It's fairy magic. Now think of your wife and children. Do you want to spend eternity in some underworld, pining along with all the other bridegrooms who've been discarded by that spoiled little bitch?'

'That's not the sort of language I'm used to expecting from you,' said Craig, stiffly.

'You'll hear worse if you don't hurry away with me,' replied Hupa, firmly. 'Stop dragging your heels.'

When they reached the brow of a hill they saw a group of people from the canoe coming towards them. There were Boy-girl, Seumas and the Farseeing-virgin, Kikamana, with several armed mariners. When Hupa reached them she said to two of the sailors, 'Get hold of this one. Don't let him go.'

Craig protested but Seumas could see she was deadly serious.

'Do as she says,' he confirmed.

On the way back to the canoe, during which Craig put up a half-hearted struggle, Hupa told Seumas, Boy-girl and Kikamana the story of Craig's capture by Uetonga's daughter. Kikamana was enthralled. She said she had never seen fairies in that number. One or two flitting through the shafts of sunbeams and shadows in a forest, playing touch-and-run in the half-light, but never a whole host of fairies.

'You are very privileged, young woman,' said the ancient Kikamana.

'It doesn't feel like it,' said the more pragmatic Hupa. 'I feel as if I've been into the jaws of sharks and have managed to escape unscathed by sheer good fortune.'

When they had Craig on board again, the canoe set sail. He stood at the mast, staring wistfully at the island as it slowly grew smaller in their wake. No one knew what was going on in his mind, but many could guess. He had fallen, or been made to fall, violently in love with one of the most beautiful creatures in the world, and was now being forced to leave her.

Seumas told his son to snap out of it.

'You're lucky you had a sensible girl like Hupa along with you.'

'I suppose so,' sighed Craig, 'but it's so hard.'

'Self-pity is something I can't stand to see,' Seumas said to Hupa. 'It sickens me to my stomach.'

'Do you mean pining over a woman you can't have?' she replied in an innocent voice. 'In the way that you languish over Dorcha?'

Seumas looked up with narrowed eyes, having been caught entirely off his guard.

'It's not the same,' he said.

'Oh, but I think it is,' replied Hupa, smiling tenderly at the old man. 'And you know it is too.'

He bent his head to his task, declining to reply.

Before she left him, Seumas asked her, 'Are the arrows really magical?'

'Of course,' said Hupa. 'At first I believed my aim had improved, but when I found I could not miss, even with my eyes closed and visualizing the target – I knew then it was not my skill, but the arrows.'

'It would be better to keep this to yourself.'

Hupa nodded. 'I agree – the fewer people know this, the better. There are forces out there which work against us. We would not want these to fall into the wrong hands.'

Seumas nodded, turning away, the guilt flooding through him.

PART FIVE

The sea raiders

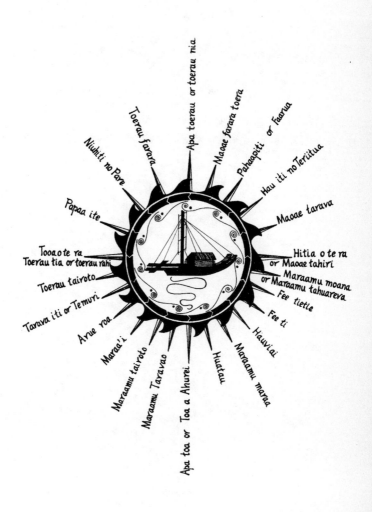

1

Maomao, God of the Winds, was busy using all his resources to get the individual fleets to arrive at Tongatapu more or less at the same time. Tangoroa, the Great Sea-God, was also fully employed in such tasks. Oro, the God of War, and others followed behind the active Maomao and Tangoroa, he reshaping and cleaning his weapons of war and the others occupied with similar tasks. Other gods, like Ara Tiotio, God of the Whirlwind and Tornado, were necessarily doing nothing at all, simply keeping themselves quiet and peaceful.

Many of the smaller and less important gods had come along with the Great and Powerful, to be part of the glorious battle with a foreign foe. Amai-te-rangi, the god who angled for humans from the sky, was there with his fishing line and wicker basket. So too was Ulupoka, the god known as The Head, though his body was elsewhere. And Paikea, the God of Sea Monsters, with his following of giant octopuses, squid and gargantuan creatures for which man had no set name.

There were also potent local gods, such as Kukailimoku, the Hawaiians' God of War, without whom they would not consider going into battle.

All these followed in the wake of the two gods who

managed the safety and direction of the Oceanian fleets, as
they ploughed their way through benign seas to their meeting place. The gods were aware that down below, on the
decks, there was martial singing and orations in progress.

Since Hiro had returned with the art of writing, there
were men and women recording the events of the voyage by
using charcoal to mark rush matting. The gods had nothing
against *writing* as an art form, though not many of them
understood it or saw the need for it, since they had given
mankind 'memory' which should have been sufficient tool
for recording purposes.

The same with poetry and song.

It was the Goddess Papa who remarked that Oceanians
would soon lose their skill at remembering, if they continued to write everything down on a rush mat tube.

Kieto's voyage was not an easy one. He was still recovering
from the shock of losing his hand. But there were enough
able captains amongst his navigators to allow him plenty of
rest. When he arrived at Tongatapu there were fleets from
more than a hundred islands throughout Oceania, averag-
ing ten canoes for every island, each canoe carrying eighty
or more warriors. Eighty thousand warriors! It was a glorious sight.

Every so often the sound of conch horns drifted over
the quiet evening waters, telling of some new arrival.

'I suppose you thought this day would never come,
Seumas,' he said to the Pict. 'Well, here it is.'

'I *hoped* it would not,' replied Seumas.

That evening Seumas took his son aside.

'Craig,' he said, 'it's time I told you something.'

The two sat down by the mast, where a lamp was lit and
threw its yellow light over their shoulders. Craig remained
silent, knowing his father had something of a serious nature
to impart.

'You are aware,' said Seumas, 'that I killed a man, the

husband of Dorcha, back in my own land of Albainn. A Scot from the Kingdom of Dalriada, in those days ruled by Aidan-the-False. The Scots have their own region, you see, and the Picts have their Pictland. The two have always been at war, since the Scots came from over the sea to settle in Albainn. There were some people called "the Britons" around, but they have been of little account since the Scots arrived.

'Anyway, this Scot had an iron sword which I coveted. A sword with a *name*, which is always considered special in my homeland. I shall not tell you what the weapon was called, because that's unimportant now. What is important is that I was a savage man in those days and when I wanted something I would go out and fight for it until it was either mine or I was defeated. This was the way amongst the clans and I doubt it's changed very much.

'I don't know whether Dorcha was especially attached to her man, or whether her clan blood ran thicker than water, but she never really forgave me for that bad act. Perhaps it was just the act itself and not those involved which saddened her? I don't know. I could never fathom her soul to its depths, though I tried often enough.

'Don't get me wrong – it wasn't murder – I fought Douglass fair. He was a Scot, not from my people the Picts, and we might have indulged in single combat anyway, just because of our differences in race and clan. There were a dozen reasons to battle without the prize of the sword. Men of our stamp did not need excuses to cut each other down.

'All that is by the by, but in later years Dorcha confessed to me that she had a son, a boy of around ten years at the time we were whisked away by the Oceanians. Dorcha had not had much to do with the recent raising of that lad, even though he was hers, since her husband took him from her at six years of age and gave him to his own parents to raise thereafter, the grandfather of the boy being a man given to brutality and wanting to train the child in violent ways.

'He was also taught to despise the weaknesses of women, especially his mother's. Whenever the boy saw his mother after that he would abuse her, to prove to his grandfather how much he had learned in the art of spurning females. Dorcha suffered mental and physical mistreatment from her own.

'There was not much wrong with all this to the thinking of some people, even perhaps Dorcha, since a man had to be strong to survive at all. One had to make sure a boy could survive hard winters out of doors, fight off wolves, kill intruders before they killed him. It would ensure the boy's future. A baby was breast-fed, weaned by the mother, but the infant was taken by the father and fed with the necessary skills of survival in a land where life outside the clan was cheap.

'In many clans of course the women were treated with respect and deference, but not in all.'

Seumas paused for thought, as if he had forgotten where he was going. Craig remained silent, waiting patiently for the point of the story. Seumas never wasted breath on simple tales, even the history of his past life.

'The trouble is,' continued the Pict, 'that boy will have grown to a man by now – grown *beyond* a man. He's about fifty winters, if he's still alive. He'll be looking for me. His whole life he'll have been looking for signs of Seumas from the Blackwater, in order to put matters to rights. The man who killed his father must be killed. Clan against clan, family against family, man against man. A blood feud.

'When you find yourself in the land of the Albanachs you must seek out Douglass son of Douglass and make your peace with him . . .'

Here Craig at last interrupted. 'You can do it yourself, Father – I shall help.'

'Certainly, if I am able, I shall do it,' replied Seumas, 'but

I am an old man. We may go into battle and lose and perhaps I may fall. Perhaps *you* may fall. What I say is, if for any reason I cannot go out and seek this man, you must do it for me. One can't leave such a bloodstain on the land without trying to rectify things. It's been a long time, perhaps Douglass son of Douglass has forgotten me – but I doubt it. I think he'll still have me in mind.'

'I'll do my best, though I'm sure you'll be able to do it yourself.'

'Just one more thing – he may call your adopted mother a *wipperjinny*. If you are there with me I command you as my son to stop me from striking him dead, as I'm most certain to do. If you are there alone, then you must swallow the insult put upon her and explain that she was never unfaithful in her head, only doing with her body what a woman with her own needs must do to live a normal life.'

'A wipperjinny?'

'A promiscuous woman.'

For the last part of this conversation, Boy-girl had been present, since there were no secrets, since there was nothing sacred, so far as she was concerned. The fact that this was between father and son meant nothing more to her than that she must be silent for much of the time. But not *all* the time.

She said, 'Seumas, if he is such a man now as you were when you came to us, he will not understand about a woman's needs. If I remember correctly, in the order of things precious, women came after cattle and dogs. Am I correct?'

'This is not to do with you, Boy-girl,' said Seumas, stiffly. 'This is between father and son.'

'Huh!' snorted Boy-girl derisively. 'What's so special about that? The fact is, you pompous old puffer fish, you're thinking of trying to impart civilized thoughts to a savage. It won't work. This Douglass will roar with laughter if Craig mentions his mother's sexual "needs". You know that, I know that, so why try to tell Craig differently?'

Seumas looked thunder at Boy-girl for a moment, then nodded his head slowly.

'Boy-girl's right, I suppose. You will simply have to suffer any insults.'

Seumas then went off to another part of the canoe. Boy-girl followed him, presumably to make her peace with the old man. Craig was left to consider his father's words.

There came a time when the whole fleet was assembled. Kieto then called all the navigators – many of them kings – to a meeting. There he laid out the route for them, to the Land-of-Mists. His memory maps, learned at the age of seven, were perfect. He was not of the new warriors, who relied on the art of writing, though he saw the immense worth of such a thing, and his recall had not suffered accordingly.

He began by telling the navigator kings the fundamental direction as discovered by Kupe when he chased the rene-gade octopus to the colder parts of the world.

'Sail to the left of the setting sun,' he said. 'This is the time of year when Kupe and myself crossed the dark, cold ocean from Tongatapu to the Land-of-Mists.'

Prince Daggan, leading the Raiatean fleet, stood up to speak. 'Through our atua we have learned that the gods approve of our great expedition,' said the prince, 'but how can they themselves know what lies in store for us? You have told us of ink-black seas, of hard cold waves, of fierce freezing currents likely to wrench a canoe off its course. What I wish to know is, are you fit enough to lead us through these deadly waters?'

Kieto said, 'I assume, Prince Daggan, you refer to my recent injury. It has healed well and good, thanks to the High Priestess Kikamana's ministrations. You need have no fear that I shall fail you at the helm. I have worked all my life towards this goal – nothing could make me pass leadership on to you or anyone else at this point.

'But,' he added, 'you may take your own fleet and return to your Faraway Heaven, if this does not meet with your approval.'

Daggan scowled. 'I shall stay,' he said, sitting down.

This interruption over, Kieto then proceeded to describe the navigational aids that the captains of each craft should look for, in case they became separated from the main fleet. There were, beside the rising and setting stars, certain wave shapes and strange swells; new types of driftwood, sea-weeds and birds; the sound of the sea in different regions, and many other smaller points of navigation.

When he had finished, Kieto told his fleet commanders to get some good rest.

'We sail in the morning.'

The next day's dawn was the colour of a chicken's wattle.

Group by group the crab-claw sails were raised and the mighty fleet began to sweep out into the ocean, on the heading of Arue roa on the windflower. Kieto had told all the captains that when they reached the Land-of-Mists they were to travel down the port coast to the bottom of the great island. There, where they had plucked Seumas from the waters, they would make their first landing. Kieto's reason for this was that Seumas knew nothing about the region of the Angles, which covered the top two thirds of Land-of-Mists. He did, however, know intimately his own landscape at the bottom-most tip of the island.

Nothing untoward occurred until the fleet reached the dark, cold waters of which Kieto foretold. Once in those hard, black waves which menaced the fleet on all sides, the leading canoes were attacked by a giant squid. Three tipairua were lost before frantic sailors managed to hack off two of the squid's tentacles and it submerged. Some said the squid was a friend of the octopus which the great Kupe had killed in these waters, but others reminded them that giant squids had no allies.

Next a school of monstrous whales plagued the fleet,
swimming and diving in and about the craft, churning the
water to a milky white froth which washed over the decks
and swept away many warriors, carrying them to a strange,
cold death below unfamiliar waves.

The horror with which the mariners regarded this unfamiliar ocean was universal. They could see no further than
the surface, below which the darkness of a deepest night
prevailed. Darkness and cold were the two aspects of the
natural world which Oceanians feared and abhorred, and
both were present in this miserable ocean in abundance.
The impenetrable nature of the waters gave vent to the
wildest imaginative terrors.

There were gargantuan monsters of immense size and
ferocity down there, it was said, which waited for victims
to enter the water before ripping them to shreds and
crunching their bones in jaws full of jagged teeth.

Some of the fish that were caught, though not of giant
size, gave a certain credence to these ideas. Lines which
went deep came up with ugly monstrosities: fish with huge
mouths, lumpy bodies and warty eyes. So repulsive were
they the fisherfolk threw them back, line and all, without
touching them.

One great eel, cold and slimy and thick as a man's thigh,
was as long as one of the canoes. It had small cold eyes
with which it regarded its captors and caused them to
believe some god of this ocean was using the eel as a *familiar* to view them at close quarters. They hacked the eel to
pieces and threw the bits back into the sea.

Although the fleet managed to avoid serious storms,
there were squalls which took canoes away in a white blizzard of scattered foam. Fierce cold winds sprang from
nowhere, counter to Maomao's efforts to help the fleet on
its path, to rip and tear at the mat sails, and sweep away
people without their hands on a lifeline. Black rocks suddenly reared up out of high seas, dripping and running

with green-white water. It was as if the ocean were alive with monstrous tors which surfaced like whales in the path of the voyagers.

Sometimes gloomy stretches of still inky water dipped and swayed before the lead canoes, harbouring sinister menace which no sailor could name.

It was on one of these oily expanses that Seumas fell sick with a chill.

'It's because I haven't been in this climate for so long,' he said to Hupa and Craig, as they sat by him, piling blankets on his thin shivering form. 'It's a shock.'

'How do you think it is for us?' said Craig, wryly. 'I've never experienced anything like it.'

'And this is summer . . .' replied Seumas, with an attempt at humour.

One morning a weak pale sun the colour of coral sand appeared in the sky. This brought with it a thick mist which swirled around the fleet, making them cling even more tightly together. They were locked together on still waters forming a massive raft, waiting for the mist to clear, when suddenly three long ships appeared off to starboard.

'Look!' cried Polahiki. 'War canoes!'

Craig, sitting by Seumas, looked up to see the three vessels, which had no outriggers, no double-hulls and a single square sail. Yet they were large, deckless craft, capable of carrying fifty or more men. They were long and sleek, with high curving prows. Weapons of war flashed in the weak sunlight as the intruders approached the raft of Oceanian canoes.

'Those canoes look like giant lizards,' gasped Craig. 'Father, look at them!'

Seumas went up on one elbow to view the oncoming craft.

The Oceanians who were watching this silent progress could see pale men manning the sleek vessels: men with dark, tawny and red hair. Burly, stone-faced men who looked like sea-washed versions of Seumas. They were wrapped in animal skins bound with leather thongs and there were thick, shiny bracelets on their forearms and upper arms. It appeared to the Oceanians that they had no necks, for their heads sat firm on their shoulders.

Suddenly the three newcomers, having assessed the situation and found themselves wanting in numbers, turned away together as if they were one craft joined by invisible spars. They disappeared into the mists again, as swiftly as they had become visible, one lone man shaking a heavy fist at the Oceanians.

'Who were they?' gasped Hupa, coming to Seumas's side. 'They looked like demons riding taniwha.'

Craig asked, 'Yes, who were they, Father?'

'Sea raiders, from the outer islands.'

'Will they inform the Celts we are coming?' asked Craig.

'Doubtful,' replied Seumas, going back down to a state of rest. 'They pillage the coastal villages themselves, so they're as much the enemy as we are.'

Hupa asked, 'Where did you say they come from?'

'There are small islands to the far south – the Rocks of Orca – which breed men like those you have just seen. They are hard men, made of nothing but muscle and tendon, with very little brain. They strip even the poorest village of its meagre stores and skins. They are merciless creatures. Have no doings with the likes of sea raiders. They would chew you up and spit you out like a piece of gristle.'

This information was duly passed on to Kieto, who regarded it with some suspicion. Seumas was known to exaggerate, especially when it came to stories of his homeland. Dorcha had confirmed that much. There was something of the tale-teller in Seumas: he could not allow the opportunity for a fine story to go by without some embroidery. Kieto thought that perhaps the sea raiders were to be avoided, but not if it meant any serious inconvenience to his mission.

Craig, on the other hand, had been very impressed by the savage looks of those seafarers. The man who had shaken his fist had had hair the colour of sunbleached driftwood. It had hung down below his shoulders in greasy tangles. On the top of his head had been a hat shaped like half a coconut, except that it had been shiny and smooth-looking. Slung across his chest had been a sword, similar to the narwhal spikes which some Oceanians made into weapons, but flat-bladed.

'He would be a difficult man to beat in single combat,' Craig told himself, staring into the thick curtains of mist before him. 'It would not be easy to take him.'

However, though Seumas was sick in body, he seemed to recover in spirit. He was all for chasing the sea raiders to the ends of the earth once the Land-of-Mists had been won or lost.

'We could take a breakaway fleet,' he said to Craig. 'You and I, son, out on our own. By the gods, it would be like the old days . . .' His eyes shone with enthusiasm. 'Just six or seven canoes. We could attack them quickly, while they were in harbour, for those longships are fast under sail. We could board them in the night and have a fine old scrap.'

'I think it would be more than a *scrap*, Father. They look formidable fighting men.'

'They are, son, they are,' cried Seumas. 'Where would the glory be if they were not? But we could beat them, I know we could. They're arrogant bastards, but they're clumsy in battle, wielding heavy axes and swords. Us Oceanians, we're light on our feet. We could be in and away before they knew what was happening to them.'

Us Oceanians? His father was one of them again. But his Pictish ancestors did not go without mention.

'. . . also I was once an Albannach. We Picts are worth three times one of those sea raiders.'

Seumas picked up a patu club and began hacking away at invisible enemies, while the mariners ceased working at the shrouds and stood to watch and cheer, some of them yelling encouragements to Seumas during his mock battle. Craig had to admit his father's old litheness was still evident. Age had not dimmed his battle spirit. Seumas had fought with monsters and had walked away laughing. He was a hero of the old school.

Seumas quickly tired, his breath becoming short, but he smiled at his son.

'Like that,' he said. 'And with you at my side.'

'Yes, Father,' grinned Craig. 'We would stand like rocks, you and I.'

'Dorcha too, if she were alive. She could be a warrior when it suited her. Oh, yes, she used to bleat a lot about war being terrible, but when it came to protecting her own kind, why she could use a weapon I can tell you. Pity she's dead.

'But there's life in this body yet. Deeds to be done, Craig. I've been a bit morose of late. That's not good. I'm happier now. I have things I want to do.'

'Rid the sea of raiders.'

'Yes, by god,' roared Seumas, delightedly, holding his son behind the neck and bellowing into the wind. 'That, and other deeds!'

Seumas never recovered from the effects of the chill. His son and his friends took turns to sit up with him at night, during the dark hours, when the fear of death overwhelms any person close to its edge. There were times when he was terrified, there were times when he was accepting of it. More than once he felt ready to go. Some believed it was because he was faced with seeing his birthplace destroyed by an invader. Craig did not subscribe to this view. Craig believed it was merely coincidence, that his father was old and unwell, that his body, not his mind, was failing him.

'The black spectre comes to make me pay for my

wrongs,' whispered Seumas to Kikamana, the Farseeing-virgin, as she watched over him alone one night. 'I have to atone.'

'If you feel remorse, then you are atoning,' she replied. 'Your wrongs are nothing beside the crimes of many men.'

'I should like my hands to have been clean, but I'm not that kind of man. If not the misdeeds I have done, then others equally as bad. I wish I had been a better made man.'

'There are many who will mourn you, be sad to see you go.'

'Then I am dying?' he said, his eyes misting over with sadness and fear. 'I am going.'

Kikamana was not one to lie. 'I shall be arriving at journey's end myself very soon,' she said. 'It will be good to stop travelling and rest.'

He grasped at this view of death like a drowning man clutches at thin air.

'Yes, yes, that's it. The end of a long journey. Not a thing to get upset about. Like stepping from a boat after a long sea voyage, eh? Not such a terrible end – more something we've been striving for, hoping to reach, all our lives?'

'That's how I see it.'

For a moment his face looked serene, then it hardened into a cynical expression.

'If you believe that, you'll believe anything. It's a bloody shame, that's what it is. Who wants to get off the boat while it's still out in the ocean?'

Seumas slipped lower and lower, until one morning grey cliffs appeared out of the mist on the starboard side. Boy-girl and Craig were with him, by his side, as was his hound Dirk. Seumas lifted a weak arm and pointed.

'Albainn,' he whispered in a voice like rustling leaves.

'Is this it, Father?' asked Craig. 'Is this your birthland?'

'This is where I was born,' confirmed Seumas. 'I climbed those cliffs, boy and man, to wring the necks of those fulmar birds you see wheeling about them. I killed them for the oil in their stomachs. Now the damn birds outlive me, for I am dying, son – slipping away fast. Listen to those bastards laughing at me. They're getting their own back. They don't see an old man dying – they see justice happening before their eyes – the Pict who killed their mates and fledglings is choking for want of air. I can hear them call to one another. They remember I used to rob their nests of their kind. Birds don't forget.'

'They're not the same birds, Father,' replied Craig, as if it were important. 'Those birds are long dead.'

'Then I've gone past my time,' sighed Seumas, his voice like the wind riffling the dry leaves of the pandanus hut. 'I should go. Yet I still cling fiercely to the world of the living. There's still a fire burning within me, which does not want to go out.' His eyes shone with an unusually bright light, as if there really were a flame behind them. 'I wanted to know more, my son, learn much more. But I had a bad start at learning. A good start at killing, but a bad start at gathering knowledge. You have a better one . . .'

'Quiet, Father – you'll tax yourself.'

'Tax myself? I'm on my way out. How strange to think that in a few moments I will no longer be in this body. No longer able to draw breath, move these lips, make these sounds which mean so much to us. One moment there is life, the next nothing but an empty shell, a discarded coconut husk.'

Craig was holding his father's hand now, gripping it hard, as if he could anchor Seumas to the living world, stop him from drifting off into oblivion.

'The darkness is coming in, boy. Where are the cliffs? I can hear the fulmars' cries but faintly in the dimness of my fading brain. Craig, Craig, are you there, son? Don't leave me now.'

Dirk whined – a mournful note.

Seumas's fingers clawed at Craig's cloak, gripping it,

pulling his son's face down close to his own. Craig could hardly feel the shallow breath on his cheek. He knew it was true, his father was dying. There was no sight in the eyes. They could see things now that no living man should see. Craig wrapped his arms around the tattooed Pict, holding him close as the lungs sighed for the final time.

In that moment, while crossing the pale of death, Seumas begged for a promise.

'Look after my people, son.'

'Yes, Father – I promise.'

Then the old man was gone – gone to join his Dorcha in the regions beyond life – where they could know each other again.

Dirk nuzzled the body, now cooling rapidly in the chill air. The dog was making strange noises in the back of its throat.

Boy-girl was weeping, her tears falling on Craig's shoulders as she reached over to touch the face of the corpse with the tips of her fingers.

'He never said goodbye to me,' she said. 'Couldn't he see me?'

'He was blind at the end – didn't you hear him?' replied Craig, wondering at her words. 'He told us so.'

'I couldn't understand a word he was saying,' sobbed Boy-girl. 'Not in that strange tongue of his.'

It was at that moment that Craig realized his father's deathbed speech had been in Gaelic. It was a shock. Craig had never learned the language from Seumas, though the old man had tried to teach him on a number of occasions.

Craig gently laid the body back down. It was as light as a straw. It was as if it had been the spirit of the man which had weighed heavy on the earth: the lifeforce which carried muscle, bone and blood. It was true, there was nothing of Seumas left but a husk. Hupa came and put her arm around Craig and he wept into her slim shoulder. She hugged him and held his head and rocked with him, imbibing much of his grief, letting it mingle with her own lesser grief, so that he could become whole again.

When Kieto learned of Seumas's death he ordered the fleet out to sea again. First he ordered that the Pict's heart be removed from the chest of the corpse and placed in a container of preservative fluid. Then he conducted the funeral of his lifelong friend and mentor, saying that Seumas was a man of two worlds and had belonged in both. The body was swaddled tightly in pandanus leaves and bound with sennit. The package was then strapped to a spar ready for a journey to some shore.

'We shall miss him greatly,' Kieto said. 'His close friends – Kikamana, Boy-girl and myself – and yes, to a certain extent, Polahiki – we shall all be the poorer for his passing.'

He paused for a moment's silent before adding one last comment.

'I-am-bereft.'

With those last three words Seumas's body was consigned to the dark ocean and the dry-eyed Kieto went into his deck hut.

Craig stared as the mummified body was taken away by the currents, wondering at his father's last request.

Look after my people!

Craig had said he would, but now that he thought about it, was unhappily confused.

Who were his father's people?

Which did he mean?

The Celts?

Or the Oceanians?

2

It was night and the watchfires of the Celts could be seen from the decks of the tipairua.

Seumas's death had left Craig with a terrible responsibility, since now their major guide and mediator had gone. It meant that Craig was the one to whom Kieto would turn for information: knowledge Craig had come by in a curious and convoluted way. Boy-girl had since told Kieto that Craig understood the language of the Picts and Scots, had learned it secretly from Seumas.

Yet Craig had not learned it, not in that way.

It seemed his visit to the fairies had been for a purpose, for now he remembered King Uetonga's gift to him on parting.

I wish to understand my father, Craig had said.

It is done, the king had replied.

Craig had of course meant that he wanted to understand his father's feelings, his thoughts, the roots of his culture, but the king had taken the words literally. He had given Craig the gift of understanding his father's *language*. Gaelic was now as much a part of Craig as it had been part of Seumas and Dorcha, who had kept the strange tongue alive in their heads between them during the years of their exile.

Other knowledge, too, was embedded in Craig's brain,

and needed but direct questions to prise it out. Often he did not himself understand what he was talking about. It was as if he were a vessel full of exotic fruits, of which he knew all the names, but none of which were familiar to him.

Boy-girl came to see Craig as he stood by the mast. Dirk was at her side. She had taken on the care of the dog now that Seumas was gone. It was something she wanted to do. When Seumas had been alive, she had derided the Pict for his love of his hounds, but now he was no longer there she wanted some part of him to remain with her. Dirk filled that role.

'We land at dawn,' said Boy-girl.

'I know,' replied Craig. 'Are you ready?'

'For this? Never. It's been Kieto's dream, not mine. What would I want with a conquered land, a conquered people? It's some notion Kieto has of warding off a future invasion. Strike first.'

'And what if we lose?'

'Then we go home like curs, with our tails between our legs, and wait for the Angles or the Celts to come to us.'

'It's a big risk. They wouldn't have come to Oceania in *our* lifetime.'

Boy-girl nodded. 'I know, but Kieto's right – we must protect the future.'

When the slow dawn came rolling in, grey and mon- strous, some time later, they made a landfall. A beach head was quickly established, then the warriors poured onto the shore, out of the cold waves that crashed on lonely grey sands covered in weed, dead birds and tangled driftwood. They made their way up craggy slopes to the land above the shore. There in the drifting fog and mists they began felling trees with flint and shell axes, to build fortified pa accord- ing to the instructions issued by Kieto.

With engineers supervising, the Oceanians worked furi- ously to give themselves some sort of protection before they were discovered. Soon there were palisades of sharpened stakes and deep ditches encircling the individual encampments. Samoans, Fijians, Raiateans, Hawaiians, all had their particular methods of getting the tasks done, and they did it with zeal.

One of the reasons for the speed of the operation was that the mist was gradually clearing. Sentries had been placed in a wide semicircle, to warn of any approach by the enemy. By noon there were reports coming back to Kieto to indicate that the natives were now aware they had foreigners on their soil.

Yet still the shock of the Oceanian arrival had not been felt seriously enough, for the Celts did not organize themselves on any large scale. What was happening was that clan members, out hunting together, would come and stare in amazement at the activity of close to a hundred thousand dark-skinned men stealing their trees to make forts, before going off again to pass on the news to chieftains and overlords. It was not until that night that the chieftains themselves began to come to the idea that they ought to discuss this invasion of their land between them.

Such was not an easy thing, for the clans were constantly at war with one another and the maintenance of blood feuds was more important than the threat of any casual visitors. Those who lived in hill cave communities hated those who lived in wee crofts in the lush glens below. Those who owned the mountain passes despised those who herded cattle around the shores of the lochs. Pict hated Scot, Scot hated Pict, both hated the Britons, all three hated those tribes of Angles who lived in Albainn and even more those Angles up in Engaland.

In short, none of them trusted one another. If anything, they wondered how they could turn to their own advantage the arrival of these brown-skins in order to kill a few more Kenzies or Leods or Phears. Some of the larger Scottish clans around their centre of Dunadd in the kingdom of Dalriada were even considering herding the lesser clans towards the newcomers, to see what occurred between them. Their chief, Ceann Mor, 'The Bighead', hardly mentioned the newcomers. The Pictland clans – the Círech, Fiobh, Moireabh, Fótla, Cé, Fortriu and Cat – warned each other to stay away in case it was a Scottish ploy to get them all in one place and wipe them out. Their present war chief, Cormac the Venomous, who had recently murdered his rival, Eochaid Redhands, chose to ignore the situation, saying it was Scotch witchery, sorcery of a Celtic kind.

In consequence, the Oceanians found themselves with a week's grace, to build their pa and settle into the Albannach earth like hard little nuggets. The tipairua were kept moored off-shore at first, but wild winds and heavy seas drove them into bays unsuitable for a long stay. Finally, Kieto sent them off northwards along the coast to find a natural harbour somewhere, hopefully on a small island away from the mainland, leaving his army without any means of escape.

'We have to make good now,' he said, grimly. 'We must vanquish or we perish.'

After a week the clans were wise enough to see that they would be overrun by a foreign army if they did not quickly get themselves together. Already companies of Kieto's men were making forays into the wild hinterland, chasing local wildmen back into their bogs. Their first encounters with the Scots and Picts gave both sides a healthy respect for each other.

Kieto organized a system of messengers, to run between pa with written instructions and orders. Obviously the fleetest runners were used for this purpose. Parties of warriors were sent out to find sources of food. There seemed to be no coconuts, breadfruit or sweet potatoes. The landscape seemed devoid of edible crops of any kind, except for root vegetables as hard as stone and tasteless into the bargain.

As for meat, wild pig was found. Birds were there in plenty, often plump and sweet-tasting. Fish in the streams were abundant and very appetizing. There were dogs too though these were not suitable for eating, since they were mangy, savage creatures, all stringy muscle. The wild dogs attacked the Oceanians savagely when approached. They were worse than Dirk, who was well known throughout Oceania for his ferocious nature, and so the creatures were given a wide berth.

Hupa and Kapu were amongst the hunting party to first come upon a herd of cattle.

'What are they?' cried Kapu. 'They look like walking huts.'

There were about a dozen of the creatures, idly grazing on grass. The cowherd had run off on seeing armed tattooed brown warriors in strange dress come out of the forest. His cows with their long shaggy coats and large horns remained where they were, unperturbed. To the Oceanians they looked formidable creatures, with their huge curved horns and muscled bulk. One of the steers lifted its head and stared at Kapu.

'It's going to charge!' cried the young man, backing towards the forest. 'Kill it quickly, Hupa.'

But the creature merely ambled forward to a greener area of grass and began ripping and chewing again, seemingly unconcerned by the presence of the warriors.

Hupa walked forward slowly and found that the cattle edged away from her rather than charged. They did not run in fear either, though they appeared slightly timid. Finally she persuaded her group to prod the beasts with their spears, driving them back to the pa. There she presented this 'find' to Kieto, who was most impressed with the animals.

'We shall spit-roast one of them tonight,' he said.

And indeed, this they did, to find the meat wholesome and absolutely delicious.

'No wonder Seumas didn't want us to invade this land,' said Polahiki, burping loudly. 'With big horned pigs like these roaming around, just waiting to be cooked.'

'The hide will go to my daughter Hupa,' said Kieto, 'for finding the beasts – it will make a fine cloak.'

'I was there too,' grumbled her twin brother, Kapu, 'don't I get a cloak?'

Hupa said, 'The skin is large enough for two cloaks at least – we'll share it between us.'

'No,' replied the petulant Kapu. 'I don't want part of yours, I want my own. Why am I always being treated like an infant? Why do you and your Whakatane get all the credit, when others do as much?'

Kieto glared at his son. 'You will share the skin, or you will get nothing. Your sister is very generous. I hear you ran away when you saw these creatures.'

Kapu scowled and denied that he had 'run'. He told his father he was naturally cautious and had moved towards the tree line, for protection in case they were charged.

'We did not know at the time whether they were dangerous or not – I think my caution does credit to me.'

The war chief softened in his attitude.

'Perhaps you are right, but you will still do as I say – you will take half of the hide – the other half going to your sister. I will hear no more dissent.'

With that the matter was closed, but a festering jealousy was growing in Kapu which others recognized might one day be his downfall. Already he was beginning to hate his sister. In recent days he was much in the company of Prince Daggan and his sorceress wife, Siko. They seemed to have a lot to talk about, considering Daggan was an enemy of the boy's family.

Traditional Oceanian sources of food were not so forthcoming as the meat. There was very little fruit to be found, except for berries on bushes. Seumas had told them of tiny nuts and small hard, bitter fruit, called 'apples', both of which grew on trees like mangoes. These were not in evidence, it being the wrong season for such bounty. There were wild flowers everywhere, and the purple and white stuff about which Seumas had waxed lyrical on many an occasion – a plant called 'heather'.

Kikamana was the person with the knowledge of fauna and flora, she being the person most interested in such things when Seumas and Dorcha were alive. From pictures drawn by those two Celts, she now recognized many of the different plants and not a few of the strange creatures of the landscape. There were deer, equally as good for eating as the cows but much fleeter of foot. There were woolly sheep and goats.

There was one fast little animal that made a good meal – provided a hunter could catch one – which Craig knew to be called a 'hare'. However, one had to be an excellent shot with a bow, like Hupa, or be clever at setting snares for the creatures. They ran like the wind in a wide curving arc and hid in little double-ended tunnels on the mountainside. The wild dogs chased them and the eagles fell on them, but their numbers seemed to be such that the loss of a whole colony did not appear to affect their ubiquitous presence on the landscape.

What with the stores they had brought with them and what they could forage from the landscape, the Oceanians were not likely to starve. Also, once they began taking prisoners, there would be meat for those Oceanians who still practised cannibalism. The Hivans and the Fijians said they could not wait to get their sharpened teeth into some nice white meat for a change.

The climate, however, was not to the Oceanians' liking. Although the season was supposed to be what Seumas called 'spring', it was still very cold on the skin of the sun-loving Oceanians. Winds swept up from the regions beyond the dark seas, the source of the world's coldness, and cut right through the warm-blooded warriors from the islands.

Nights were brisk affairs to be passed under thick blankets, cuddled up to some loved one if at all possible. Mornings were always draped in mist and sometimes the warriors woke to find themselves chilled to the marrow by a covering of hoar frost on the ground.

'Where does Ra go to in this awful place?' asked Polahiki of Kikamana. 'Is he ashamed to show his face?'

'You forget, this is not Ra's domain, but that of another sun god,' replied the Farseeing-virgin. 'Even now our gods are gathering on the fringes of this land, ready to enter and do battle with strange deities for whom we have no names.'

'Craig knows some of the names,' replied Polahiki, shivering, and looking about him at the dreary aspect of a misty evening closing in. 'He told me some of them. One of the most important is a goddess called Brighid, who taught the Celts smithcraft and metalwork – that is how to use that iron stuff which Seumas regarded so highly. And Taranis, a thunder god, who no doubt will fight with Tawhaki when the time comes. Manannan mac lir, the Great Sea-God of this place, who will battle with Tangoroa for supremacy of the ocean . . .'

'I am unable even to find a place for such gods in my mind,' said Kikamana. 'Their names are so utterly alien to me.'

'I know what you mean,' replied Polahiki, as the twilight wore unendingly on. 'Here in this land even the dusk takes for ever to disappear into its own gloomy hut.'

'Speaking of huts, yesterday Craig and I went out together. We were looking for streams with fish, but came upon a rocky place deep in a valley where there was a small dwelling made completely of unhewn stone slabs. I could not approach the place, for there were dark spirits there, glaring out at me. A *dolmen* Craig called it in the language of his father.'

'How did Craig know what to call it?'

'He has this gift of knowing, given to him by King Uetonga of the fairies.'

'Is this dolmen a dwelling place for the dead?'

Kikamana said she did not know for sure, but that it felt such a place.

Thus the Oceanians, with the help of Craig, grappled with their new environment and struggled with the strange atmospheres of Land-of-Mists, which disturbed some more than others.

There were certainly fairies and monsters here and other supernatural beings, which for the moment were holding their powerful forces in check. The Oceanians were as strange to the indigenous spirits of the place, whether fair or foul, as they themselves were to the newcomers.

There was a kind of magical stalemate while assessments were carried out.

The Celts finally managed to put traditional grievances aside and formed what they called an army, but was better described by Craig as a horde. One sunless morning thousands of them came charging down out of the hills, yelling and screaming, their wild hair streaming in the damp morning air. The Picts were recognizable by their tattooed bodies, but the Scots had also painted themselves with various dyes.

They were all completely naked except for a weapon belt around their waists.

The sight of naked hairy bodies and freely-swinging genitals shocked and unnerved the prudish Oceanians behind their defences.

'It's to do with going into battle unencumbered,' Craig explained to them. 'Weapons catch on clothes, and cloth can be driven into wounds by blades and make them fester . . .'

But this explanation went over the heads of the Oceanian warriors, as some of the Celts stopped dead not far from the palisades and used their left hands to waggle their genitals in an obscene and insulting gesture at the enemy, while making strange gaseous noises with their tongues. Some of them actually turned to bend over and fart with bare arses at the shocked newcomers. Others pissed on the ground in front of them with a look of disdain on their features. Then the naked Celts threw themselves at the high fences, while the stunned Oceanian spearmen had to gather their wits before they could hurl their missiles down on them from platforms above.

Oceanians beat out battle rhythms on their drums, but the enemy responded with fearsome music.

'The screaming of dying pigs,' wailed some of those Oceanians who had never heard Seumas play his pipes. 'They have evil spirits trapped in those bags!'

Craig quickly sent messengers between the pa to inform the warriors as to the exact nature of the bagpipes and to tell them to put wax in their ears if they could not stand the sound.

Since there were no siege weapons the attack was not a great success, except for the opportunity for the two sides to get a good look at one another. It was an especially frustrating day for the Celts, who desperately wanted to get at the enemy and give them a good thrashing. The Oceanians on the other hand were impressed by those few Celts who were on horseback. To ride an animal like that obviously took great skill and man and creature would have been a formidable set of opponents on an open battlefield.

As it was the Celt horsemen could do nothing but ride up and down in front of the pa, waving their iron swords. There were grisly round objects suspiciously like human heads dangling from the manes of their mounts. Their horses, strong-looking muscled creatures with thick legs, wore masks of wicker and bark, which made them appear devilish creatures.

Kieto realized now why Seumas had warned them about the horses, for the mad-eyed, snorting, hoofed beasts with their clashing teeth were like something out of a nightmare.

When the Celts saw that they were throwing themselves against virtually impregnable defences, they tried to burn those defences down. Kieto, having lived with the Maori who invented the fortified pa, had foreseen this and seawater was available to douse the flames. At the end of the day the Celts went home, taking their dead and wounded with them. The Oceanians too had lost men, but the casualties were light on both sides.

'What now?' Craig asked Kieto. 'Do we follow them?'

Kieto considered this. It was a good tactic to creep in the path of retreating warriors and fall upon them in the dark, just when they thought they were safe. They would be busy building fires and making camp. Many of them could be slaughtered this way. But somehow, after seeing the Celts in battle, Kieto got the idea that the natives would regard this as a rather dishonourable way to conduct a battle.

'No, we'll see what tomorrow brings. Let's replenish our water supplies tonight and prepare ourselves for another day of fighting . . .'

The following day's fighting produced more or less the same results, so that evening a deputation of Celts – some six or seven of them dressed in coarse clothing – came unarmed up to the gates of one of the pa and indicated with sign language that they would like to talk. Kieto was actually in another pa, but the fortifications were all linked by fenced passages. He arrived with Craig as the visitors were being sat down in front of a fire.

The leader of the Celts was a big bole-chested man with thick shoulders and one eye. He had a hound with him that was almost as ugly as its master. The cur lay with its belly to the earth, regarding everything around it through suspicious, narrowed eyes. It clearly did not like the smell of this place or the people in it and would, for less than the rib of a rat, deliver a few flesh wounds amongst these unwholesome strangers.

One-eye spat into the flames as he glared at the two

Oceanians with his single orb. The phlegm sizzled on one of the logs as Craig opened negotiations.

'Greetings, chieftains,' said Craig in Gaelic, 'you have nothing to fear while you come to us unarmed.'

'Fear ye?' growled One-eye. 'I fear my dog more than I fear you.'

'A wise choice,' said Craig, looking at the ferocious beast. 'It is a fearsome creature.'

One of the other Celts, a thin man with whitish hair, smiled at this remark. This man cleared his throat now, ready to speak, and Craig gave him his attention.

'Ye speak our language,' said White-hair. 'How is this?'

'I am half Pict,' explained Craig, 'though this is the first time I have seen the land of my forefathers. My father was Seumas-from-the-Blackwater . . .'

This speech was interrupted by a cry of anguish from one of the visitors, a thick-set man with black hair. The Celt leapt to his feet, snatched a club from one of the Oceanians guarding him, and rushed forward to strike Craig. One-eye grabbed his ankle as he passed and wrenched his legs from under him. The warrior, not a young man, went crashing on his face in the fire. The smell of singed hair filled Craig's nostrils. His attacker was back on his feet in an instant, still brandishing the weapon, but was felled from behind by One-eye with a log from the woodpile at the side of the fire.

'Get him out of here,' said the chieftain to two of his men, as the warrior lay unmoving. 'Lug the fool away.'

When the unconscious man was removed from the pa, White-hair continued to question Craig.

'Ye are the son of Seumas. I do not know this man. Is he amongst us?'

'Clearly your friend knew him, but no, he is not here. He died on the voyage to this land. And before you start thinking "traitor", it was not Seumas who led the Oceanians here. They found their own way many years ago and took Seumas captive along with a woman called Dorcha.'

Something registered on the old man's face.

'Ah, now I think I understand – Dorcha is the mother of Douglass Barelegs, son of Douglass . . .'

'Stop this gabble,' interrupted One-eye, impatiently, 'and let's get down to what we came here for.' He turned to Kieto, recognizing him as the leader of the invaders. 'We cannot fight while you hide behind skirts of bark. Come out into the field and we shall see who is strongest. Are ye cowards to cringe and cower behind these wooden walls?'

With Craig acting as interpreter, Kieto learned what was being said and made reply.

'No, we're not cowards, we're sensible men. You know the lay of the land, we do not. You know the nature of your weather, we do not. We must use every advantage open to us, or you'll overrun us.'

'Overrun you? We are a tenth your number.'

'For the moment,' replied Kieto, 'but I am not so stupid as to think your numbers will not increase by the day, as word goes out to more of your tribes. Even as we speak they must be flocking towards this place, eager for a good battle with outsiders.'

One-eye exchanged looks with White-hair and Craig realized that Kieto's guesses were accurate.

'My name is Cormac,' said One-eye. 'They call me Cormac the Venomous. What is yours?'

'Kieto.'

'Listen then, Key-toe – give us one good battle, the morn's morn. I'll be on the field with double the numbers I have today, but that's still a fifth of what you can put out. One good battle, eh? To get each other's measure.'

Kieto considered this proposal for a long time, then he nodded slowly. 'One good battle in the open – then we fight as best we know how. You will see that Oceanians are superior warriors and capitulate thereafter. But no horses.'

'No horses?' cried the chieftain, his bushy eyebrows arching.

'There must be a trade. You do not get something for nothing. We are giving up our pa, you must give up your horses. If you promise the beasts will be kept off the field, then we will meet you and do battle.'

Cormac nodded thoughtfully, reaching down to stroke his hound while he considered the matter. Kieto stared at the dog. Its hackles rose and it growled in the back of its throat as its head came up.

'I know you,' said Kieto to the cur. 'I have seen your kind before.'

The dog snarled, but its master held it by the ruff.

'I agree,' said Cormac, finally.

'Good.'

'Ye will see you waste your time attacking Celts, who will bite off your heads and chew your skulls to mush.'

After the Celts had gone, Craig followed his leader into a hut and sat with him.

'Is this a good thing, Kieto? I thought the idea was to wear them down first, by letting them exhaust themselves on the pa? But to go out there while they are fresh?'

'We must prove our worth on the open field, or we'll never get them to capitulate. You heard the veiled reference to hiding behind women. If they believe we are timid creatures afraid to come out of our villages, they'll simply keep on fighting until they exterminate us, no matter how many battles they lose. If, however, we put it in their minds that we are bold invaders, proud warriors who love the art of war – then we shall see a different frame of mind.'

Craig went to his bed thinking about the man they called Douglass son of Douglass, realizing this was one of those who his father wished him to befriend. It did not look a likely proposition at this point in time. To make his peace with such a man he would first have to knock him down, then tie him to a stake to render him harmless. Otherwise the Celt would open up Craig's skull at the first opportunity.

Craig sighed. It was not going to be easy.

*

The following day the two armies met on the open plain between the mountains and the shore. The moaning tones of conch shells drifting over the Albannach hills mingled with the sound of metal horns. Celtic drum beats melded with the rhythm of Oceanian sticks on hollow logs. There was a feeling in the air, the anticipation of battle, as warriors ululated, calling to one another from hill to hill, ground to ground.

This feeling increased amongst the naked Celts, many of them with combat erections, until they were delirious with battle-joy, rushing forwards without waiting for commands, thoroughly disorganized but eager to bite flesh with iron. The Oceanians were rigid. They had their set pieces and they awaited the command for the day.

Craig looked out on the battle lines of his own people, before the roaring Celts reached them. There were the gay feathered helmets, the magnificent cloaks of dogskin decorated with parrot feathers, the banners and standards of the chiefs flowing in the wind, the polished ironwood clubs glinting in the sunlight, the decorated white, brown and black kilts of tapa bark with their geometric designs. The wonderful tattooed shoulders of the warriors. How colourful they were! How brilliant to the eye! What a stirring picturesque vision they made.

The Celts themselves were drab in comparison, despite the blue and red dyes and the tattoos on the bodies of the Picts. Their naked bodies were quite offensive to Craig's eyes, their black iron swords looked rough and sinister, their sweat-stained, cracked leather weapon-harnesses quite ugly. The only real colour about them was the variety of hair types, that billowed red, brown, blond and black in the ripe wind from the coast.

They were like their own landscape, their own seascape and their own skies: rugged grey rocks below with mournful grey skies above. Yes, there was green and purple in there somewhere, with the occasional patch of blue, but swamped by grey.

Yet these too were his people, on his father's side!

The Oceanians were light on their feet, graceful, full of the flame of youth, closer to the sun and the stars, richer in skin tones, delicate, more spiritual in aspect!

The Celts were heavy on their feet, bulky in stature, strong-boned, ruddy-complexioned, big thundering fellows with big forearms and big thighs, full of savage courage that hurled them into battle with no thought of defeat or the safety of their lives and limbs.

Kieto, on seeing the wave of unruly, wilful Celts tumble in a torrent down the sides of the hills and wash out onto the plain, gave the order for paitoa: to stand like a rock and allow the enemy to hurl themselves at them. The messengers fanned out from Kieto carrying their prepared slates with the order scratched on them, using the 'writing' which Hiro had brought back to the peoples of Oceania from his travels.

The runners reached Samoans, Fijians, Hawaiians, Rarotongans, Raiateans, Hivans, and many other Oceanian islanders who then knew to stand unwavering, with weapons at the ready, while the wild Celts came charging forwards. They had received tapu from the priests and were full of the lust for battle. Victory would give them much mana, fill their heads with the potency of manhood and magic. Their faces were blackened with charcoal to make them appear that much more ferocious to the enemy. They were eager, hopping from one foot to another, as the drums pounded out blood-rushing rhythms.

Craig remained frustrated behind the lines, witnessing the action, his skills as an interpreter too valuable for Kieto to lose at such an early stage.

The land on the two sides of the plain consisted of brown peat bogs, with weather-scoured deep ditches. In order to avoid these, the Celts pouring across the plain were channelled naturally towards the centre of their front. Craig saw a thick wedge of naked Celts drive into the middle of the Oceanians, their iron swords wreaking havoc. The line of Oceanians gave at that point and almost let the Celts through, just managing to hold with a second line of reinforcements holding firm.

But the Celts' undisciplined attack worked against them as they pushed and shoved against each other in a massive tight knot of bodies, arms and legs, trying to get at the enemy. The Hawaiians, fighting in their traditional crescent-shaped front, closed their flanks round the foe, so the Celts were effectively caught in a passage lined by two walls of their brown-skinned enemies, whose battle clubs, some of them almost as tall as a man, cracked skulls and took off heads at the neck.

This meant there were some Celts caught in the middle of the mass of their comrades, Celts who were unable to use weapons on the foe for fear of striking friend. Spears and arrows rained down on these unfortunates hemmed in by their own confederates. They naturally tried to force their way out of the middle, thus propelling those on the outside of the column into the clubs of the Oceanians, eager to pay back in kind.

The eagerness of the Oceanians worked against them, however, as they drove the enemy back to firmer ground. Once outside the bottleneck the Celts were able to spread sideways and form a more cohesive and orderly battle line. However, this meant that the front had thinned and a group of impetuous Hivans broke through the line, which then closed behind them. These Hivan warriors, some fifty men, found themselves battling behind the Celtic front line. With more space available both iron sword and ironwood club were wielded with more swing and thus more force.

Although it was metal against wood, the metal was not of the highest quality and the wood was one of the hardest

on the earth, thus sword broke against club almost as often
as club was hacked in half. In the main, both weapons held
up well. The fighting in this small pocket of the field was
heavy and furious, the warriors on each side seeing a
chance to distinguish themselves on an isolated stage in
front of their war chiefs.

The tattooed Hivans rolled their eyes, lolled their
tongues and growled at their foes, clubbing this way and
that, felling Celts with crashing blows of their great ironwood weapons.

The painted Picts did likewise with their swords, hacking
away at the enemy, hooting when one went down under the
wide curving slashes of their swords.

Craig, seeing the Hivans were in trouble, as more and
more Celts fell back from the front line to settle their frustrated wrath on this isolated group of Oceanians, motioned
to a group of elite warriors, originally Samoan before they
had co-settled the island of Rarotonga under their king
Karika. With this small force of disciplined fighting men
Craig attacked the Celt line with a wedge-shaped formation. With much cracking of skulls and chopping of legs
they managed to push through and reach the now depleted
group of Hivans.

'Fall back,' cried Craig into the ears of the nearest
Hivans, 'drop back through the channel.'

His own men had formed an avenue between the Celt
warriors on both sides. The Hivans slipped down this protected passage to rejoin the main force. Once the Hivans
were back in the Oceanian ranks the channel closed at the
front, went wedge-shaped again and the Rarotongans
themselves dropped back, with the loss of only a few of
their number.

However, this movement had aroused the ire of those
Celts who thought they had a bunch of the enemy amongst
them which they could chop down at leisure. They attacked
Craig's retreat with great venom and strength. Craig found

himself looking into faces twisted with battle-anger, just a nose in front of his own. Hot breath was on his cheek as the knot of men struggled with each other. Sharp light-blue eyes stared into his own, startling in their intensity. Broad faces with blond stubble grimaced. He could smell the rank sweat under their armpits as they raised their swords and tried to strike in the solid knot of warriors that heaved and grunted, trying to get in a good blow amongst the tangle of arms and legs.

Then Craig fell, was in danger of being trampled by the thick-legged Celts. A foot crashed down on his chest, robbing him of wind. A heel struck him in the thigh, dangerously close to his testicles. Any moment he expected a sword to come down and divorce his head from his shoulders. Then he felt hands on his ankles and he was dragged unceremoniously out of the mêlée, back into his own lines. When he rolled over and looked up, he saw the face of Boy-girl smiling down at him.

'You naughty boy,' she said, wagging a finger. 'No heroics now – you've been told to save your tongue. Do as you're bid next time.'

'Thanks, Boy-girl,' he said, getting his breath. 'Here, help me to my feet. I'm winded.'

She did so and the pair dropped back a little, behind some stocky Fijians whose distinctive woolly-haired heads made them look a good deal taller to the enemy than they actually were, thus adding to their stature and ferociousness. Once more the fighting was at close-quarters, with muscled, pale-skinned men locked limb and trunk with dark-skinned warriors. There was much grunting and heaving amongst men who smelt differently from each other, looked strange to each other's eyes, and found the idea of touching a little distasteful. Dark men were slightly revolted by the fish-belly skin of the pale men. The freckled warriors were vaguely uneasy at grappling with shadows. The two groups found themselves fighting to get away from each other, rather than attempting to overrun and conquer those in their path.

The filed teeth of the Fijians and Hivans gave their wide faces a shark-like appearance. This aspect filled more than one Celt with terror when he looked into a mouth full of sharpened incisors. More than once a beleaguered Fijian or Hivan, whose weapon arm was trapped in the crush, simply sank his pointed teeth into the Celt warrior nearest to him.

'Nae biting! Nae biting!' screamed a young Pict, the first to be subject to this unfair tactic, soon to be spoken of as monstrously infamous by the Celts around their post-battle camp fires. Fear and dread swept through Scot and Pict. The Oceanians heard the gabble and guessed it was protest, but paid no heed. Great chunks of shoulder went missing, or an ear, or in some cases a few fingers. The Celts howled their dismay at such barbarism, renewing with vigour their attempts to hack themselves some space away from this ugly method of fighting.

Then one Scot, a brawler from the west coast, nutted a Fijian in the face, surprising that man. A howl of horror went up from the Fijian, who dropped his weapon to clutch his precious broken nose. Blood poured from his nostrils, soaking his triumphant attacker who saw that the Oceanian was not used to this kind of treatment and happily turned and nutted a second man.

Soon, many of the Celts who found themselves in this close-combat, hand-to-hand situation, used their broad foreheads to crack the noses of the Oceanians whose faces were closest.

'Use the nut, use the nut,' cried the Celts, realizing they too had a bare-body weapon to which the enemy were unused. 'Crack a few heeds, man!'

The Oceanians, who were not used to fists being used as weapons, let alone great-domed heads, began to back away as the Celts cracked skulls with their brows. The Oceanians could not understand how the Celts did not hurt *them-selves* with this method of fighting and began to kick out at the bare testicles they could see waving obscenely in front of them. The Celts were on to this, however, being quite good at such foot-to-balls village fighting themselves, and gave as good as they got during this deplorable brawl in the thick of the battle.

Suddenly, to the astonishment of the pale-skinned Celts, Kieto gave the signal for the Oceanians to retire quickly, back to the pa. The runners went out with their slates, then at a sign from Kieto the whole Oceanian army turned almost as one man and swiftly ran to safety, leaving the Celts bewildered and upset, swinging at air. Scots and Picts alike were incensed at this cowardly action, just when the fight was warming up. They had never witnessed anything like it in their lives and screamed taunts after the fleeing brown-skinned warriors, calling them old women, children and mice, and yelling at them to stand and fight like real men.

Hupa covered the retreat with a line of her bow-women, ladies of the Whakatane, whose deadly accurate fire prevented the faster runners amongst the Celts from catching stragglers. She and her archers picked off the more adventurous of the enemy, whose blood lust was greater than their common sense. Some of them were so high on battle passion they did not stop running even with an arrow through the head or heart.

While Oceanians congratulated one another on the speed of their feet, the Celts gathered themselves and ran pell-mell at the fortifications, only to receive the same treatment which had been meted out over the last two days of fighting. They turned in frustration and began walking back to the hills, complaining loudly about 'yellow-bellied brown-skins' who ran from the field just when the fight was becoming interesting.

They were about halfway back when the Oceanians

poured out of the pa, assumed fatatia, or long, straight combat lines, and began sweeping across the plain towards backs of the enemy.

Many of the Celts turned to meet them again, but were in disarray, their ranks shot with men who still believed they were on their way back to their camp to rest. They found themselves awkwardly placed at the bottom of the foothills, struggling to get up the same slopes they had rolled down so easily earlier in the day. Craig saw the pain of irritation and annoyance on their faces as they grappled with these peculiar tactics of fighting, then not-fighting, then fighting again. He could imagine they would be asking themselves what kind of creatures they were at war with, who, just when the outcome of the battle was about to be decided, turned and ran then came back when it was all supposed to be over and done with for the day.

Hand-to-hand fighting resumed, with both sides scoring minor victories.

Then Kieto gave the order for Ropa tahi.

Concentrate on killing the chieftains!

Although the Celts were naked, their chiefs displayed their wealth with shiny bronze amulets and torcs, decorated with spirals and centripetals. These were recognizable as the light caught their ornaments and signalled the rank of their wearers as surely as if they were helmets and cloaks. Oceanian warriors turned on these chieftains, ignoring fights with all others, and the slaughter of the Celt clan leaders began in earnest.

When those chieftains who were not at the forefront of the fighting saw what was happening, they began to panic. It was one thing to be part of a battle, but quite another to be selected out of the mass and have some thirty thousand savage warriors after your skin alone. One or two of the less courageous – or rather more sensible – of the chiefs turned and fled from the scene of the conflict.

Their clan members, on seeing their leaders flee, also decided to relinquish ground to the invaders.

Why should they stand firm when their supposedly most able warriors had shown them their heels?

Craig watched grimly as the whole army of Celts was in flight, racing back to the hills, while the Oceanians stood silently watching, gathering mana unto themselves. The day was won for the Oceanians, though Kieto was not quite so foolish as to think that there was an end to it. He knew this would only whet the appetite of the Celts, who would be back again with their numbers replenished.

3

That night Craig was sent up into the hills with a small escort to inform the Celts they could come down and collect their dead and severely wounded. He crossed the battle plain with Hupa and a dozen of her archers. When they sighted the fires of the enemy camps, Craig called out in Gaelic that he was entering under the sign of truce, to impart information. They were taken by escort to the Celtic war chief, Cormac, in his tent of animal skins high on the ridge.

Cormac regarded Craig sourly with his one eye.

'Why have ye come here, half-breed?' he asked with folded arms. 'To ask us not to use horses? Never again. Cowards are easily caught by men on horseback, for that's what ye are, damn ye. Ye run even when the battle's going your way.'

'I have come to ask for no favours, nor give any,' replied Craig. 'I come to tell you that you can collect your dead and wounded without fear of attack.'

'How is that?' snarled the one-eyed Cormac. 'Surely ye don't think we'll trust you after today? You'll probably fall on us like scavengers on sick deer and bite us like wee 'uns fighting at play with they sharp teeth. Probably when we've our backs turned, ye snivelling gilleans.'

'Why should you not trust us? We broke no agreements. We did nothing wrong.'

'Ye *ran*, damn ye!'

'This is not considered cowardly by our people, it is thought right and proper. A warrior must have fleet legs as well as strong arms. A warrior is judged on his skill in out-running the enemy, as well as whether he can kill that enemy. You must understand our ways are not the same as yours – what is considered cowardly by you is considered bold and skilful by us . . .'

'NEVER!' roared Cormac. 'He who runs is a coward, wherever ye hail from. He who attacks an enemy from the rear while he's walking back to his home is a treacherous cur. The brown-skins are both cowards and treacherous curs. I say it to your face, ye twixt-and-tweener.'

Craig was determined to ignore insults like 'half-breed' and 'twixt-and-tweener', references to his mixed blood.

'If you say that,' he replied in a firm, even voice, 'you're a liar and a man without honour.'

Cormac started forward, his one eye blazing, but he was checked by two of his fellow chieftains.

'Careful, Cormac – don't give them grounds for this man's accusations,' said one of his allies.

Cormac had his sword half out of its sheath and he snapped it back in again reluctantly.

'And what about that there today! We lost the chieftains of seven clans in that last ruckus. What a way to fight. D'ye hate us chieftains, laddie? Is that what it is? Do ye want to slaughter us all because we're born to lead?'

'It's one of the ways we fight – to single out the chiefs and attack them alone – ignoring all others. It puts confusion in the enemy. It makes them wonder who is next – maybe those with red hair, or black beards?' Craig folded his arms and stared at Cormac, adding softly, 'Why, were you scared?'

'Scared?' roared Cormac. 'Scared? I was shitting myself.

I could feel my arsehole pinching with fear – what would you do if ten, maybe twenty thousand men were after *your* guts alone? You'd bloody shite yerself, laddie, and no mistake.'

Craig grinned, seeing his father in these hairy men of war, who stank of grease and animal fat.

'Yes, I would – I'd do that all right – and it smells just the same coming from us – same colour too – and its just as humiliating to do it in front of comrades.'

Several of the Celtic chiefs present roared with laughter and Cormac could not help but join in.

'You're a strange one,' said the Celt war chief, 'but not as strange as the rest of them devils. Well, we'll collect our dead and wounded, but watch out tomorrow. The morn's morn we'll cut ye down like corn . . .'

As he was leaving, Cormac called after Craig.

'Listen, laddie, I like ye. You're the only one of them brown-skins I trust. Maybe it's because you're half-Celt, or maybe it's because your fether was a Pict, or maybe it's just because I think ye an honest man. Tell that chief o' yours that any dealings will be through you, an' naybody else.'

Craig felt elated. If he was to do his father's bidding, of attempting to reconcile the two peoples, then both sides had to trust in him. Kieto knew and trusted him. Now Cormac had said he did too. There were those who thought him a fence-sitter, neither one nor the other, and mistrusted him for that reason alone, but it was the two chiefs who were important. 'Thank you,' replied Craig. 'I'll tell him.'

The following day the fighting was renewed. This time the Scots and Picts used their horses, though since these were highland clans and none too rich, there were not enough horsemen to make any difference to the outcome of the battles. Oceanians then thought it fair to use their fortifications more, throwing rocks down on the Celts who struggled to get over the ditches and dykes, raining arrows on the massed warriors who tried to storm the pa and climb the wooden palisades. Each new battle brought both sides nearer to the conclusion that they were not going to get beyond a stalemate.

Some of the lowland Scots and borderers arrived on the scene and threw a certain amount of panic into the Oceanians.

The lowlanders were better equipped, better armed, than the highlanders. There was more organization about them, more discipline. The borderers came with large wheeled chariots and sometimes six horses to a team. Oceanians had never had much use for the wheel, which they knew only in the form of the rolling log, but they saw its worth in those chariots.

The Oceanians watched in amazement as the charioteers, one man in a canoe on wheels, came hurtling at their battle line clutching a bunch of spears. When the charioteer was a certain distance from the line he leapt over the front of his chariot, ran down the centre pole between the six horses, threw two or three of his spears into the mob of Oceanians, then ran back up the pole and into his place again, just in time to turn his horses. It was an awesome feat of control and judgement, not to forget the skill and balance required to run up and down the pole.

'Those men are as quick and nimble on their feet as any Oceanian,' said Craig to Kieto. 'No wonder my father admired horsemen so much.'

'If they had two hundred of them, we would be done for,' agreed Kieto. 'We're lucky they can only muster a dozen or so of those war machines.'

The battles were exhausting for both sides, but especially for the Oceanians not used to the chill weather. There was disease in both camps too, taking its toll on lives. Then, as spring turned to early summer, the Oceanians saw the true colours of this land. Some blue skies, some white clouds, and a green landscape with foamy tops to the distant mountains.

Wild flowers and herbs came out in profusion: such dainty alpine flowers with delicate colours. The sun showed itself three days in a row, albeit a rather more fragile sun than the islanders were familiar with. Nevertheless it produced hot days on the moors and in the foothills, with midges in their millions, biting the unprotected and ignorant Oceanians. In the dusk the irritating insects arrived in such thick clouds men and women could hardly breathe without filling their lungs with them.

'What mad god invented these?' cried Hupa to Craig as she was being bitten on her face, breasts and thighs one evening, and tried to keep them out of her hair with a flaming brand. 'What cruel deity would dream up such an insanity?'

The midges got into every piece of clothing, past every fishnet-covered doorway, into every room. Nowhere was safe from them. When the midges and their cousins the mosquitoes were not around there were the clegs, huge things that Craig's father had called 'horse flies', which had almost as nasty a bite as a flying shark. The Oceanians tried burning all sorts of materials and produced a variety of perfumes to get rid of the insects, but every one of them failed, if not wholly then in part.

With the early summer the deer emerged from the forests to add more meat to the baskets.

Fighting in the oppressive hinterland heat became a chore and more often than not the Oceanians preferred to remain inside their wooden walls, while the Scots and Picts drifted away back to their homes in the highlands and lowlands, leaving only the diehards to man the watch platforms and call names from the plains below. Sea raiders summoned by the Celts came in from the ocean side, to try to attack the Oceanians from the rear, but by this time the invaders had completed their pa and waggled their fingers at the men from the wild sea.

Kieto sent a clutch of canoes homewards, to the islands, with instructions to recruit more men. These duly arrived to fill the places of those who had died in battle or of sickness. Of the gods nothing was heard, but the thunder storms and wind storms and sea storms were many, testifying to the fact that the battles amongst supernatural lords and ladies was still raging. Kikamana and the other kahuna and tohunga tried to reach the gods through their atua, but were not successful.

During a great lull in the fighting, Craig took a message to the chiefs amongst the Celts, suggesting that the two sides swap entertainers for an evening. It was one of those gestures which occur in the middle of a war, which helps to form a better understanding between opponents. Craig, through his gift from Uetonga, was able to understand the Gaelic language, the nuances of Albannach culture, but his fellow warriors could not.

He persuaded Kieto that it would be good for both sides to have a truce, during which they could entertain one another, much like fighting stopped for the Arioi in Oceania when they arrived during a war betweeen two islands.

Craig confronted Cormac.

'You send your best people to us one evening, and the following evening we will come to you.'

Cormac viewed this scheme with great suspicion, as he did everything proposed by the Oceanians.

'What? Will ye fall on us to a man, after getting us drunk on that rotgut ye call *kava*? Will ye murder us in our seats, while we watch ye dancing like pretty wee fairies in the firelight, eh? Damn ye – you come to *us* for the first evening – then we'll come to you.'

Craig shrugged his shoulders.

'Fair enough. It doesn't matter to us which way round we do it. You can get us drunk on that stomach poison you call *wiskie*, and then chop us to pieces with your iron swords while we watch two oily Celts wrestling in the firelight and pretending they aren't enjoying touching each other's bodies.'

'They *don't* enjoy it, damn your eyes and liver,' roared the one-eyed Scot. 'It's a manly sport of strength and skill.'

'So you say,' sniffed Craig. 'We'll reserve judgement.'

When Prince Daggan heard about the entertainment, he called his wife Siko to his side.

'This is our chance,' he said. 'Tell me what I should do.'

'I have been sending my spies amongst the Celts, to learn of things which might be advantageous to us. There is a Scot who is not in tune with his nation at this present time. His name is Douglass son of Douglass. It was his father who was killed by Seumas and he thus bears a grudge against Craig, being the son of his father's killer.

'He and his clan have been banished by the war chief, Cormac, but they have sympathizers amongst others in the Celtic camp. We must contact one of these people and arrange something for tonight, or tomorrow night, when Kieto is vulnerable. Leave it to me. There must be no suspicion attached to you. You must be untainted when they come to you and ask you to take the dead Kieto's place as chief of chiefs.'

'I'm happy to leave things in your hands, my wife – but tell me – these agents, these spies of yours – are they human?'

Siko gave her husband a tight smile. 'Of course they aren't – I conjured them from other regions. Have you not seen the balepa, floating above the hills at night? Have you not felt the coldness of the kabu, lurking in the shadows? Or the marks in the dust of the putuperereko's great bollocks, where he's been dragging them around the battle plains? You should watch for these signs more closely, my husband.'

'Ah,' replied Daggan, shuddering, 'I thought so.'

Daggan left his wife, going off into the night. He had a

meeting with Kapu, who was assisting the prince with his plans to become leader of the expedition. It was not that Kapu hated his father, or wanted his downfall, but he was frustrated by his father's lack of faith in him. He wanted to be made a chief, to lead Rarotongans into battle, himself at their head. Kieto would have none of it. He told his son he was too inexperienced to be made a general: that he would have to wait some years.

Kapu was impatient. He needed recognition *now*. He was fed up with being second to his sister, who though not lifted up by her father grasped the thing she wanted with both hands. She lead her Whakatane, albeit unsanctioned by her father, while Kapu could not raise more than two or three men under his command. The older warriors laughed at his efforts to organize a secret society with him at the head. The younger ones were too impressed by his dismissal by the veterans to follow Kapu. Unlike the young women, they were afraid of losing their mana by following an unseasoned warrior.

So he had thrown his lot in with Daggan, who promised that the whole Rarotongan contingent would be given to Kapu, should Daggan ever become war chief.

PART SIX

Island of the Wondrous Beast

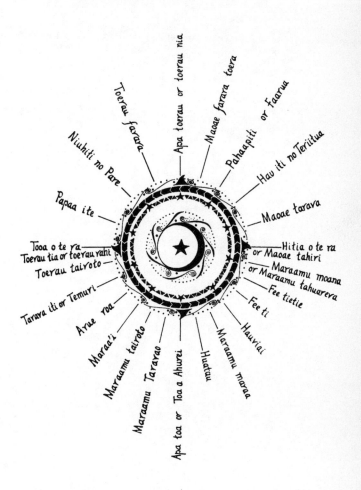

1

It occurred to Craig, through knowledge of his father's ways, that one aspect of their two separate cultures was the love of island stories. Seumas had often told his son that though the Celts were not a great sea-going nation, they were just as fascinated by individual voyages out on the ocean as were the Oceanians themselves. As with all nations there was amongst the Albannachs those men who built boats and went out to explore the unknown.

'Why have none come this far?' Craig had asked his father. 'How is it they have not washed up on the shores of our islands?'

'The boats they build are not like your ocean-going voyagers,' Seumas had replied. 'They are small one-man craft – little reed boats, or even a thing we call a coracle, a small round framework covered in animal skin barely large enough to contain a man – and they would not be able to make the distances to these islands. Our exploring mariners tended to leave from the far shores of Albainn, on the other side. They visit nearer islands in colder seas than these . . .'

But there was this love of island stories amongst both peoples and Craig informed Boy-girl, who was to be the tale teller for the evening, of this fact. She caused a bit of a sensation amongst the rough Scots and Picts, when she stepped into the firelight to do her act. The word was passed to them, by Craig, that Boy-girl was a man brought up as a woman. He knew this would both shock and fascinate them, help to ensure and hold their attention, while Boy-girl related the tale.

Craig, for the most part, translated the words for the benefit of the Celts. However, many of the kahuna and tohunga had begun to learn the language of the Celts, through captured warriors, and being people of magic they were progressing at a rapid rate. Thus people like the Farseeing-virgin Kikamana were able to assist Craig in his endeavours to make the stories available to the ears of the Scots and Picts.

'This is the story of the Island of the Poukai Bird and involves two people – Pungarehu, an Oceanian warrior, and Seumas-the-Black, a Celt like yourselves. These two between them, with equal merit, helped to slay the monstrous Poukai Bird which had attacked, killed and eaten so many unfortunate castaways on its strange and magical island . . .'

The Celtic audience stared at Boy-girl with wide eyes, taking in the shells and ribbons with which she decorated her long greying hair, noting the flamboyant and colourful dress she wore, observing her tall graceful figure and her complexion kept smooth over the years by sweet-smelling ointments, aware of the perfumes she exuded and her fragrant breath. Not one of them dare look at another, for fear they would reveal something about themselves which would forever be used to ridicule them.

They were held, too, by her strange words, for Boy-girl was like most Oceanian, and indeed Celtic, storytellers – she was a priest of that profession – and her words were sacred no matter what the language or understanding.

When she had finished her tale the Celts turned to one another and nodded gravely, mentioning that it was good that one of themselves was involved in such an heroic incident. They studiously avoided any reference to Boy-girl's gender, preferring instead to switch the subject of conversation to hunting, while giving each other hearty thumps on the shoulder.

Next Craig himself entertained them with a magnificent display of talent on the drums. At the end of this they cheered wildly and called for more wiskie. After Craig came acrobats, archery displays, poets, wrestling and dancing. The Oceanians avoided doing the hura, knowing it would offend their audience in the extreme to see two dancers actually copulating, albeit through grass skirts.

Craig remarked to Kieto that there was in both races this ambiguity. The Celts would come into battle naked, but they would have regarded the hura as distasteful. The Oceanians were prudish about nudity, but allowed themselves to be carried off by the sexuality of a dance.

The haka was a different thing and the Celts had seen the Oceanians do this before a battle. They witnessed it now at close quarters, finding the lolling tongues, the rolling eyes, and the strutting tattooed legs and jutting jaws just as awesome, just as intimidating, as they had been on the battlefield. Some of the younger men wanted to join in at the end.

Finally, when the show was almost over, one burly young crofter with sandy hair jumped into the circle and challenged any Oceanian wrestler to take him on. His comrades cheered and spat into the flames of the fire. The young man wore just his breeks and nothing else, stomping around the ring, yelling for an opponent to dare to step forward out of the 'brown-skins'.

Craig translated all this for the Oceanians.

Boy-girl stepped into the ring, removed her top and stared pointedly at the bulge in the front of the young man's breeks.

'Sorry I've been so long,' she said, 'I've been smearing my body with coconut oil and powdering my naughty bits.

You need to do that before wrestling, you know. Look how my arms gleam in the firelight. Exciting, isn't it? I'm ready now.'

She stood languidly waiting for the young man to understand her words as Kikamana repeated all this in Gaelic.

The lad gawped at her, shifted his feet awkwardly, stared at his now quiet comrades, then mumbled an excuse before rushing off into the night.

At first the silence continued, then a sudden roar of laughter from both Oceanians and Celts ripped into the night air, while Boy-girl smiled sweetly and pranced around the ring, offering a fresh challenge to the Celts.

No one took her up on the proposal.

Before the Oceanians left the Celtic encampment, Craig asked Cormac-the-Venomous a question.

'When you first came to us there was a man called Douglass Barelegs, son of Douglass, who wanted to kill me. I know why he wishes to do so and my father charged me to make my peace with him. Where is the man now?'

Cormac said, 'Banished. He would have struck ye down the next time he saw you. He hates you and your family and would slaughter you to a man – or woman. I've no love for you, ye wee bastard, but you're too valuable to us as a go-between – there is no one else. I exiled him.'

Cormac folded his arms and looked out into the night.

'He's gone to join the Angles, damn his hide. It would have been better for him to go to the Bride Isles, but he's gone to seek the assistance of our traditional enemies. I would stay well clear of that one, Craig-the-Black, for he'll have your testicles drying on the end of his cromach stick else.'

'I've heard of the Angles, and another people, the Jutes.'

'Aye, well, the Angles and us don't see eye to eye – we make very poor neighbours if you get my meaning. The Jutes, well, there's not so many of them – just a wee area right up the top end of this place ye call Land-o'-Mists. The

Angles steal Jute babies and raise them as if they were dogs. If ye go into battle against the Angles, ye'll see these naked men on the end o' leashes – savage, mindless creatures brought up without the meaning of language, kept like dogs, fed like dogs, running on all fours and snarling and snapping. They'll tear your head off if they catch you, those Jute curs . . .'

The following night the entertainment was returned when the Celts came to the campfires outside the pa. As the Oceanians had the night before, they brought with them their women and children, to enjoy the fun. There was much chatter in both languages which took some time for the clan chiefs on both sides to quell.

Finally, Kieto stepped into the area ringed by torches on posts, to welcome the enemy to the Oceanian night fires.

'. . . we know you will match, and probably even surpass, our attempts at entertainment yesterday evening,' he told the Celts politely, 'and as for wrestling . . .' he got no further than these words, however, for suddenly one of Cormac's bodyguards leapt from his seat on a log beside the great chieftain.

'ASSASSIN!' he yelled.

Before anyone knew what was happening this man had thrown a double-bladed battle-axe towards Kieto.

There was a shocked silence amongst the crowd as the axe swished through the air.

The weapon went spinning over Kieto's left shoulder, into a crowd of Celts on the far side. The blade buried itself in the chest of a slim blond warrior, who was at that moment drawing a bow. The loosed arrow went skimming erratically across the ground to bury itself in one of the campfires, kicking up clouds of sparks.

As he fell forwards, blood spurted like mountainside spring water from the chest of the mortally wounded Scot, his heart split in twain.

There was pandemonium, with Celtic clansmen leaping into the ring with drawn swords, and Oceanians instantly forming a guard around Kieto, waving their clubs and brandishing daggers. Warriors from both sides were yelling and snatching flaming brands from their holders. They were all looking to their leaders for guidance. Should they fight? Should they begin striking down the enemy? Who should make the first move?

Fortunately, the crush of people was such that few of the hotheads amongst both armies had room to use their weapons. They were hemmed in on all sides by those warriors at the rear pushing forwards, trying to find out what was happening. Many had no idea what was going on at all, being too far at the back to see what had occurred, and merely excited by the noise and movement around them. On top of all this, children were crying, caught up in the milling confusion of bodies.

Craig called for calm in both languages. Cormac took up his cry, as did Kieto. After a period of jostling and threatening, peace was finally restored. Celt had killed Celt and the truce had not actually been broken.

'One of Douglass's men,' growled Cormac, when the dead archer's body was brought to him. He kicked the corpse savagely and looked around the faces of his warriors. 'Who let thon bastard into my camp?'

Whichever clan was responsible, they were not saying.

Cormac had his enemies within as well as outside his camp. He had bonded together all clansmen for a common purpose, but that did not make him the idol of all. There were still those who would disrupt Cormac's efforts to unite the clans.

'Well,' said Kieto, 'I have to thank your bodyguard for his sharp eyes and the quickness of his hands. If it had not been for him I would probably be dead.'

'My people know better than to break the sanctity of a truce,' replied Cormac through the interpreters. 'I gave express orders to kill any man who looked like doing so. Ye have my deepest apology for this outrage. I'll not have ye thinking we are uncivilized barbarians who can't keep their word, nor have any sense of honour.'

'The thought never crossed my mind. There are always rotten fruit amongst the good. Your apology is unnecessary. The deed was not yours.'

Cormac looked down at the archer.

'I doubt this stupid *luch* would have killed ye though. Douglass's archers couldna hit a mountain if they were climbing up the sides . . .'

While the chiefs were talking thus, helping to pacify their separate peoples, Hupa had gone to the fire and retrieved the arrowhead, the haft having burned away. She had discovered what she feared, that this was one of Lioumere's teeth. Had the assassin been allowed to fire his arrow at Kieto, the Oceanian chieftain would be lying dead on the ground instead of the archer.

'Where did the Celts get this?' she asked Craig, when he came to her side. 'And how did they know its power?'

'Obviously we have a traitor in our midst.'

'Or traitors,' replied Hupa. 'I'll speak to my father after the night's entertainment.'

With some semblence of calm restored, the evening's entertainments were allowed to begin.

There were feats of strength, with men lifting great stones and throwing them over a high wooden bar; tree trunks were tossed around as if they were kindling; there was horsemanship, bagpipe playing and running. For the most part the Celtic entertainment consisted of showing feats of prowess. There were sweet flute players though and drummers and others of a musical turn.

There was poetry too – a strong lilting poetry which spoke of heroic deeds – which Craig tried to do justice to in his translation.

Then came the storyteller for the Celts, who was a

pugfaced, short, stocky man with deep blue eyes and flaxen hair. He stamped about the ground in front of the listeners, not only re-enacting the scene, playing several roles, but speaking as if he were actually there, witnessing what had taken place.

'As you all know,' said the storyteller, 'the voyager in this story is called Maeldune, who built himself a coracle of animal skins and set out one blustery day. He found many magical islands on his travels, but the one I am going to tell you about is the Island of the Wondrous Beast.

'There came a day when Maeldune needed to replenish his stores and he came to an island which was nothing but bare rock and sparse vegetation. Around this island was built a stone barrier, constructed either to keep people out, or to keep something else inside. Maeldune knew immediately, when he saw the sluggish water swilling around the island, and the sombre aspect of the gloomy landscape, that this was a magical island. He knew he should not go ashore.

'Unfortunately, Maeldune's fresh water was so low he could not continue without taking on more. He beached his coracle and climbed the stone wall. Once on the other side he took his goatskins to the nearest burn and began to fill them. All the while he kept his eyes peeled for anything unusual.

'Sure enough, when he was halfway through his task, he saw a strange creature emerge from the rocks. When the creature noticed Maeldune it went as mad as a loon and began running around the landscape, pausing occasionally to make sure the handsome Maeldune was still watching it.

'Every so often the beast would turn in its own skin, so that its hide remained still and the body inside reversed itself. Then on other occasions its body would remain still, but its skin would flow around it like water over a stone.

'Once Maeldune had filled his water bags, he ran back down to his coracle. The beast appeared to be annoyed that he was leaving and began to launch sharp stones at him. One of these missiles hit the coracle, sending it spinning around in circles on the surface of the sea. It spun right out into the ocean, with Maeldune feeling sick to his stomach, but having escaped the beast by the creature's own hand.'

There were sounds of appreciation from the Oceanian audience at the end of this story. It was true, they said to each other, the Albannachs had some similarities with themselves. They both enjoyed the same type of magical island story.

What happened next, however, perturbed the Oceanians.

The storyteller began strutting around the circle, making rude gestures with his fingers at the Oceanians. He called them old women and said they were not fit to scrub under the arms of his vest, let alone share the same air. He said their penises were the size of bone needles, their balls were like apple pips and their arseholes the size of bear caves, through frequent misuse by their fellow warriors. Craig decided to translate the storyteller's obscenities and insults, just as he had related the story the man had told.

This incensed Kieto and his men, who looked askance at each other wondering what it was all about.

Finally the storyteller told them he was not just a teller of tales, but also a famous barefist fighter from the border country, where the land raiders came from. Did the Oceanians know anything about barefist fighting? He doubted it. They all looked like pansy-faced wrestlers to him! Barefist fighting was the sport of *real* men. Let one of the brown-skins step into the circle and he would knock them down in an instant.

All the Celts cheered and stamped their feet at these words, adding their own insults to those of the pugfaced storyteller's. The hounds which had accompanied many of the Celts came up on their muscled haunches and howled into the night air. Foxes in the mountains around the plain took up the cry and began singing too. For a moment the whole world seemed to be in discord, with humans, dogs and foxes in full cry.

Now the Oceanians looked up at the moon, down at their own feet, and everywhere except into each other's eyes. They had never heard of boxing and thought it a strange thing to do. Were they actually expected to ball their hands into a fist, then strike another man's face with it? It did not seem right. It was a barbaric, grotesque, and unwholesome sport.

'What, are ye babies that ye can't fight with your fists?' cried Cormac. 'Is my man here expected to go home unchallenged by these brave brown-skinned warriors?'

As this was translated by Craig at last one of the Oceanians had had enough of the taunts. He stepped forward and removed his cloak, to bare his upper body. There was a great cheer from his own people, followed by one from the Albannachs. Watching out of the corner of his eye the Oceanian saw his opponent practising punches on the air in front of him.

So the Oceanian did the same, much to the mirth of the Scots and Picts, who cried out in amusement that he looked like a fairy picking blossoms from the branches of a cherry tree.

Finally, when the shadow boxing was over, the Celt removed his cloak to face his would-be opponent.

At this the Oceanian gave out a cry of surprise, for his Celtic adversary was clearly a woman, with large flattish breasts which had been hidden by the thick sheepskin cloak. She faced him with a grin on her broad features, her muscular shoulders gleaming palely in the firelight. She swung a right hook at his jaw which he managed to avoid only by leaping back with all the agility of a frightened deer.

Coming stolidly forward she threw a straight left which grazed past his startled nose, just nicking the end of it and causing his eyes to water. Then another right, this time to his stomach taking all the wind out of him. Finally he let out a cry and went running off into the night, with the jeers of the Albannachs loud in his ears.

The barefist-fighting-storyteller put on her cloak and with a great smirk on her face left the circle.

The Celts all rose to go, gathering up their hounds and their children, laughing quietly to themselves. As they went off into the night, Cormac turned and called to Craig, 'Tit for tat, ye bastards. Tit for bloody tat! And that's the truth of the matter, eh? In fact *two* bloody tits for one skinny tat. Ye don't get the better of an Albannach that easily!'

After the evening's entertainment was over and the Celts had all but gone, the Oceanians began to drift back to their several pa. Kieto had deliberately not let the Albannachs inside the pa, or they would have noted the weak spots and used the knowledge to advantage. The following day the truce would be over, they would be at war again, and men would be out on the plains battling for supremacy over their adversaries.

Since the war had reached such a stalemate, it was mostly a case of Celtic champions walking up to one pa or another and throwing down a challenge. Eventually someone would go out to meet the challenger and single combat would take place under the eyes of those on the fighting platforms of the pa, and those of the enemy standing on the slopes which formed a natural amphitheatre for the Albannachs.

One or the other combatant would eventually triumph, and someone's body would get dragged through the dust by its heels; there would be cheers and jeers from one side or the other, and by that time everyone would be hungry and the morning's conflict would cease in favour of eating and drinking.

In the afternoon there would be a repeat of the morning's action, with different protagonists.

There was one warrior from the Celts, a giant of a man called Guirk, who advanced to the walls of the pa every day and called for Kieto to come out and fight him. This Guirk, who had a bright sword and shield of metal, would fight no other opponents, rejecting anyone else who answered his challenge. When Kieto did not emerge after three challenges, Guirk would call the Oceanian general a coward, a whining cur, and many other insults, before trudging back to his own camp and leaving the field free for others.

The one-armed Kieto was not so stupid as to allow this to anger him to the point of accepting the challenge. He guessed it to be a Celtic ploy. While he did not consider himself entirely irreplaceable, this was his war and he was the spirit of the invasion. Without him he knew the Oceanians would lose heart and return to their canoes. They would sail back home to their islands, then sometime in the future the Albannachs, or the Angles, or both, would form their own fleet and follow the Oceanians to their islands, and subjugate them.

Kieto was not going to risk all this simply for the sake of vanity and pride.

'Let him yell all he likes,' he told his advisers, some of whom were for and some against answering the challenge. 'I am a symbol to my people and I am not going to get drawn or sidetracked into a petty brawl with some bone-headed warrior out to make a name for himself.'

Though his son Kapu was incensed at this decision by his father, saying all men and women would call him and his family cowards, his daughter Hupa approved. She believed the Celt had been sent by the chiefs on the other side, in order to disrupt the Oceanians and get them arguing amongst themselves.

Once, she had waited on a fighting platform of the pa, until Guirk came to within archer distance to shout his dare. She let loose an arrow at the man and was astonished when it was deflected by his black metal shield.

Guirk removed himself from range and Kieto admonished his daughter, telling her the rules of single combat did not allow intervention by third parties.

'You are impugning the honour of all Oceanians by employing such sneak action,' he had told her. 'It is fortunate the man was not struck – you must not do such a thing again.'

Hupa had begged her father's forgiveness and was left wondering how she had missed with her magic arrow.

'There must be other magical forces at work,' she told Craig. 'Lioumere's teeth *never* miss.'

Kieto had sent a message of regret to Guirk, apologizing for the incident and saying it would not occur again.

The following day the giant Guirk had come back again, daring Kieto to meet him face to face in single combat.

Craig had thought about all this, after the incident with the Celtic archer earlier in the evening, and wondered whether the two occurrences had anything to do with one another.

Now it was dark, with the cold distant stars fixed in their places on the roof of voyaging. These frozen stars seemed to Craig to be further away than they had been on Rarotonga, and the heavens less fluid. The face of Marama, God of the Moon, husband of Hine-keha, appeared sterner here. Or was it indeed Marama, who peered down on the landscape of Albainn? Perhaps it was the moon god of the Celts? Was it because the two opposing gods were locked in immortal combat, that the face on the moonscape appeared so severe and forbidding?

Craig had begun to walk back to the pa when Kieto called him over.

'Craig,' said Kieto, 'I have come to a decision. The Farseeing-virgin, high priestess Kikamana, has been looking into the future. She tells me that it is not the Celts we have to fear, but the Angles and other tribes from above the border. *These* are the warriors who will one day build ships of war and sail to Oceania, to try to destroy our peoples. It is the Angles who must be taught a lesson in warfare – who must be discouraged from ever attempting such an invasion on Oceania.

'Therefore I have decided to sue for peace with the Celts, so that we might concentrate our forces on the Angles. It would seem the Celts have no love for them either. But you must be the mediator between ourselves and the Celts. Cormac would listen to no other. It is essential you make yourself available tomorrow. You will go to Cormac and put the proposal to him, so that we might not waste the summer in this futile fighting between two peoples who need have no fear of one another.'

Craig was elated. His father's work was bearing fruit. If the Celts and Oceanians could join forces, one swift battle might be enough to subdue the Angles. Then they could go home before this terrible thing called 'winter' was upon the land.

'I'll go to Cormac at first light,' said Craig. 'He trusts me. We'll have peace before the sun warms the soil.'

'Good.'

Kieto left Craig then, the war chief going back with his bodyguard towards the pa.

Craig stood for a few moments, thinking about what had been said, obviously delighted with Kieto's decision. It was while he was thus engaged in thought that suddenly Kapu appeared out of the darkness. He seemed to be in an agitated state.

'Quickly, Craig,' said the boy. 'Someone has abducted my sister Hupa. Two Celts. I saw them drag her off into that clump of trees over there . . .'

'What?' cried Craig, peering in the direction of a dark patch just definable as a spinney in the starlight. 'We must get some more men.'

'No, there isn't time,' said the young man, plucking at Craig's arm. 'We must rescue her – you and I. Everyone else has gone back to the pa.'

Craig stared around him. There was enough starlight to make out shapes in the gloom. The youth was right. The two of them were now alone. Valuable time would be wasted by running back to the pa. He turned to Kapu.

'Right – let's go,' he said. 'You get behind me. I don't want to take you back to your father with a broken skull.'

For once Kapu did not argue. He slipped behind Craig and followed him up to the treeline.

At the edge of the copse, Craig paused, but he heard a strange noise. A low whistling was coming from the centre of the clump of trees.

'I can hear something,' he told Kapu. 'You keep a few paces to the rear. If I'm attacked, you must come up swiftly behind my attackers and deal with them best you can. Between the two of us we should be able to cope with them.'

Craig began to creep forward. He followed the sound with his ear. It seemed to get lower and less distinct the nearer he got to it.

Brambles snatched at his clothing. Roots tried to trip him. The undergrowth became denser and less easy to navigate nearer the middle of the wood. Finally he reached a spot from which he was positive the sound originated. Parting the leaves of a tall shrub, he stared down to see a man. The fellow was squatting on his haunches. He had a blade of grass between cupped hands and was busy blowing through it, making the sound Craig had heard. On sensing someone's presence the man looked up into Craig's face – and then smiled broadly.

'Got you!' he said.

At that moment Craig felt a thump on the back of the neck as if from a club. Those stars he had believed so distant were now swimming immediately around his head.

He staggered forward a couple of paces. Then a second blow landed right where a lump was already forming. Craig son of Seumas slipped quietly to the woodland floor and lost consciousness.

The man who had struck Craig with a heavy cudgel stood over his body for a moment, looking down on his work with some satisfaction. His aide and brother nodded at a good job done between the two of them. Then the brown-skin, the minion of Daggan, Douglass Barelegs' spy, came out of the bushes to stare down on the body of his father's friend. Also, out of the far side of the copse came Prince Daggan.

'He's not dead, is he?' whispered Kapu in a frightened voice. 'You haven't killed him?'

'No, he's just sleeping,' said Daggan. 'You did well, Kapu – we will soon have you raised above your sister. Once I am war chief your status will be that of my right hand man. How does that sound?'

Kapu seemed to be having a change of heart, now that the deed had been done. His worried expression did not change. He continued to fret over Craig's body.

'I wish it didn't have to be like this. You promised we would avoid bloodshed. You said Craig would be taken without undue force and sold into slavery in the north. I wouldn't want to be responsible for his death. I mean, as a slave he would at least be alive, and maybe one day set free again. He looks dead to me. Are you sure you didn't kill him . . .?'

'He's not dead,' growled Daggan. 'Stop chattering, boy.'

But Kapu's voice was becoming shriller and he was wringing his hands now.

'We shouldn't have done this thing. My father will be absolutely furious. Look, can't we find some other way of making you war chief? Perhaps if I persuaded my father to retire from the position . . .?'

Daggan shook his head slowly, looking at the trembling

youth with tight lips. Then he nodded sharply to the two rough-looking characters who had felled Craig. A knife was produced and instantly plunged into the unsuspecting Kapu's throat, thus quenching any cry of alarm.

The boy fell to his knees, gargling, his hands trying to staunch the blood. Two swift and savage blows with the club on the back of his neck broke his spinal cord. Kapu fell dead at the feet of the three men.

Without anything further being said, the brother of the man with the cudgel lifted the body and carried it to a spot further in the trees. There was a prepared grave. He tossed Kapu's corpse into the hole and immediately filled it in. Afterwards dead leaves and fallen branches disguised the fresh earth. Then the man walked back to his two companions. He made a gesture of affirmation. Prince Daggan left the spinney.

Punga had been in the middle of a great battle when he heard Craig's silent call for help. The Oceanian gods had joined in battle with the Celtic gods, at much the same time that Kieto's army had first confronted Cormac's. Since then Punga had been wounded in a thousand places, but gods are not like men, they can withstand such injuries and still find the strength to fight.

Punga's thick feathered helmet had been split, his shield cracked, but he still wielded his club with energy. Several Celtic deities had felt its blows on their backs and heads, and respected the strength of the god behind those strikes.

Leaving the battlefield for a moment, the God of Ugly Creatures looked upon the scene below and witnessed Craig's abduction. Seeing the girl Hupa nearby he directed her attention to the scene and was satisfied to see that she followed the men who had Craig in their hands. It was the best Punga could do for the time being. He went back into the fray, avoiding a blow from a savage Celtic mountain god, and attempting to deliver one of his own.

All around him was fire and flood – mayhem – as the rival gods fought for space in the minds of men.

When Craig came to he found he was bound hand and foot. He was in some sort of cart drawn by an animal very much like a horse, except that this creature was smaller, stockier and not quite so handsome. Sitting up on the cart with him was the man he had seen blowing on the blade of grass. On foot, holding a strap on the jaws of the beast of burden, was another man. Craig did not recall seeing either one before this night.

These were rough-looking fellows in wolfskin cloaks, with leggings held on by long, criss-crossed leather sandal straps. Both men had shaven scalps around a hairy patch from which hung single long plaits. When they saw he was awake, they began speaking a guttural language which Craig did not understand. One of them said something to Craig but he remained silent, not knowing in the slightest what was going on.

'Ah,' said the one on the cart, in Gaelic now, 'don't understand our tongue, eh?'

'Who are you?' asked Craig. 'Why am I here?'

'Why, as to that, me and my companion here are what they call Jutes, so called because we hail from a piece of land which juts out into the sea. Not on this island, but in another great place, far away across the cold sea to the south-east.'

'South-east? What does that mean?'

The man grinned at him through a charcoal beard.

'Bottom end, right hand side, keep on going.'

Craig did not understand but let it drop.

'Where are you taking me?'

'There's a man wants to see you, down below the border. Says he's going to hang you, then draw you, and then have you quartered by four sturdy cart horses. That means they'll dangle you by your neck from a rope until you're half dead, cut open your stomach to let out your entrails, then have your limbs torn out of your torso. How does that sound?'

'Painful,' replied Craig.

The man grinned again, savagely, revealing several broken teeth behind a scarred lip.

'I've heard it's that all right. It's painful. They say you never forget the screaming of a hung, drawn and quartered man. They say it haunts you to the death . . .'

The man leading the peculiar-looking horse said something in his own tongue and got a sharp reply from the one on the cart.

'Wants to know what we're saying to each other,' said broken-teeth. 'Doesn't trust either of us.'

'Does he not speak Gaelic?' asked Craig, thinking everyone in the Land-of-Mists spoke the language of the Celts.

'Naw, he only speaks Anglish – he's an ignorant man. He's not as bright as that donkey he's guiding. You got to make allowances for him though, for he helped his brother murder his mother and father when he was ten. Sort of sticks the brain together that kind of experience – hasn't moved on much since that time.' The man gave Craig another lopsided grin. 'I ought to know – I'm his brother, see.'

Whether this man was telling the truth or not, Craig knew he was in the hands of two evil characters.

'Who is this person who wishes to have me at his mercy – let me guess – Douglass Barelegs?'

'Ow, you're a clever one and no mistake,' cried his delighted companion. 'The very man. He's prepared to be generous too. Paying us well, he is. And you'd never guess it, he's got a couple of you invaders helping him. A man and his wife. A very pompous fellow they call Prince Daggan. And the woman's called Siko. Wouldn't mind humping that dark ewe, don't mind saying so, even to a man who's about to die.'

'Daggan and Siko are with Douglass?'

'Shouldn't have told you that, should I? Still, even if we can't deliver you for some reason, we've been ordered not to let you go. I think a red-hot iron poker up the arsehole was mentioned in dispatches? Ow! Makes you clench your buttocks when you think of it, don't it? Nasty way to die. Almost as bad as the triple-torture I mentioned – not quite – almost. Now you get some sleep, build your stength up for the big day ahead of you – weve got a long way to go yet, my lad.'

'Glad to hear it,' replied Craig, determined not to slip into a state of despair. His main concern was that, until he was able to escape, the war between the Oceanians and the Celts would continue. Cormac would not listen to any other messenger from the Oceanians. Craig had to get back, so that peace talks could start between the two peoples. In the meantime things might deteriorate between the Celts and Oceanians, to the point where reparations would not be possible. A great wave of despair and frustration swept through Craig. He had to get back, or all his father's work would come to nothing.

They hurried past a single great tree, from which dangled bleached rags and ribbons which fluttered in the dawn breezes. The tree's bole was thick, hollowed in places, and reminiscent of a human face. The two men glanced nervously at this shrine to some unknown cluster of spirits. Clearly they were not a couple who could laugh away the superstitions of others, nor tread easily over landscapes upon which they trespassed.

2

Seven days and seven nights the abductors carried Craig across country. Craig might have despaired did he not believe some god or other was watching over him. He felt, deep in his heart, that some deity was caring for his welfare. Thus the hope of release did not die in his breast.

For the most part they kept to lonely highways, mere tracks such as an animal might make, through moor and weald, through forest and field, over beck and gushing torrent, around hills and hollows. Until on the eighth day they came to a wide lake, where Broken-teeth told his brother, whom Craig had now named Big-nose, that they should rest. They settled on the grass at the edge of the lake with a dark wood to their back and the shining waters to their front.

For the past week it had been raining. They had trudged through muck and mire until all three men were sick of being wet and plastered with mud. Broken-teeth said it was good for him and his brother, for it meant that not many people were abroad. As Jutes they had to avoid coming into contact with both highland and lowland clans while in Albainn. Now that they were in border country he told

Craig, there were still bands of thieves, cut-throats and raiders roaming around.

'If we see any I shall yell for assistance,' Craig told his captors. 'Then perhaps the red-hot poker for you too, eh?'

Broken-teeth, tending a peat fire on which he was boiling pigeon's eggs, gave a little shudder.

'In this part of the world they use starving rats,' said Broken-teeth. 'They strap them in a cage to your stomach, so the only way out for the hungry beasts is to gnaw their way through your belly and past your backbone. If you're going to yell, you might think on that before you open your mouth.'

Craig did not think there was a great deal to choose between any of the forms of death he was being offered, so he reserved his decision until the time came when he had the opportunity to use it. As it was the two brothers seemed expert at avoiding company, so there was not much point in worrying about it. In the meantime his bonds were cutting into his limbs, chafing his skin, and his immediate concern was the use of his legs.

'Can I be allowed to walk around?' asked Craig. 'My legs feel like someone else's.'

Broken-teeth said something to Big-nose and the other brother came and undid Craig's feet. He left his hands bound tightly behind his back, but tied another long rope in a noose around his throat, the end of which he attached to his wrist.

Broken-teeth said, 'My brother will strangle you if you try to run – he's not too fussy about things like that.'

'I'm sure he's not,' said Craig.

Craig tried to climb to his feet, but his legs were like dead eels. There was no strength in them and hardly any feeling. He fell over several times, much to the merriment of the two brothers. Their sense of humour was extraordinarily rich and bountiful. Finally, he asked them if they would untie his hands, so that he could rub his legs and feet.

'Oh, yes, we're likely to do that, aren't we?' replied Broken-teeth.

'I give you my word I will not try to escape on this occasion.'

'Your word? You a man of honour then? Are we supposed to trust your word?'

'Yes.'

Broken-teeth surprised him then by shrugging and saying, 'All right, but if you do run, remember we know the country, you don't.'

Once his hands had been untied Craig set to massaging his ankles and calves. When the blood came back into his limbs it was excruciatingly painful. This was cause for another few guffaws from the brothers. Finally, Craig managed to get to his feet and totter around the campsite, crashing into the bivouac Big-nose had built. After a while he regained use of his legs and was able to stagger down to the lake, on the end of the long leash, to drink the cool waters.

On the way down the bank he fell once again, on to ground extraordinarily soft. He looked down, expecting to see moss, but instead found a patch of flattened thistles. This surprised him but before he could discover what was going on, he was jerked to his feet by Broken-teeth, tugging on the other end of the rope.

'Are you going to lie there, or go down for a drink?' demanded his captor.

'Drink,' replied Craig, staring at the spot in front of his feet.

'Well, get on with it then.'

With a shrug of his shoulders Craig did as he was told, staggering the last few yards down to the edge of the lake.

It was as he was drinking, looking down into the clear waters, that he saw the horse. His first wild thought was that he could use the creature to escape. He had seen them ridden by the Celts and it did not look too difficult to him.

You simply sat on the beast's back and gripped its mane with your right hand, slapping its rump with your left. The horse always seemed to do as it was told without too much fuss.

But then Craig suddenly realized that this horse was actually on the bottom of the lake, racing through a forest of green waving fronds. He jerked upright. Horses were quite new and magical creatures to him, but this did not seem right at all. No one had told him they were aquatic beasts. So far as he knew they were air-breathing creatures fit only for the land.

Yet here was this wild magnificent beast charging through the weeds on the bed of a lake, looking like a demon with its blazing eyes.

'Hey!' he called excitedly to Broken-teeth. 'Come over here, quickly.'

Now the creature below wheeled, stopped and then stared at the sound of the voice. Craig could see its flaxen mane floating in the currents, its beautiful tail drifting out behind it. It curled back its lips and revealed its teeth. Its eyes were like bright suns which burned in its head. Its nostrils flared and blew plumes of tiny bubbles. One hoof began scraping the muddy bottom, raising swirling clouds of mud. Craig tried to tear his gaze from that of the creature's, but found it impossible to turn away. Craig felt a growing urge to join the beast on the bottom of the lake.

'What is it?' snapped Broken-teeth, testily, not moving from his place at the fire. 'Your legs gone again?'

'No, come here – there's a horse on the bottom of the lake. It's looking at me. I think it wants me to dive down to it. I've never seen a creature like it. It seems to have stars for eyes . . .'

Broken-teeth went pale and came hurrying over to where Craig was kneeling. He looked once down into the waters of the lake, saw the horse, and immediately looked away. Then without a second glance, he grabbed Craig by the rope around his neck and dragged him quickly from the bank.

Broken-teeth's breath was coming out in short, sharp gasps. When he had brought Craig back to the fireside, he stared at the edge of the lake for a long time, finally giving out a quick shudder before saying something to his brother. The two men were clearly ill at ease. Without saying anything more they bound Craig's hands behind his back again.

'What is it? What was that creature?'

'A bloody kelpie, you fool. If you'd have kept looking at it, you would have jumped in and drown yourself. Don't ask me why, because I don't know. All I know is let one of those creatures latch on to you, and you're done for.' He stared about him with a look of concern on his features, before adding, 'This must be a magical place. We'd better move on quickly. There'll be other creatures like that kelpie about, that's certain enough.'

The two brothers began to pack up camp swiftly, but before they were ready to leave a group of very short, stocky people came out of the forest.

The strangers had small square bodies fitted with large square heads. They wore hard serious expressions on their weatherbeaten faces. Their eyes were tiny glittering jewels pushed deep into clay-coloured complexions. Each of them was armed with a sword, stuck sheathless into a wide leather belt with a huge buckle. The buckles had various designs, but all involved beasts of the forest in their patterns.

Golden ornaments dripped from their chunky necks and wrists, were fixed to their cloaks: bracelets, torcs, brooches, pins, clasps. Several of them had golden teeth which flashed in the sunlight. Others had mouths of black rotten molars and incisors. On their heads they wore colourful floppy caps which fell to forked points at waist level on one side of their bodies. A big sweeping feather decorated each one of these marvellous hats. Most wore red or blue jerkins, with white and black striped pantaloons. On their feet were equally colourful slippers, the toes of which curled exotically up and over to touch their kneecaps.

Broken-teeth immediately went pale and he nudged Big-nose energetically. One of the little people came marching directly up to Broken-teeth and stood before him, arms akimbo, and stared him directly in the face.

'You know who I am?'

Broken-teeth gave out a nervous laugh.

'Why, sir, I do believe you're Laurin, King of the Dwarves.'

'I am indeed Laurin. What are you people doing here? Do you not know this is a sacred place? Sacred to me and my kind? Are you trying to provoke us into doing something rash? This lake is ours, this grove is ours. You trespass.'

Broken-teeth made an attempt at a smile.

'I've only just realized that, Laurin. As soon as my slave here saw the kelpie, I knew we shouldn't be here. You see, we've packed up camp already. We were just about to leave when you came out of the trees. I'm sorry.'

The small square Laurin studied the three humans carefully, muttering, 'A slave, eh?' Then he proceeded to look beyond Broken-teeth and Big-nose, as if searching for something, either on the ground or hanging in a tree.

'Did you feel something like a cobweb brushing your face as you walked under any trees?' asked Laurin, sharply. 'Come on, out with it now.'

Broken-teeth looked genuinely surprised.

'No, Laurin. What would that be?'

'Why, it would be Hel Keplein, my mantle of invisibility of course. I put it down somewhere and now I've lost it.' He looked with suspicion at Craig. 'Your slave hasn't stolen it, has he?'

By this time the other dwarves were walking through

grass with large bare feet. They had removed their slippers and were feeling with their toes. Others were marching under trees waving their hands about. Others still were thrusting their arms down rabbit holes.

'If he has, I don't know anything about it.'

Craig said to the king, 'It must be very difficult to find an invisible cloak once you've forgotten where you've placed it.'

For a moment the king looked quite miserable.

'Well nigh impossible. You have to come across it by accident,' he sighed. He was now staring about him in despair. 'I'm sure I had it when I was last here. Now my enemies will be gathering in the hills. How shall I avoid them without Hel Keplein?'

The dwarf-king looked so upset that Craig felt he had to reveal something he had been holding back for the appropriate moment.

'King Laurin – I know where the mantle is.'

All the dwarves stopped their search and began murmuring like a swarm of bees. The king looked quickly at Craig's face. He stared hard into his eyes. Craig knew that Laurin was searching in them for the truth. He held his head high, staring back at the king.

'Where is it then?' demanded Laurin.

'First we must bargain,' replied Craig. 'Do you promise to make these men set me free if I show you where to find your Hel Keplein?'

'Set you free? It will be done in an instant.'

Broken-teeth looked upset at these words and glanced away over his right shoulder, as if forcing back some comment.

'In that case, you'll find the mantle down by the lake. There's a patch of thistles which appeared to have been flattened by some heavy weight. I suspect it's Hel Keplein that's pressing them down. I knelt on it when I fell over a short while ago. I'm sure that's where you'll find it.'

Dwarves rushed down to the lake, yelling excitedly. Eventually, after scouring the bank for a short while, one of them let out a yell and held up his arm.

'It's here, my liege. I have it in my hand. Your own Hel Keplein.'

A look of great relief came over Laurin's wide features. His body seemed to slump for a moment and tears came to his eyes. Reaching out he grasped Craig's arm for a moment in a gesture of gratefulness. Then the cloak was restored to him by the finder.

He draped it over his shoulders. The effect was startling: only his head was now visible, seemingly floating at waist-height to Craig, off the ground. The king nodded gravely.

'How can I ever thank you?' Laurin said to Craig.

'Why,' said Craig, 'by keeping your promise.'

Craig, on hearing a stifled laugh behind him, turned to find Broken-teeth sniggering to himself.

'What are you looking so pleased about?' asked Craig, surprised.

'You'll see.'

A feeling of alarm flooded through Craig. He turned back to face the king.

'Will you have your dwarves cut me loose now? You promised to set me free if you remember, as a reward for finding the mantle. I should like to be on my way . . .'

'Alas,' cried the king, a small stubby-fingered disembod-ied hand appearing out of nowhere and grasping Craig's arm again. 'How I wish I could do that.'

'But you promised,' cried the astonished Craig. 'Have you dwarves no honour?'

'Honour is not what we lack,' replied Laurin, sadly, 'but the means. We cannot meddle in human affairs. It is against our laws. If a human does something wrong, such as you three trespassing, why, then we can kill them stone dead. But we cannot interfere between the three of you. You are a slave, my friend – be satisfied with your station in life.

Your master here looks like a kindly man. Be happy with your lot.'

'I can't believe you're doing this,' Craig cried. 'You *promised* to help me.'

Broken-teeth laughed and pulled on the rope, tightening the noose around Craig's neck.

'Come on, you. Let's not bother the king with our little problems. We'll be on our way then, Laurin. You watch that kelpie.' Broken-teeth nodded towards the lake. 'I hear it's a savage one. Tore the throat out of one of my friends with its teeth. Almost took his head off in one bite. Well, look after that mantle of yours – we'll be off.'

Craig was dragged away on the end of the line. Broken-teeth and Big-nose now took it in turns to ride the donkey, while Craig was forced to trot behind, his feet becoming bloody and raw in the process. They travelled over dark rough country, stopping occasionally at villages now they were over that wide stretch of land of border country. Up here in the 'north' it seemed Broken-teeth and Big-nose were made welcome, no questions asked about the man on the end of the rope. They simply paid their way, sleeping in houses made of timber plugged with clay.

Deeper and deeper they went above the border, until at last Craig asked the question, 'Where are you taking me? You said Douglass was waiting just beyond the land of the Celts. We are now in the country of the Angles.'

Broken-teeth looked at his brother Big-nose and then sniffed loudly.

'Well, as to that, we decided to hold on to you for a bit longer. Douglass is a mean bastard. He thought to get away with giving us just a few of his scrawny sheep, but now we're in a position to bargain with him. We've got the goods he wants. I'm sure he'll pay us a tidy bit more for you, once we let him know that you're for sale at a higher price.'

Craig fell into an even more weighty state of despair. Even should he manage to escape now he would have the greatest difficulty in getting back to his people alive. He was on a huge island full of savages – the tribes of Angles seemed even less civilized than the Celts – and he would have to pass through or around them. His memory maps were good, but he realized that sometimes he would have to deviate from them, in order to skirt a village or travel through the territory of a less hostile tribe. It would be easy to become lost in an unknown land.

Broken-teeth was smiling at him.

'What's the matter?' said that man. 'You missing some-one?'

'You pig's arse,' replied Craig, releasing some venom, 'you have bird shit for brains . . .'

This earned him a cuff around the head, which set his ears ringing. Over the past few days Craig had been kicked and punched, not just by his two captors, but by anyone who felt the need to rid themselves of spleen. Often tied to a post in the middle of the village as he was, all sorts of tough men and women, and children, had given him the benefit of their strength. He now felt thoroughly aban-doned and abused.

That night they camped by a river. Craig could smell a damp mustiness carried on the cool wind. He could see the ruffling of the water on the river, from which came the occasional 'plop' of a fish breaking the surface of the water. The trout were after the storm flies which heralded rain. Otherwise the night was quiet.

Big-nose made a fire by striking flints together. Yellow flames were soon licking at the darkness around them. Big-nose sat hunched over a hearth made with smooth river stones, staring out into the blackness. He looked uneasy and from the tone of his brother's voice, Broken-teeth was trying to console him. It seemed the dim one of the two was not happy with something.

'What's the matter with your brother?' asked Craig. 'Conscience bothering him?'

'Conscience? What's that?' said Broken-teeth, looking in his brother's direction, 'a wasp or something?'

Craig realized that Broken-teeth was genuinely ignorant regarding any feelings of guilt or remorse he was supposed to be having concerning Craig's abduction. The Oceanian saw then just how dangerous was this man. He was an intrinsically bad man – born not made – who simply did not know the difference between good and evil, only between poverty and riches.

At that moment Big-nose threw some woodshavings from his whittling on the fire, which flared brightly, lighting up the faces of the men. There was a very small sound out in the darkness which attracted Craig's attention. Broken-teeth was saying, 'You shadow-skins, you don't know a dwarf from a horse's arse. Why I – gaaahhhhhhh . . .'

Craig sensed that Broken-teeth was now partially standing. The Oceanian prisoner turned back to see that his main captor's face was ugly with contortion, his eyes staring wildly at Craig. The strange crouch gave the impression he had been halfway through a crap when he had been interrupted. There was something wrong with his throat and his hands scrabbled at a projection which had appeared there, as if it had grown out of the sides of his thick neck.

It was a good second or two before Craig realized that what Broken-teeth was trying to remove from his neck was in fact an arrow. The mysterious missile had pierced from one side and gone right though.

The arrow must have smashed through Broken-teeth's spinal column, where it met his head. At the next moment the fatally wounded man fell on the floor with his body twitching and jerking, his tongue lolling out. His brother was now yelling and trying to wrench the arrow from flesh and bone. Broken-teeth's feet kicked spasmodically at the fire, scattering bits of flaming wood and bark in all directions.

Just as Broken-teeth's breath bubbled its last in a strangled effort to force air down a severed windpipe, Big-nose fell backwards with a stunned look on his features. A second arrow had come out of the darkness and now protruded from the big man's chest, just left of the breastbone. Big-nose coughed once and a great gobbet of blood came from his mouth to flop in the embers of the fire where it sizzled. Then he too fell backwards, to lie with his great foot rammed in his brother's open mouth, neither man being conscious of the indignity of the position.

'Who's there?' cried Craig, concerned that he would be next on the archer's list of victims. 'Do you speak Gaelic?'

'Cut that demon tongue,' replied a familiar, cheerful female voice, as Hupa stepped out of the shadows on the edge of the forest. 'I hate to hear you talk like a goblin.'

'Hupa? Thank the gods!' cried Craig, feeling the fear drain from him. 'Where are the others?'

Hupa knelt down beside him and cut his bonds with an obsidian knife. She rubbed the red, raw places where the ropes had chafed him. Craig climbed unsteadily to his feet, having to place a hand on her shoulder to steady himself. He wanted to hug her for her timely entrance. All his reserve had gone from him and the spark of his spirit had been about to go out.

While he was thus attempting to gain his balance she told him something he had not wanted to hear.

'I'm alone, Craig. No one came with me. I noticed you go into the copse after the entertainments. When you didn't come out again, I went in to look for you, thinking you might have had an accident. I found signs of a struggle and some tracks. I hoped to reach you quickly, so I didn't go back to the pa for help, I simply tracked you.

'But it was difficult following spoor in the darkness, and I lost a lot of time. Since then I've been tracking you night and day, over the landscape, sometimes losing the trail and having to patiently search for signs again. Finally, tonight, I caught up with you – and there you see the result.'

They both stared at the dead men, lying on the mossy bank of the river, and it was hard for Craig to feel sorry for them.

PART SEVEN

The Celtic Otherworld

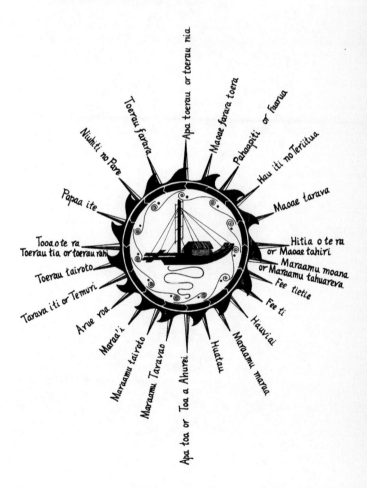

1

When his two agents did not meet him at the agreed point in the southern hills of Umberland, Douglass knew that they had betrayed him. The only balm for his wrath over the next few days was devising ways of killing them both when they did surface. He had no doubt they would contact him with a demand for more payment. That would be typical of those two Jutes.

Douglass was a man rich in cattle, sheep and horses, but he was not one to squander his wealth. It would be a pleasure to make a bargain, then break it and grab the pair of them. Douglass knew a torturer, an artist of pain, amongst the Angles. This expert's particular genius was to turn men inside out while the body remained alive – almost alive – enough to feel agony and distress, which was enough for Douglass.

'I'll get him to reverse one of them, then I'll hang the carcass for a day or so from a tree, before cooking him like a hare.' He smiled to himself. *Jugged human.* 'Then I'll force the other brother to eat him. That will be a suitable end for one of them at least.'

There was a third brother, a much younger man, who was now Douglass's hostage. Some satisfaction had been gained by cutting off two of the fingers of the youth's left hand, at the second knuckle, when those pair of renegades out on the trail had failed to appear at the meeting place. These had been used to plug the boy's nose while Douglass clamped a broad palm over his mouth, demanding to know the whereabouts of his kin.

However, since the young man had not talked, even after passing out several times with the pain wracking his chest, it had to be assumed their non-appearance had not been planned beforehand, but was a spontaneous action.

In the meantime he had to attempt to find them. He was at the moment a guest of the Wuffingas tribe – the 'wolf people' – but only because he was paying their chief a tribute. The Wuffingas were a clan within the greater tribe of the Angles, who lived in Albainn. The Angles and the Jutes had come originally from a huge land mass in the cold seas to the south-east of Albainn.

It seemed invasions from this place never ceased. Already there was another people beginning to make tentative forays into Albainn and what was now called Engaland. They too came from this cold vast land to the south-east. They were the sea raiders now on the small outer islands and they called themselves Saxons.

In truth Douglass was more concerned about the Saxons than he was the Oceanians. He did not believe the brown-skins would stay. He had heard they came from a place of warm seas, vertical suns, lush vegetation and colourful wild life. Why would they want to stay in a climate which pissed rain and snow alternately from the skies for half the year? One winter in Albainn would send them scuttling back to Oceania, and it would be as if they had never come at all.

The Oceanians would leave and all trace of their ever having been there would be gone. The Celts would burn their wooden fortresses and no one would ever know they had set foot on this sacred land of Albainn.

This was what the witch had told him and he believed her – she had been right about everything so far. She had also told him that the Celtic gods were at war above, under and around the island, with those who had accompanied the Oceanians. She did not know who was winning this ethereal war, but some of the terrible storms attested to the struggle going on.

The victors will be *our* gods, thought Douglass, for they are warriors of great might. They will crush these invaders with lightning and thunderbolts, strangle them with their bare hands, stamp them into oblivion with their feet. These foreign gods will follow their people back to Oceania, with their tails between their legs like the curs they be.

He paused in his thoughts as he saw two of his subchiefs talking with local women.

'Dunan, Conall, get ye here by me.'

The two men in deer-skin cloaks came running at his call.

'Aye, Douglass, what will you have of us?'

'Take some men and post them in the hills around. There'll be a messenger arriving for me soon. I want to know which direction he comes from. I'll have those two Jute bastards as well as the half-breed, Craig, or whatever he calls himself. They may think they'll get the better of Douglass Barelegs, but they're as wrong as they could ever be. Get to it.'

'Aye, Douglass.'

'And the pick of my sheep for the man who first spots the messenger.'

Dunan grinned. 'Would it be the pretty ewe, the one with the glossy fleece, Douglass?'

'Get out of here, ye debauched man,' laughed Conall. 'Are ye no satisfied with the Wuffingas women?'

'They're too ugly. They all look like sows.'

Douglass did not have a great sense of humour and he roared at his men to get on with what they were supposed to be about, then stomped back into the village through a gate in the thorn-bush defences, already changing his mind about jugging one of the brothers, thinking instead he might cut off their testicles and have them sewn inside their mouths . . .

Punga, having lost his weapons, had been locked in a wrestling embrace with a god named Oenghus mac in Og, who was a worthy opponent for the profusely bleeding God of Ugly Creatures. Now he had escaped the clutches of Oenghus and was going to the assistance of Tangaroa, the Great Sea God, who was being flailed by Manannan mac Lir, the Celtic God of the Sea. Nearby, Tawhaki, the God of Thunder, was battling with lightning lances against Taranis, his opposite number.

While he staggered across the battlefield, where many gods lay wounded and dying, Punga had time to glance down to see that his charge, Craig, was now safe from the hands of his abductors. Punga had guided Hupa, the archer, to the site where Craig was being held by the two Jutes, and now she had performed her task of freeing the young man. All was well there, though Craig had to be returned to the pa of his people.

'Punga, you ugly creature!' roared Tangaroa, in his pain and suffering. 'Why so slow? Leap upon the back of this Taranis, Lord of the Cold Seas, while I take his flail . . .'

The loyal Punga did as he was bid, suffering some savage blows which stripped the skin from his shoulders in so doing.

Like many of the gods he was gradually being torn to pieces and those pieces were being scattered about the earth. He wondered for how much longer he could keep going . . .

That night Hupa and Craig buried the bodies of the two Jutes under a great tree with spreading boughs. The leaves of the tree had scalloped edges and the nuts were like small coconuts in shape, but protruding from a half-husk.

Hupa said she sensed tree spirits in this place and the souls of the men would have company on their journey to the land of the dead, wherever that was for people of their kind.

'We have triumphed over the evil of these men,' said Hupa, 'and whoever sent them.'

Craig, however, felt there was someone else who should be thanked for their deliverance. An ancestor perhaps? Or a god? Some supernatural being was taking time out to watch over the whereabouts of the son of Seumas. He could feel it in the very wind which blew across this cursed land.

Craig said to Hupa, 'I must get back to the pa as quickly as possible. The night I was abducted, Kieto told me he wanted to sue for peace with the Celts and concentrate on a war with the Angles. It can't happen without me. Cormac-the-Venomous will trust no other Oceanian.'

'Now we must get some rest,' she told Craig. 'In the morning we'll retrace our journey as best we can. Although, it's as you said, we'll need to go around villages. Perhaps there's a river we can follow? It might be easier to travel by water than over land?'

'We'll see,' replied Craig. 'In the meantime, I am so weary I could drop. Is this a safe place to sleep, do you think?'

'We'll have to risk it,' replied Hupa. 'I sense rock spirits, river spirits and tree spirits all round us, but they seem harmless creatures.'

'How come you sense them and I don't?'

'Because you're a man. Women have a greater sensitivity to such things.'

Before either of them could fall asleep, however, there was a howling in the night around them. Both sat bolt upright and stared out into the darkness. Hupa took up her bow and quiver of arrows. The howling was a haunting sound which it might seem came from the mouths of the dead. It was mournful, it was cold and distant, and it chilled one to the marrow.

'I think that is a messenger from the world of the dead,' Hupa said, shivering. 'Come to collect the souls of those two Jutes I killed.'

'Sensitive female!' snorted Craig, putting more dead branches on the fire to build up the flames. 'That's an animal they call a wolf. The two Jutes spoke about it all the time. It roams in packs. You've seen their skins – the Celts make cloaks out of them. Coarse grey pelts. A wolf is like a dog only much fiercer in aspect and in behaviour.'

'Foxes, dogs, deer, horses, badgers, otters – I even saw a creature much like a rat only longer and sleeker, with very sharp teeth – killing one of those rats with long ears they call hares. A baby hare, it looked like. There are so many more animals here than on our own islands.'

Some pictures came into Craig's mind: descriptions from his father when he was alive.

'What you saw was either a weasel, stoat, polecat or tree marten – something of that kind. There are many variations on a theme here. Let's get some sleep. The fire will keep the wolves away. I hope.'

Craig did at last manage to fall asleep, but he seemed to wake in the middle of the night. The fire had gone cold and the wolves were calling all around. He climbed to his feet and looked about him, sensing something different about the landscape in the emerging light of the coming dawn. There was a chill breeze from somewhere, like a draught from an open door, and on it was the whisper of his father's voice.

Come to me, Craig – bring a weapon with you – an iron sword if you can – if not, even a stone axe will do.

An intense-looking hunched bird, a white owl, suddenly appeared on the branch of a nearby tree and hooted at Craig and stared hard at him. When Craig approached the owl, its head swivelled round back to front. It seemed to be telling him to follow where it went. Then it took off, silently flying towards some foothills, and Craig proceeded to go in the same direction, pausing only to pick up one of the daggers left by the Jutes.

Craig found he was walking in the direction from which the cold wind was coming. Hupa remained asleep by the remnants of the fire as he strode away from their camp in the wake of the night-hunting owl. His journey across the country, which he seemed to cover remarkably quickly, was through forested foothills, and once he passed between some wolves.

The wolf pack regarded both him and the owl but casually, as if they were only half there, letting him weave his way through their midst without a murmur. One of their number was on a crag, calling in hollow tones as if to a listener on the moon. Looking into their strange hazel-coloured eyes, he saw other distant places, other lands, stranger even than the misty regions of the island which he now traversed.

Finally, he and the owl came to a cave, whereupon the owl disappeared inside it. Craig entered without a second thought, as his father's voice became stronger in his head. Within the cave it was quite cold and he wished he had brought a thicker cloak with him. Finally, after many hours walking in the darkness, he saw a grey light in the distance. It seemed he was coming to the end of his journey. When he drew nearer, there was a creature guarding the exit, a monster with three heads.

'I have come to see my father,' said Craig.

These seemed to be the right words, for the monster remained unmoving as Craig passed between it and one wall of the cave, then out into a swirling, hazy world of half-light. If he thought he had been cold before, he was wrong. In this place there were the substances called ice and snow, which his father had told him about. There was also a wind which carried sharp invisible shark's-teeth in its jaws. Craig felt as if his flesh were being stripped from his bones.

Never in his life had he experienced such a feeling of coldness. His lungs hurt him when he drew in oxygen. Freezing air made his mouth numb as he tried to suck it down. His nose, ears, indeed all his extremities, felt as if they were about to snap away from his body. The channels within him – his nostrils, his windpipe – had shrivelled.

'The sun god has abandoned this place,' he told no one in particular. 'Here the light comes from within this ice.'

He wrapped his cloak around himself and walked out into the crashing whirlwind blizzard which raged around him. It was like a tempest out in the ocean, a typhoon, which turned the world upside down and whipped its whiteness from the foaming mouths of waves. Except here was not wetness but solid light, battering his body with tiny chips of translucent gravel, stinging his eyes and cheeks with their sharpness.

And here the snow his father had told him about was not just of one whiteness, but many different shades, even down to a kind of blueness. Everything seemed impenetrable. There was no clear sight to the centre of things. All was opaque, frosted, cracked and veined. Everything had a layer of solid wind upon its surface, almost thick enough to cut with an axe.

Just as his eyes were becoming used to the white darkness, a hideous monster rose out of the snow in front of him. It was twice as tall as Craig, and covered in white fur. Standing on its hind legs it opened its mouth to reveal two terrible rows of teeth which could tear raw flesh from bone. Its eyes blazed in fury, as if Craig had trespassed on some holy place, and its forelegs, tipped with long claws, opened wide as if about to enfold the Oceanian in a embrace of death.

The monster roared and stumbled forwards, but out of the vortex of snow came another shape, which hurled itself at the monster and gripped it by the throat. This creature was in the shape of a naked man whose powerful arms began to strangle the giant. Craig could see ridges of muscle and sinew standing proud on those large forearms. The man's legs were wrapped around the beast's chest, attempting to crush its ribs.

The creature bellowed and thrashed around, trying to get those claws to rip open its assailant, but the man, almost buried beneath the thick fur, was protected by the beast's pelt, and their points were ineffectual. Its slavering jaws with those dreadful teeth were utterly useless to it, so long as the man was locked around its throat choking the life from it.

Gradually the moaning beast sank to the ground, yet still the naked man remained fastened to its head, strangling the life from its body. Eventually, after a very long time, the struggle ceased, and the creature lay still. It was dead.

'Thank you,' said Craig, stepping forward. 'You saved my life.'

'Only your dream-life, Craig,' replied the man, getting to his feet, 'for you are not really here in body.'

Now Craig recognized his saviour and it was his own father, Seumas, though much younger, in perfect form.

'Father?' he cried. 'You're still alive!'

He went forward to embrace Seumas, only to be warned away by a thrusting hand.

'No, my son – here you cannot. This is Ifurin, the Otherworld of the Celts, which has me in its thrall. I asked you to come to me because I neglected to bring a weapon with which to defend myself. Had I not been years in Oceania I would have remembered to die with a weapon in my hand. There are many monsters in this place, some of which cannot be killed by these two hands, strong as they may now be. I have been reborn in the best condition I owned when in the world of the living, but I must have something with which to defend myself.

'Did you bring your father a sword, Craig? I must have some metal about me. I must fend off the dark creatures of this world until I can find your step-mother.'

Craig shrugged his shoulders, feeling he had failed his father.

'Only this iron dagger. The Jutes who abducted me had no swords. You may have the knife, Father.'

'A dagger will do for now,' replied Seumas, 'thank you, my son – but when you are able, you must find a sword and cast it into the depths of the nearest loch. I will retrieve it from there, though it be locked under thick ice, for the Otherworld is but a reflection of the one you now inhabit.'

'Not for long,' replied Craig, hugging himself. 'After this, I shall wish to go home to the islands. Is the Otherworld of the Celts always so cold and brittle?'

'Winter in Albainn is not much warmer,' replied his father, with a phantom of a smile. 'I told you your mother's people were soft and womanish.'

'Dorcha's people?'

'Your real mother.'

Craig studied the ghost of his father before him, seeing something substantial yet sensing there was but a shadow there. He had never seen Seumas as a young man and he was astonished how much he looked like the man Craig saw when he looked into a reflecting surface. He was his father's son, there could be no doubt about that. Perhaps one day there might be an opportunity for him to visit the Otherworld of the Oceanians, and meet his mother for the first time? If one had happened, then why not the other?

Seumas said to him, 'What of Douglass's son?'

'Douglass Barelegs? He tries to kill me, Father. I am told he will not rest until the death of his father has been avenged.'

'You *must* try to make your peace with him,' Seumas insisted. 'He has been wronged.'

Craig replied, 'I have promised to try, Father, but this is

a thing of *your* making, not mine. I will risk my life, but I will not throw it away because you could not control your temper as a young man. That would be a foolish thing to do. I will attempt to repair the damage you caused, but I can't be held responsible for it. You understand?'

The ghost of his father stared at him for a long time, before saying, 'You have grown wiser, my son.'

'What of the other Douglass, the one you killed for his sword? He must be here too.'

'Why, he is long gone, his soul eaten by a supernatural creature similar to the Shark-God, Dakuwanga. He had no weapon with which to defend himself, and so he was taken, as I will be eventually if you do not send me a sword.'

'Why did he not send for his son, as you have done, to bring him a weapon?'

Seumas shook his head. 'He did, but Douglass son of Douglass panicked when he saw the three-headed creature guarding the entrance to this world. He ran back. It was not long after that his father met one of the largest and fiercest of the monsters in Ifurin, the Icharacha, a creature like a lobster with a thousand legs, each leg bristling with sharp pincers large enough to snip a man's limbs from his body. Douglass could not defend himself. He was first pruned and then eaten.'

'Now I must go.'

'Now you must go. Go quickly. We cannot embrace in this place.'

'Will you be here for ever, Father?'

'I think not, for the spiritual world is changing. The old gods, the Otherworlds, these seem to be fading. There is a place where Dorcha has gone, not yet open to a heathen like me. I hope to join her when this is settled.'

Craig nodded, then turned and hurried towards the cave. He looked back once, to see a swirling shape of mist and snow, which might have been his father's ghost, then entered the cave. The three-headed monster was still there.

Craig slipped past it and down the long passage to the real world. When he arrived back at the campsite, Hupa was still asleep.

He lay down on the other side of the fire, conscious that she was a beautiful young woman and he a married man.

2

On waking the following morning, Hupa went to the river to wash. Unused to the dirt and squalor which seemed part of the Land-of-Mists, she stripped and entered the water to bathe all over, wearing only the shark's-tooth necklace which proclaimed her ariki rank. Since she had been on this foreign island she had never felt physically clean. The Celts themselves were often covered in mud, smelled of oily peatbog-water and animal dung, and carried about them various foodstuffs that either dripped, or mouldered, or rotted in some way.

She tried to imagine what it would be like to be married to a Pict or Scot, and shuddered as she splashed water between her legs, getting in those crevices which harboured the odours of young womanhood. It was her time of month and having no tapa bark pads with her she was having to use an awkward combination of dry moss and grasses. Still, she prided herself on being inventive enough to overcome these inconveniences.

No, to be married to *anyone* from this island would be quite horrible. She was an Oceanian ariki, a virgin of noble rank, and her husband should be likewise. He should be noble, a great warrior, a man of learning, good, kind and gentle, with a dry sense of humour. In short, he should be

quite perfect, for she knew herself to be a prize to be trea-
sured. The idea of being attached to a stinking lump of
lard in a poorly cured wolfskin was quite abhorrent to her.

Yet – yet – she would like to be married to one who carried Pictish blood in his veins. She glanced guiltily towards
the spot where the red-haired man who was her companion
slept. Hupa had loved Craig since she was fourteen, when
she first realized he was not such an old man as she had
always thought. Now she was eighteen and ready for a
man, yet the one person she wanted was not available, was
already married.

'I shall stay a virgin all my life,' she told the trees, the
river, the grassy banks dotted with wild flowers. 'I shall be
like Kikamana, pure in body and spirit.'

Yes, but her heart ached, for she thought Craig perfect in
every way for her. True, he was not a virgin, but that was of
small account. Hupa hated it when pictures of Craig
making love to Linloa, his wife, entered her mind, but she
usually managed to change faces with Linloa before any
great hurt was felt.

She imagined that tattooed limb, the painted leg, nestling
between hers after making love, while he whispered wonderful words into her ear, telling her how beautiful she was,
how much he adored her, how he would die for her.

A silver fish came near as she bathed, darting through
the green weeds at the bottom of the clear water. Her bow
and quiver were on the bank. She wondered if she could get
to the weapon before the fish went away, but it shot off
along the gravelled bed into a nest of fronds in the next
moment. It had been frightened by a shadow falling on the
surface.

She looked up, startled to see Craig had awoken and
come down to the riverside. He stood there, staring at her
nude body, his eyes soft and blue. Troubled a little by his
quietness, she covered her small breasts with her hands.

He turned away, quickly.

'I'm sorry,' he said, 'that was unforgivable of me – but you looked so – so pretty. My thoughts were innocent. It was like catching a young faun unawares. It will not happen again – I'll – I'll go and stir the ashes of the fire . . .'

He walked away and she found herself wishing he would not go, catching the words in her throat. The look in his eyes told her his thoughts had not been entirely innocent, as he had maintained. It would have taken but a word or a gesture, to have encouraged him. When it came to it though, Hupa could not rid her mind of Linloa, that quiet modest woman who had stayed at home to raise his children.

Next time though, thought Hupa fiercely as she dressed, I will not hold back. I deserve the man I love as much as anyone else. Why should she have him just because she saw him first? It is about who loves the most, not about who grabs who before anyone else can get to them. Watch out, Linloa, I will not let a second opportunity pass me by.

Once dressed she took her bow and went wading again, searching for that large silver fish. She found it, or its twin, in the shallows further up. Her aim was true and very soon she returned to the fire, which was now in a state for cooking her catch. Craig stared in admiration.

'By the gods,' he said, 'you're a fine hunter, Hupa – you'll make some great hero a fine partner in life, if that's what you choose.'

You, she thought, the pit of her stomach aching. *You*.

They roasted and ate the fish, then started on their journey south. Since the river must have been flowing towards the sea, they decided to follow it. Once they reached the coast it would simply be a matter of following that, too, until they reached the pa which they knew to have the sea at its back.

'So long as the river goes to the right side of the island,' replied Hupa. 'Are you sure it does?'

'It must do. We have never been that far from the sea,

wherever we were. I can smell the salt air. Besides, I took
the direction from the sun.'

Their progress was slow, due to the nature of the braided
river, which meandered over a vast area, causing them to
make deviations to previous dry rocky beds which were difficult to walk across. Towards the first evening it was
obvious by the blackness above that a storm was coming in.
There was already a growling in the throat of the sky.
Almost simultaneously, they saw some smoke curling above
a patch of woodland.

It was only one column, which meant a single dwelling
rather than a village.

'Let's go and see,' said Hupa. 'We can remain hidden if it
looks dangerous.'

In a clearing, in the middle of the wood, they saw a huge
green mound like a grave. It was from a hole in the top of
this mound that the smoke drifted. There were two other
squarish holes in the turf which seemed to serve as windows. These were close to the ground and framed by thick
wooden logs. Thin dirty rags covered the windows, preventing anyone from peering inside. Up against one sloping
turf wall – or roof, for it served as both – was a stack of
broken branches and kindling, but no axe. In a pen made of
wands, were some birds with flattish beaks that made a
monotonous kind of *quak-quak-quak* sound.

Beyond this ugly little hovel stood an earthen well, lined
with stones. Not long after the pair had ventured into the
glade and had hidden themselves in bushes, someone came
out of the stone, timber and turf dwelling to draw water at
this well. It was a child, hunched, with wild black hair and
smoke-darkened, wrinkled skin: a child with an old man's
face.

She was accompanied by a small animal. A tame creature, much like the wild one Hupa had earlier described as
sucking the blood of a baby hare. It flowed in, around and

between the child's legs as she walked. It seemed to be caressing her ankles with its soft-looking, furry, serpentine form.

While she was at the well, Craig hurried over to one of the windows, lifted the covering rag and peered inside. Then he crept back to where Hupa was hidden.

'No one else there,' he whispered.

The child-with-the-old-man's-face was on her way back to her hovel. She suddenly stopped and stiffened, putting down her obviously heavy wooden bucket for a moment. She stared hard at where the two were lying. Her pet immediately went up on its hind legs, staring in the same direction, but whether it was doing so because it had heard, seen or smelled something, or whether it was just copying the child, was not really evident.

But then the child-with-the-old-man's-face took up the bucket again, her pet now back on all fours and weaving its strange patterns through her legs, and the two of them went back into her dwelling. At that moment large drops of rain began to fall, splattering on the leaves above Hupa's head. Somewhere in the distance a sharp crack sounded and there was a flash.

'The storm,' she said, looking up.

'She's alone in that dwelling,' whispered Craig. 'We could spend the night here. One small child can't hurt us. What do you think?'

'I agree there's no need to fear a person of her stature.'

'Let's do it then.'

They went down to the thick wooden door of the hovel and Craig yelled to the child in Gaelic, hoping she spoke the tongue of the Celts.

'Hallo in there!'

To his relief she replied in kind. 'What do you want?' Her voice was low and rasping, like that of an elderly woman racked with some respiratory disease.

'We are two weary strangers. May we spend the night

under your roof? A heavy storm is coming up. We'll be caught out here and may be killed by a struck tree. There's already squalling rain, which is soaking us to the roots of our hair.'

'How can I trust ye?'

'There's nothing to fear. We are . . .' Craig looked pointedly at Hupa, 'we are a man and his wife. We are travelling south to the land of the Celts. You sound like a Celt yourself . . .'

'I am,' said the child-with-the-old-man's-face, beginning to open the door now, 'they're not all south of the border.' Once she laid eyes on them, however, she started backwards in alarm, crying, 'But look at you! Ye have the skins of demons. And strange stripes across your face! What's this? Are you from some Otherworld? Do I need magic to send ye hence?'

'We are – castaways,' replied Craig. 'We come from another land. Our skins are dark because we live always in the sun. And these bars across my face are only tattoos, such as those Picts decorate themselves with. But have no fear, we are not supernatural. If we were, why would we be afraid of a storm? Why would we need to call to you to open your door? If we were demons we would come down your chimney, or slide under your window rags.'

'These things are true,' replied the child, peering hard into his face. 'Ye do not look like a demon. Ye look like something born of man, but with a strange darkness to you.'

When Craig translated this for Hupa, the girl became incensed.

'Better than having skin the colour of the belly of a fish,' she snapped.

The child-with-the-old-man's-face clearly knew an insult had been flung, even though she did not understand the language. Instead of shutting the door in their faces, the child smiled.

'Fiery strumpet, ain't she? What kind of tongue is that? It sounds like the speech of bogles, hobgoblins, boggarts and other such creatures of an unnatural stamp. Are ye from the world of such beings? Come on, speak up. Tell me the truth.'

'I have no idea what you mean.'

'Have ye not, then,' she said, peering into his eyes. 'What a pity. What a pity. I always hope for visitors from such regions. Once they might have clustered at my window, but I killed an elf you see, it drowned in a pail of milk, and now they won't come any more, except to plague me. Today I am a child, tomorrow an old man, then next a young woman – sometimes even betwixt and between, when they feel at their most cruel.'

'Today you are between,' said Craig.

'Am I?' shrieked the child, running her hands over her face and head, looking down at her body. 'Damn those fairies!'

'I don't know what an elf is,' confessed Craig. 'Is it some kind of a butterfly or moth?'

Her face changed again and she laughed and leaned on the doorpost.

'Butterflies and moths – some folks see them as such . . .'

Craig studied the child's face as she spoke, unable to determine her age. Her skin was careworn and dry, with deep wrinkles, but the eyes were young and very alive. They flicked from feature to feature, quickly, taking in everything about these visitors at her door. They were so bright those eyes, and the blue in them washed to such a fascinating hue, that he found it hard to look into them.

'Well, are ye coming in, or do you stand in the doorway and gawp at me?'

She stood aside, letting them enter.

The inside of the hovel was not much different from the outside. There was a hard dirt floor, a ring of stones in the middle of the one room which served as a hearth, a bed of straw in a far corner, and thick logs to sit on. In a pile on one side were rotting cabbage stalks, bits of offal and other remnants of past meals. Flies covered this heap and were evident in most other parts of the room too.

From the beamed ceiling, plugged with clay, hung bunches of dried herbs, dried animal parts and smoked fish. She took down one of the fish, which looked as brittle as bark, and broke it into pieces, offering the pair a piece each. Craig took his and began chewing on it. Hupa did likewise. The child dipped hers in the bucket of water for a time, before sucking on it.

'My teeth are loose,' she explained. 'One falls out every day or so. It's some sickness of the gums.'

Just as the three of them sat down on thick, up-ended logs, around the fire, the thunderstorm broke outside. Rain came hissing down onto the turf roof above. There were almost deafening explosions as thunder punched the belly out of the sky, right above their heads. Lightning blasted through the clouds as if it were splitting giant trees, making Hupa jump.

'Frightened, strumpet?' laughed the child-with-the-old-man's-face. 'Frightened *and* fiery – there's a combination.'

Outside, the downpour increased in fury, smacking into the hovel like a flood. Water began to run under the door and down the walls on either sides of the windows. There was dampness in the air. Just then, Craig himself started, but not with the thunder and lightning, for things began to move in various parts of the room. Something snaked out of a woodpile, something else crept from the darkness of a corner, yet another creature appeared from out of the straw of the bed.

'What? What is it?' cried the child, sensing his discomfort. 'Oh, my *beasties*. They'll not hurt you, boy. They're my children, my precious ones.'

There was a weasel, and some kind of a rat, and a short, slim snake. They were clearly disturbed by the storm and went to the child. She lifted the hem of her ragged shift and they went under her skirts, hiding there. Hupa shuddered, making the child laugh huskily, before throwing a log on the fire.

'Fiery, frightened and fussy!'

The storm outside built itself to a terrible fury, crashing and blundering about in the woods like an insane giant. Inside the hovel the group were at least safe from being struck by lightning. Craig went into a doze, swaying on his log seat as he sat by the fire looking into the flames. Hupa too was lolling on his shoulder. Some time later the child and her pets went to her bed in the corner and Craig, finding Hupa asleep on his arm, lifted her up and carried her to a dry spot to lay her down.

Then he himself found another suitable patch on the earthen floor and slept fitfully as the storm continued.

In the middle of the night they were all woken suddenly by a crashing sound. Beams on the ceiling fractured and the whole structure bulged inwards. A huge broken branch, still attached to a trunk, speared the roof and buried its point in the dirt floor. It was this branch which saved their lives and prevented the tree to which it was joined from smashing through the roof. Had the branch not been there a massive trunk would have crushed the hovel and possibly those in it. As it was the water came pouring in, through the hole in the roof and down the branch, causing Hupa to move her position.

'Ferret's shit!' swore the child from the corner. 'My little home . . .'

But there was clearly nothing to be done until the morning, so everyone went back to sleep.

When daybreak came, Craig woke to find a child-with-a-child's-face examining Hupa's bow and quiver of arrows. She seemed to find the points of the arrows particularly interesting, running a finger over one of them, murmuring to herself.

'What are you doing?' asked Craig, and at that moment

Hupa woke and, seeing what was happening, snatched her arrow from the child's grasp.

'Manners!' murmured the child.

'I asked you what you were doing,' Craig said again. 'Why did you take that arrow without permission?'

'Don't fash yourself, boy,' she snapped back. 'I was just looking. Can't a person look at something in her own home, without being treated like a thief? You carry too much on yourself. Here, I'll break our fast with some cooked food, while you see what is to be done about the roof.'

It seemed it was an order, rather than a request.

Craig decided it was best to let the matter drop. It seemed a harmless enough piece of curiosity. He then set about examining the structure of the hovel. The beams were fractured all right and clay and stones had been dislodged, but the tree that had fallen, breaking the back of the roof, could not be moved. It would have taken an army of strong people to lift that wooden giant out of its present position.

'You'd best patch round it, leave the tree where it is,' he advised. 'It's quite secure now, resting on that broken bough. Over the next year or so I should build yourself a new place, because eventually the branch will rot and the tree will sink lower and lower into the room.'

'That's your advice, is it?'

'You asked me for it.'

She nodded, thoughtfully, and continued with her cooking.

After the meal, as they were preparing to leave, the child asked them for payment for a night's lodging and food.

'Payment?' said Craig. 'What do you mean?'

'Night's lodgings. You owe me.'

Hupa said, 'What does she want?'

'She wants to be paid, for giving us shelter and food.'

Hupa expressed her repugnance of such behaviour. In

Oceania, you shared what you had with neighbours and strangers alike. It was not unknown for a childless couple to ask parents of a large family for one of their offspring and expect to be offered a baby or an infant. Certainly if you had food and someone asked for some, you gave it without question. If a person asked for hospitality, you gave it willingly and would not dream of requesting payment for it.

Craig turned to the child. 'It is not in our nature to pay for such services.'

Her face twisted and she went back on her heels.

'Ho, I see, it's not in your nature to pay for such services, is it? Well, I'm not asking you to act natural. Treat it as a peculiar request if ye will. Think on me as quirky and unusual. Because in this part of this great island we expect to be paid when we hand over hard-earned food and open up our homes to passing outlanders. Now give up.'

'I refuse,' replied Craig, annoyed. 'In any case, what would we give you? We have nothing.'

The child's eyes narrowed. 'Ye got them bow and arrows. Them there arrowheads is magic, I can tell. I can *feel* the magic flowing from 'em. Give me one. Or better still, give me them all. What do you want in exchange? I'll do anything for arrows with such magical properties.'

'We don't need anything. All we want is to get back to our people.'

'I can do that for you too,' said the child-with-a-child's-face. 'I can help you get back to 'em quicker than that.'

'How?'

'I'm what ye might call an enchantress. I can change you into a deer, fleet of foot, for one whole day. So long as you are willing. So long as ye give me such permissions as I ask. Or a wolf? Ye could cross the country twice as fast if you were a deer or wolf. But I can't do it against your nature – it must be with ye, not against ye – what say ye, eh?'

'A shapechanger?'

'D'ye not see the weasel?' sniggered the child. 'He used to be a man, a woodcutter. And the others my distant neighbour's sons. I change 'em back when I need something only they can give me, but they're less of a nuisance this way. Later they can move the tree from my little house. I can keep 'em better in hand in the form of beasts.'

Craig raised his eyebrows at this.

'They *let* you turn them into animals?'

'In this way they don't have to serve any clan chief. Such great bullies are always coming through here, looking for men to do their killin' for them, to recover some lost fief or other. My man stays with me – and my boys too – they stay with their cook and bedmaker. They recognize no fealty to this one or that one, so-called lords who march through the land looking for vassals.'

'Is this approved, by the clans?'

She laughed. 'See how I trust you, stranger? They would burn me if they knew of my powers. Yet, I confess it to you, because I want those arrows so much. What would ye have me change you into? Come on, speak.'

'Birds,' said Craig, as he saw the possibilities. 'What about birds?'

'Aye – pigeons then? They have a good sense of direction. Pigeons I can recommend.'

'No, we'd be killed by the first hawk. What about those large black birds, I've seen hereabouts. No hawk would attack one of *them*.'

'Crows, ye mean? Twa corbies? I could do that.'

Craig turned to Hupa. 'Give the child your weapon – the bow and quiver.'

Hupa clutched her bow tighter. 'What? What's going on? I'm not surrendering my weapon to anyone. Are you mad?'

'Just give them to her. She's promised to change us into birds – those black creatures – she calls them crows. We can get back to the pa more quickly that way. You have to give up your bow and quiver of arrows. Another bow can be made and there are still a few more of Lioumere's teeth, in your father's possession, back at the pa.'

Hupa was quiet for a moment, then she argued with Craig.

'If she can change us into birds or beasts, I would rather be a wolf. I don't like the look of those crow birds. They look shifty and mean. Tell her to change us into wolves and I'll agree to let her have the bow and quiver.'

Craig saw a certain amount of sense in what Hupa was suggesting. As wolves they could follow their own scent, back to the pa. Such creatures could travel across the countryside swiftly, fearing nothing but meeting men. These they could avoid, as wolves can, using their superior instincts, camouflage and wild-country skills. It was probably better to be a wolf than a crow, since neither he nor Hupa knew what it was like to fly and how things looked from a bird's perspective.

'All right then,' he agreed, and told the child-with-the-child's-face of the change of choice.

She said that changing them into wolves would be just as easy as transfiguring them into crows.

Still suspicious, Hupa removed the string from her bow and tied it around her own waist.

Turning to Craig, she said, 'Tell her she can string the bow again later. I have no wish to be shot by my own weapon, as a running wolf.'

The child seemed to understand why Hupa had done as she had and scowled at her.

Craig said in Gaelic, 'I'm placing the bow and quiver at your feet – don't touch them until you've changed us into wolves – you may begin.'

'Tell the girl to stare into my eyes. You too. Both of ye look deeply into my eyes . . .'

3

They were not wolves but wild dogs. Afraid of the child-with-the-child's-face now that they were undomesticated beasts, animals of field and woodland, they ran off in panic. Somehow they managed to stay together, by scent and sound more than by sight, and paused in the high grasses of an open stretch of land to get their breath. Unable to communicate with the use of spoken language, Craig managed to convey to Hupa that he would still remain friendly towards her, so long as she remained submissive to him. He nipped her rump and shouldered her.

Hupa retaliated immediately, not at all sure that the hierarchy had been established. She bit his jaw, making him back off with his eyes watering. In fact it was clear to Craig that his female companion was not prepared to roll over, belly-up, in submissive pose just because he was a male. It was bulk which counted here and Hupa's size as a bitch was not much different to that of Craig's as a dog.

All this was quite frustrating to Craig, who felt they were wasting time by trying to establish the dominant animal, especially when there were only two of them. However, he was not going to assume that position without a contest. It was not in his animal nature to do so.

The pair of them began a mock fight, which turned

serious occasionally. After much rolling in the dust, side attacks at hairy flanks, chewing of tails, and growling, snapping and snarling, Hupa's canine spirit overcame that of Craig's, and she assumed the role of leader. Craig flipped over onto his back, exposing his vulnerable throat and belly. He rolled his eyes showing the whites and twisted his jaw to give it a lopsided look.

In effect he was saying: *I give in – you can be the dominant member of our small pack – until I make another challenge against your authority. Then we'll have to go through all this again, perhaps with the same result, but hopefully with me taking responsibility for the pack.*

Once she had established her superiority, Hupa went off in search of food, her prime consideration as a wild dog. Craig had some vague idea they should be following a scent trail, but having given way to her as the master, he trotted obediently behind, stopping to sniff things occasionally – grass clumps, trees roots, river banks, the genitals of his companion – finding each interesting in its way but not satisfying any of the primal drives which now ruled his canine life.

Suddenly, as they approached a wooded area, Hupa stopped and stiffened. The hackles rose on her neck. She began growling softly and menacingly in the back of her throat. A few moments later another wild dog came out of the grasses in front and stopped to stare curiously at the pair. Craig sniffed the air and immediately scented bitch on heat. He went bounding off towards the female in front, only to come to a skidding halt when yet another dog, and another, came out of the tall weeds.

There was a pack of six or seven, including a puppy. One big male came up from behind the pack and made straight for Hupa and Craig, his hair bristling and his mouth a snarling red cavern of teeth. They both hunched in the grass for a moment, watching to see if he would swerve away, then when he looked like coming on they bolted for the nearest hill. The big dark male followed them for some way, then turned and joined his pack, who were waiting either for his victory or his retreat.

After that incident the pair moved more warily onwards, not really knowing where they were heading except that their nostrils were tuned to smells of fresh meat. Occasionally they stopped to drink in a puddle, or sniff some interesting animal's urine marking its territorial border, but for the most part it was a kind of meandering progress across country, towards some distant mountainous region. These mountains seemed to be pulling Craig towards them, urging him to enter their domain.

Once, they saw a herd of deer and both animals, inexperienced as they were, set off in pursuit. They did not stand an earthly chance of catching the beasts, which sprang away like lightning and sped across the plains powered by long athletic legs. Another time they actually saw some wolves – the creatures they had wanted to be – and wisely kept a great distance between themselves and the large grey beasts. Even the scent of these creatures from a long way away was enough to strike a terrible fear in the heart of Craig.

Towards evening they heard a great noise and at last smelled the fresh meat for which they had been searching. Coming to the top of a ridge they looked down to see clusters of humans running and clashing together, yelling from their mouths, the shiny things in their hands making high clinking sounds as they came together. There were humans on the ground, some lying still, others moving but making groaning sounds. Here and there were severed limbs and broken heads, eyes that stared from dead skulls, blood seeping into the grasses. Yet still the humans screamed at each other and swished through the air with strips of something which flashed like the sun on a fast-flowing stream.

One man came running towards the two dogs, as they hunched in the grasses, watching this carnage. He managed to get halfway up the embankment, when a straight piece of wood struck him in the back, the point coming through and out of his chest. He looked down and gave a great cry of dismay and despair, then fell to the ground, his legs twitching and jerking.

Still the dogs remained where they were, knowing that if they went down amongst those blood-crazy humans, they themselves might be cut to pieces. When the twilight drained from the sky and the darkness began moving in, the human activity gradually ceased, until there were men strolling away from the scene in bloody rags, or carrying a broken comrade, or simply staggering dazed and blind in the direction of the rising moon.

Food, Craig sensed Hupa saying with her canine gestures. *Fresh meat.*

Once the darkness folded over the plain, they went down and began feeding on the bodies. Other creatures came out of their hidden holes and secret places, also to feed on the fresh meat. Weasels, stoats, polecats, martens, foxes, wolves, rats, mice. Birds came too – carrion. There was plenty to be had. A kind of truce existed between the creatures, now that there was ample food to be had, all in one place. Occasionally a larger beast would move a smaller creature on, to some other feeding ground, or warning growls would ripple from a throat or two, but for the most part they were equal. Even the birds.

Craig gorged on the soft lights of a man whose belly had been sliced open and whose innards were exposed.

When he was glutted he went looking for Hupa, finding her gnawing on the shoulder of another fallen man. He waited patiently for her to finish, then the pair of them went away into the night, to find a place to rest until the morning. Craig was conscious of the thought that the food would still be there the next day. They could eat again, once the sun came up. Unless the humans returned to fight each other again.

When the sun came up, the pair went down again to feed. Again there were others there, but everyone scattered when the humans returned to carry off their dead. The humans carried clubs with them and began to beat off the wild beasts, shouting in anger. Hupa and Craig left the field again, running through some marshland, to stop on the other side.

Craig lay down on his back, exhausted, staring at the sky. There were small storm flies coming from the oily marsh water, settling on his sweaty skin. He swatted them, then scratched the places where they had bitten him with his nails. When the lethargy left him a little, he rolled over on to his side, to stare at Hupa. She was kneeling, looking down at her hands, her nails thick with dried blood and mud.

'We're back,' he said, suddenly realizing he was no longer covered in fur. 'We've changed back.'

'If we ever went away,' replied Hupa, wiping the blood away from her mouth. She seemed to find a bit of gristle between her teeth and hooked it out with a fingernail. Then she turned away and began heaving and retching, being sick on the grass. Craig, realizing she was having a reaction against what they had eaten, sat and watched her, feeling sympathetic.

When she had finished, she looked at him.

'How is it that you're not sick?' she asked. 'Do you have a tough constitution?'

'You mean because of what we ate? Why, you Rarotongans haven't fought many enemies in the past, have you? Don't forget I was raised a Hivan. There were wars between the islands all the time. We ate our foes for breakfast after the battle.'

Hupa looked at him and was then sick again.

He continued, saying, 'Your father has probably done the same in his time.'

'I don't *care*,' she said. 'I haven't. I found it disgusting.

We ate those people because we were *hungry*, not because we wanted their mana. Not because we wanted to debase and humiliate them, prevent their atua from receiving reward after death . . .'

Craig shrugged. Except that the meat had been raw, he did not see what to get in a fuss about. Nowadays, he would not eat his enemies, because those rituals were slightly out of fashion with Rarotongans, but he saw nothing disgusting about it. The Hivans, Fijians and Tongans still did it. He felt that Hupa was making a bother about nothing.

'What did you mean – *if we ever went away*?' he asked her, when he felt she was able to reply.

'I meant that perhaps we only thought we were dogs.'

Craig considered this very carefully. Hypnotism, he knew, was a very powerful tool. Boy-girl could hypnotize. It was always better, he had been told, if the victim is willing and allows the hypnotist inside his or her head. Well, they had done that, with the sorceress. Perhaps it was true? Maybe they had been running on their knuckles and toes? After all, they were still wearing clothes, which were now covered in the blood of a people he assumed were two Angle tribes, who had been battling over some quarrel or other.

He inspected his hands and feet.

'I still think we were really transformed into wild dogs,' he said at last.

'It doesn't really matter now, does it? We're well and truly lost. If I ever get my hands on that child again, I'll strangle her with my bow. Now we have no weapons and we're deep in the hinterland of a vast foreign land. What shall we do now? Fall on our knees and beg our ancestors to guide us out?'

'I am a navigator. I can never be thoroughly lost. The sun will go down behind those mountains,' said Craig. 'That's the way we have to point our chins. I agree it's not a very accurate way to navigate, but it's better than heading in the wrong direction altogether. Come on. Pick yourself up. You can wash off that blood and gore at the next stream, but for now just lick your chops and get your feet moving.'

What he had not told Hupa was the fact that he felt an overwhelming attraction coming from the mountains. It was as if they were pulling him into their heart. He was now, and had been since first laying eyes on them, vaguely conscious that some destiny awaited him in those mountains. Somehow this whole episode, including being abducted and finding the home of the child-with-the-old-man's-face, had a feeling of a manipulative power behind it, as if unseen forces were directing his movements, urging him gently along a prepared path.

Perhaps there was a task for him to perform, for which he alone was suitable?

PART EIGHT

Over the Magic Mountains

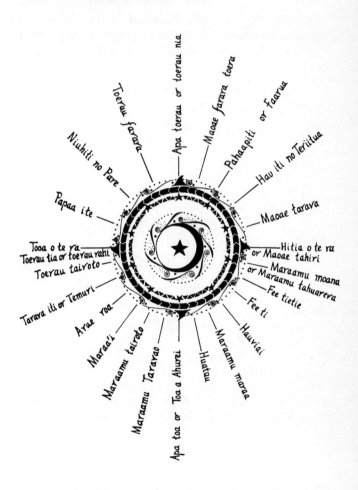

1

Before the two companions went up into the mountains, Craig had an urge to go back to the battlefield below. Given a few moments in the early morning, Craig had said his usual prayers to Punga, the God of Ugly Creatures, and had heard something in the wind as it blew through the trees. He had been *told* by Punga to return to the site of the bloody fight. Punga was his household deity and Craig could no more have ignored the faint call of this god than he could have rejected a plea from his own mother.

The Angles had gathered their dead and had gone. After searching a long time amongst the blood-soaked long grasses he found what he was looking for: an iron broadsword. This was the weapon which his father desired in order to be able to defend himself in Ifurin.

However, there was no loch in this part of the country, in which to fling the sword as instructed, so Craig stuck the weapon in his waistband and went back to Hupa. She grumbled at him, saying that it was all right for him, he had a weapon now, but she felt naked without her bow and quiver.

'We'll make you a bow as soon as we find a suitable kind of tree,' he said. 'And some arrows.'

He felt uncomfortable. She had chosen the wrong words

to describe her state. Her talk of feeling naked made him come over hot and embarrassed. Such words from her mouth filled his head with forbidden pictures. He hoped that nothing had happened between them, while they had been dogs – or worse – if they had not been dogs. Certainly the animal lust had been upon him during that time. She was (he hoped *still*) a virgin of high rank and he was married to a woman who loved him deeply. Violation would be unforgivable.

'How do you feel?' he asked her casually. 'In yourself I mean?'

Hupa stared back as he gazed at her. She was small, neatly proportioned, and youthful. An athlete. There were no feminine wiles, no frilly edges. What he saw was plain and simple Hupa: without artifice. Her gender was secondary to most people who knew her. Yet to him she seemed totally desirable.

'Me? I feel sick. I've never eaten raw people before – what do you expect? But I'll get over it.'

'That wasn't what I meant. You see, we spent time as wild dogs – or at least, *thought* we were dogs. Something – something could have happened which we might regret later.'

Hupa looked him directly in the eyes. She might have been wholly inexperienced sexually, but she was not naive. She knew immediately what he was talking about.

'Fat chance,' she muttered. 'You've made it plain how you feel about – about us.'

'I may have done that,' he said, frustrated and angry with himself and her, 'but did the bloody dog in me remember to respect this vow of celibacy?'

'I remember everything,' replied Hupa. 'Don't you?'

He was miserable. 'No, not all of it. There are bits caught up in the heat of hunting – bits which are not clear. There's a kind of hot blood haze over some of it. How come you have such clarity of memory?'

'Because I was cool,' she said, smiling in a superior way at him. 'I was cool and calm, while you were hot and bothered. Perhaps you're not the holy man you pretend to be? Perhaps you do have strong feelings for me? If I was better at being a woman I could probably get you easily, couldn't I? If I was good at those alluring little tricks which some women use to capture a man, I could have you just like that.'

'I don't know what you're talking about,' he replied, huffily. 'I think you've got a strong imagination.'

She laughed.

Disconcerted, he began to stride out, into the foothills of the mountains, knowing she would follow.

'Don't leave me behind,' she called. 'I've nothing with which to defend myself.'

'Keep up then,' he replied, uncharitably.

They began to climb, first up gradients which were easily scaled, and then into the mountains proper. Craig found trails, not well worn, but certainly more than goat trails. Up and up they went, past the vegetation line, through tall stacks and onto steeper paths beyond.

The air grew colder and the pair realized they should have gathered more clothing from the battlefield below.

When they were well into the crags and sheer walls of the mountains, they met a traveller coming the other way. This was a man of middle age with a huge hooked nose. On his back was a framework of sticks with an animal skin pack.

Craig gripped his sword as the man approached, but then with head down the stranger passed them by, not even glancing up, let alone offering a greeting. This surprised both Craig and Hupa, who had been expecting acknowledgement of their presence.

They caught a strong whiff of animal fat from the man's clothing, which were not much more than partially cured skins tied together. His feet were bound in hide, as was his head. He appeared to be dressed in no particular clannish style and Craig wondered if he were an outcast.

'Hey, you!' cried Craig in Gaelic. 'Stop a minute.'

For a short while it appeared the man might run on, rather than obey the summons, but in the end he turned round. His face was as brown as those of the two Oceanians. There were places where a blue dye had stained his skin. Above the great eagle-beak nose brown eyes regarded the pair with suspicion.

'Are you real?' he asked. 'Or is it the loneliness of these mountains? I often see things. I sometimes hear things. True the two do not usually come together, but I'm sure the solitude of the mountains can arrange anything it wishes.'

'We're real, and we're not mountain goblins or anything of that sort,' replied Craig, walking up to the man. 'Take no notice of these tattoos on my face, they make me look fiercer than I am. We're strangers from another land. Castaways. Now we're lost in these mountains. Can you help us?'

The man continued to regard the pair for a few more moments, then he removed his heavy pack. There were creases where the straps had cut into his shoulders. His weathered features cracked into a smile which produced crow's feet in the corners of his eyes and his mouth.

'You don't look fierce. I thought you was a player – a travelling performer. That's an interesting leg you have there, friend – I've never seen one so heavily tattooed. Looks almost black from a distance. Now I'm close up though, I can see the patterns. It must have hurt. Oh, yes – who am I? Hookey Walker at your service.' He touched his nose to show where his first name had come from. 'How can I help you?' he asked. 'Do you wish to buy?'

'Buy? Buy what?'

'Goods. I'm a pedlar.'

'What's a pedlar?'

The man laughed and sat on his pack.

'You really are strangers, aren't you? I'm a traveller, I go between villages and towns, selling my wares.'

'Are you not murdered for your goods?' said Craig, surprised. 'I would not trust the people hereabouts.'

'A pedlar has some protection, at least from those who are not out-and-out robbers and thieves. If I am attacked and killed, then villages will have no go-between to carry their news to each other, to bring them goods they cannot make themselves. Of course,' he stared up at the crags, 'there are those who respect no common laws and who would slit my throat in a moment, but I can protect myself. I have been a warrior.'

He pointed to a faded patch of blue dye on his forearm, which looked as if it had resisted attempts to wash it off.

'This attests to my former occupation. Woad. I fought for the Fraser clan in the south, and for a Cymru tribe in the north-east, though I am an Angle born. Old Hookey was a paid warrior, fighting for the side which fed him best. No, no, my friend, I have greater fear of wild beasts than I do of any man I might meet on the road.'

Craig translated all this briefly for Hupa's sake.

'He fights for material rewards? Oceanians fight for honour!' she said, emphatically.

Craig told Hookey what she had said.

He smiled and shook his head. 'We both fight for what we have not got,' he replied.

Craig decided not to translate this, or Hupa would probably leap on the man and scratch out his eyes.

'What have you in your pack?' asked Craig.

The man glanced at his huge deerskin bundle.

'Clay pots, wooden spoons, daggers, hand axes, spear-heads, arrowheads . . .'

'Arrowheads? Made of what?'

'Of metal of course. Not iron, but bronze. Magic works better with bronze. Would you like to see some?'

Craig indicated that they would like to see them, though

privately he wondered how he would pay for them, if Hupa wanted them.

'You say they are magic?' said Craig.

The pedlar nodded and began sorting through his pack.

'They have been dipped in the Tarn-of-the-neverlost, a high lake in the mountains of Ud. A witch sold them to me for a bag of dried blackthorn sloes. Witches in those high places never get anything to eat, which is why they're so scrawny.'

'If they don't eat, they should die.'

'And so they would, if they weren't witches and stuffed full of magic. It's a known fact that witches are never hungry, yet this one liked to chew on something. She said it was a habit with her and that it helped her to think. She also put dried grasses in her mouth, lit them and sucked down the smoke. Witches are unfathomable creatures, my friend.'

Finally the pedlar took a small soft-leather pouch from his pack and undid it to reveal the arrowheads. Hupa predictably gave a shout and picked one up to inspect it.

'Nicely made,' she said. 'Good balance. With these and some eagle's feathers to fletch the hafts, I could have my weapon back.'

When this was translated, Hookey Walker said he would throw in a couple of golden eagle feathers and some cord.

Craig told Hupa the history of the arrowheads and she asked, 'What's the signifance of them being dipped in this pool, this Tarn-of-the-neverlost?'

The pedlar smiled at the enquiry, when it was passed on by Craig.

'Why, I'll show you.'

He picked up one of the bronze arrowheads and skimmed it away from him like a child will fling a stone into the ocean. It fell on a slope of scree amongst thousands of stone shards, instantly lost to their eyes.

'Go and look for it,' he said to Craig.

Craig, thinking there was not a hope in earth and sky of finding the arrowhead amongst the scree, found it immediately he reached the general area. He had not been guided by anything shiny, for the arrowhead was dull, almost black in appearance, not having been polished after leaving its mould. It had simply been a case of walking right up to it.

'You'll never lose another arrow in the trees or grasses – not with these heads,' said the pedlar, grinning.

Hupa tried it next, two or three throws, and it worked every time.

'Once dipped in the magic tarn,' said the pedlar, 'it is never lost.'

'I like these arrowheads,' Hupa said.

'With a very different kind of magic,' reminded Craig. 'You may not hit the target now.'

'My archery does not *need* that kind of magic – it's helpful but it's not necessary. I am accurate enough without it.'

'Such a modest maiden,' sighed Craig. 'Now, how do we pay for these. How many do you want? Four? Six?'

'Six would be better than four. Offer him this necklace of shark's-teeth,' she said, removing the ornament from around her slim throat.

Craig was a little concerned by this. 'But the necklace warns others of your rank, as an ariki. How will they know not to touch you? Your mana, your tapu – these may be harmful to tutua who do not know you are of noble rank.'

'If being high-born means I cannot have you,' she pouted, 'then I'd rather not be one anyway. Look, Craig, how many tutua will we meet on this trail? As soon as I see my father again, he will give me another such badge of rank. In the meantime, give this pedlar fellow the necklace. Tell him they're magic teeth, that the wearer will experience good health for the rest of his life.'

'That's a good one,' said the pedlar, inspecting the necklace. 'If the wearer does fall into poor health, he thinks he is going to die – and most people when they're convinced they are dying, they usually do.'

'Well, what about the trade?'

'The necklace is unusual. Two arrowheads.'

'Five.'

'Three.'

'Four.'

'A bargain,' finished the pedlar. 'Four arrowheads.'

He began to sort four out when Hupa pounced and chose her own, to much sighing from the pedlar. Then Hookey Walker fastened his deerskin pack, lifted the frame onto his back, and gave them a farewell wave.

'Be careful, my friends,' he called. 'There are distractions on your route. Leave them be, is Old Hookey's advice. These mountains are not as ordinary as they appear – they have their secrets which are best left uncovered. Go without curiosity and you may get to the other side unharmed.'

'What sort of distractions?'

The pedlar walked on, hidden behind his load, calling back that this was for him to keep and for them to find out, for if he told them of one thing, they might come across another and think it harmless.

'Be wary of *every*thing,' he warned. 'Let no one thing lure you from the path. And be especially careful not to tarry near a tower if you see one.'

Craig's heart began to beat faster for no explicable reason on hearing the last sentence.

'What tower?'

'You'll see – or not.'

'Where?'

'Who knows?' said Hookey, enigmatically. 'It appears – sometimes here, sometimes there. On a moor, in the mountains, down by a bleak seashore. No one knows why, but I've learned one thing in my life – keep clear of towers that appear like mushrooms overnight. They can only lead to trouble.'

They had to be satisfied with this and went on up into the coldness of the mountains. The wind had an edge like that of a lei-o-mano and howled in their faces. Clouds were almost within touching distance as they swirled about the peaks like mad atua. There were strange gods up here, in the crags and buttresses of the high mountains. Craig could sense their incomprehensible forms lurking amongst the tall stones, in the crevices and caves, around the sheer drops. Craig wanted to be over the pass and down amongst the green valleys again. They were not his valleys, but they were preferable to alien mountains.

Towards the top of one saddle they came to a huge pile of stones. This Craig knew from his father's tales of the mountains to be called a cairn. Not far from the cairn was a sight which both Oceanians gawped at: a tall circular tower made of drystones with what appeared to be a room made of solid chalk blocks right at its head. There were no windows to this structure, nor any doors that Craig could see, once he had walked around it. Simply a hollow tower of roughly hewn blocks of granite with the top third of dazzling white chalk.

'What is this place?' he asked, more of himself than Hupa. 'Why would anyone build a tower up here?'

'The pedlar said not to give way to curiosity.'

'True – he did warn us.'

At that moment the voice of a woman came floating down from the white room. It filled Craig's head. With a sudden chill Craig recognized the voice. It was that of his dead step-mother, Dorcha. She was giving him an order.

'*Open the tower, Craig. It is time. The world is ready for the creature within. The old gods are destroying one another. The beast in the chalk room will bring about the final change. Hereafter women and men will make their own destiny, without interference from supernatural beings or forces. The fate of humankind will be in the hands of humankind.*'

'Did you hear that?' asked Craig of Hupa, looking up. 'There's someone in there.'

'I heard nothing . . .'

'They were asking for asssistance,' Craig interrupted her. 'It was – it sounded like Dorcha. Dorcha's spirit is trapped in this tower. We have to let her out.'

He realized he was talking feverishly and frighting Hupa, but he could not control his words.

'We have to ignore it,' argued Hupa. 'The pedlar warned us against things like this. Do not get involved. These are magical mountains, much like those we have on islands like Moorea, near Tahiti. Would you go climbing up into the heights on Moorea? And if you did, would you interfere with what you might find there?'

Craig insisted, 'This is different. Listen, I hear her call again.'

'*Open the tower, Craig. You promised your father you would look after his people. His people were the Oceanians and the Albannachs. Open the tower to help them both.*'

'I have to do this thing. I have to let her out. Dorcha's soul is imprisoned in this stone tower without windows on the cold hillside of this barren landscape. I tell you, we have to do something, Hupa. That could be your soul trapped in there.'

The force of his words were such that Hupa knew he could not be turned from this task. She watched as he carefully scaled the outside of the round wall, choosing handholds in which to insert his fingers and toes. It did not appear an impossible task, for though Craig was not an especially good climber, the stones appeared to have been cut and shaped by maladroit giants, and there were plenty of gaps.

When he reached the chalk room at the top, there were no more handholds. It had been weathered smooth by the rain and wind, the gaps sealing together to form one solid hollow cap of chalk. He moved around the tower carefully, in frustration, trying to find some chink in the wall of chalk, and all the time the woman within pleaded with him to release her.

Craig climbed down again, to where Hupa waited.

'Well,' she said, 'are you satisfied?'

Craig shook his head and again inspected the base of the tower. There he found something he had not previously noticed, because it was indistinct, weathered. At first he thought they were symbols, but then realized that it was an inscription which encircled the granite tower. It was in a stylized form of Hiro's writing, the letters linking each other like fishhooks to form a complete circle around the stone structure. The writing was so faint and so swirlingly curlicued he had great difficulty in reading it, but finally the words came to him:

}{In time the Natural laws of the world must triumph over Preternatural forces just as Good will eventually subdue Evil}{It takes but one man to break the chain and release from bondage the Agent within}{You Stranger standing before this tower}{Banish the element of Chaos and give mankind a natural Order}{

Craig did not really understand the meaning of these words, but he saw the significance in the way they had been written. They formed a chain around the tower. Chains, he knew from his father, were metal ropes used to keep men fettered, hold them captive, so that they might never escape. If one broke the chain, then the imprisoned might go free. What he had to do was make a break in this chain which encircled the tower.

'Stand back,' he said to Hupa, 'I'm going to try something.'

He took his sword from his waistband and struck the granite where it projected slightly, chipping out a single piece which carried but one word. The word, which was Chaos, went spinning away into the scree, leaving a gap in the chain. Immediately the stones began to crumble at the base. The chalk room dropped as the mighty granite blocks slipped from under each other, tumbling away from their places. It was as if Craig had removed the keystone. With no mortar to bind them together, once the blocks began to fall they came down in a landslide.

'RUN!' cried Craig, and he and Hupa raced away from the tower as it came crashing down upon the mountain top. Fortunately they reached a safe distance and turned to see the chalk room perched on a pile of rubble. Still this white structure which had sat on the top of the tower remained whole and complete, without a crack or fissure.

Now a wind, a natural agent of the weather, came up from nowhere out of the valleys and passes below. It brought with it a fine grit, a sand, which cut into the skins of the two watchers. They fell to the ground and crawled into a nearby cave, there burying their heads in their arms, while the wind howled and screamed around the entrance. The duststorm continued for half a day before it abated.

When the pair finally emerged from the cave, the chalk room had been worn away, leaving but an open shell like a molar which has been hollowed and scoured.

Out of this shell emerged not Dorcha's soul, but a strange dark cloud of dust as fine as woodfire smoke.

This cloud drifted here and there, shaping and reshaping itself into nebulous beasts, creatures neither Craig nor Hupa could recognize. There was one with eagle's claws for its feet and a dog's head with pointed ears. There was another with thick lithe and supple legs attached to a mus-cled torso and a face with strange flattened features. One like a horse with a straight horn from its forehead.

Fuzzy, drifting contours floated over the mountainside, forming, re-forming, growing almost imperceptibly as it rolled away like a thundercloud with a purpose.

'What was that?' cried Hupa. 'What have you let out of the tower?'

Craig was upset. 'I don't know.'

'You were warned not to interfere, Craig. That – that *thing* could be something terrible. You may have released Plague, or Famine, or something equally as bad. What have you sent out into the world, Craig?'

'I don't know,' he confessed, 'but it is an agent of order, not chaos, so it won't be either of those you mentioned. It – it must be something for the common good. Look at us! We are not struck down by some deadly disease, are we?'

Hupa admitted this was true.

'Well then, let's not fret over something from which the world may benefit. Come on, let's make our way down now. Look, there are green valleys below. We can make you a bow and some hafts for your arrowheads. Let's not dwell on what can't be changed . . .'

He strode off, down the mountain track, appearing light-hearted to Hupa, but within he was fearful of what he had done, wondering if she was right and that he had released something awful on the unsuspecting world.

2

Every day at noon, rain or sun, wind or calm, Guirk came down to the walls of the pa and called for Kieto to meet him in single combat. When no one appeared for the period over which he waited, Guirk did not seem too disappointed. He shouted his taunts – someone had taught him insults in Oceanian – then turned and trudged back to the Celt encampment. There was always tomorrow. He would be there whatever the weather. It had become a habit – a ritual.

The day came when Kieto's elder brother, Totua, could stand it no longer. He called a tohunga and asked the priest to accompany him outside the pa. The priest looked worried, but Totua told the man he was only needed as an interpreter. The young man looked relieved and nodded his assent.

'Must I listen to my family being maligned,' cried the elderly Totua, aggrieved, as Guirk's ringing tones penetrated the noon air of the pa. 'Do I have to stand here while our mother is called ugly names and our father's honour is impugned? I will kill this Guirk with my own hands.'

With the priest at his heels Totua, already wearing his helmet of scarlet feathers and his dogskin war cloak, snatched a war club, one made of ironwood and obsidian, and went out to meet the challenge from Guirk. Totua swept the cloak away from his shoulders to reveal the tattoos on his chest: badges of his manhood and courage cut into his dark wrinkled skin.

Family pride was at stake and he could take no more from this upstart.

Totua's son, idling by the gate, was surprised to see his elderly father go striding past on his way out of the pa.

'Where are you going, Papa Totua?' asked the youth, surprised. 'Have you been called to a challenge?'

'I am going to smash the skull of that mouth they call Guirk,' snarled his father. 'Our family has stood enough insults. If my brother can't go out because he's too precious to the nation, then I must silence the liar.'

The boy snatched at Totua's arm.

'Don't go out there, Papa Totua,' he hissed. 'They say that Guirk has a magic shield and sword. You can't kill him while he has those . . .'

'Who says?' asked his father, his eyes narrowing.

'Why – why Daggan and Siko. They say the Celt has weapons made from Lioumere's iron teeth. That's what they say, my father. Go back, now. Don't go out to fight this man.'

'Where would a Celt get such iron?'

'I – I don't know – it's what they say. I'm sure it's true. Please stay here.'

Totua snorted in contempt and marched past the youth, the priest trotting behind.

He stood in front of the Celt, who was stripped to the skin except for a thick leather belt and copper arm braces. As always Guirk bore his shield and sword. He looked Totua up and down in disgust. It was clear that the Celt did not think much of his opponent. Totua was no mean warrior and this further incensed him, causing his blood to burn in his veins.

'I am Kieto,' he told thick-set Guirk, using the interpreter. 'I have come to silence your lying tongue.'

'Seems to me,' said Guirk, staring at Totua's magnificent tall helmet, 'that the liar here is wearing a chicken on
his head.'

'A chicken?' cried Totua.

'You wouldn't catch me wearing one of those things –
they crap all over you, don't they? Look, yours has shit blue
turds onto your chest.'

Guirk pointed with his sword at Totua's tattoos.

'*I-am-Kieto*,' shrieked Totua.

'Not unless you grew an arm overnight,' smirked the
Celt. 'I saw this Kieto at the campfire entertainments. You
are not he. You are some old fart with an addled brain. Go
home to grandma and get her to tuck you into bed with a
nice warm glass of milk, grandpa.'

When this was translated by the priest, who had been
told by the high priestess always faithfully to reproduce
the Gaelic in his mother tongue, Totua cried that he was
Kieto's older brother and therefore entitled to take up challenges on his behalf.

With these words he took a swing with his two-handed
club at the head of Guirk.

Guirk held up his shield and the nokonoko club with the
stone edge glanced away swiftly, not even touching
the shield, as if there was a buffer of air between it and the
metal. Totua shook his head in anger and tried again, only
to see and feel the club bounce away as it struck an invisible barrier. Several more blows, serving to exhaust the old
man, were treated with the same contempt by Guirk and
his magic shield.

Then the Celt began to ridicule the old man further,
telling him he was as weak as a puppy, that he should be
back on weaning milk again, for he was but a baby. Guirk
belittled him by knocking off his helmet with the flat of his
sword, then obscenely waggling his testicles at the old man

when Totua began weeping in frustration. When Totua bent to pick up his headgear, Guirk farted in his face.

Totua stood up straight again and gathered a gob of spit in his mouth. This he launched accurately into his adversary's face, satisfied at seeing it splatter in Guirk's eyes and drip from his nose and chin.

'Magic shields don't ward off a good slab of phlegm,' laughed the old man. 'You'll probably get some nasty disease from that . . .'

Guirk's eyes opened wide with fury. In that moment he forgot his instructions from Cormac-the-Venomous, which was to fight only Kieto and no other warrior. Guirk swept down with his sword at Totua's head. The old man had lost little of his swiftness in battle over the years. Instantly the club was held up like a staff, protecting his head. To no avail. Incredibly the sword cut through the ironwood without a pause. It continued in its descent to split the old man's head in two, and on down to the middle of his chest.

The priest gave out a strangled cry of horror and turned and ran back to the pa like a chicken with a dog behind it.

Even Guirk was amazed at what he had done. The Celt had put the minimum of strength behind the blow. Now he could see the Oceanian's heart still beating inside his chest. There were lungs exposed like pulsating grey balloons. Totua fell to the floor, his brains and other matter spilling over the dust. His precious helmet fell into two neat halves like the split husk of a coconut.

'Now look at what you've made me do, you fucking old sheep-shagger,' cried Guirk. 'You made me kill you.'

He shook his head in annoyance at the leaking body, as if Totua could still hear and see him.

Guirk decided he had to make a show of it. Now the deed was done some use might be made of it. He signalled for a horse from one of his clansmen. A man came riding up. Guirk cut off the two halves of Totua's head at the neck, spooned out the brains, scraped the inside of the

hemi-skulls clean and then tied them one either side of the
horse's mane by the hair. They dangled there in the company of other heads, dead clansmen from another war.
Then Guirk fastened the feet of the headless corpse to the
horse's tail and swung himself up onto the beast's back.

Guirk next galloped the horse three times around the
pa, dragging Totua's remains behind in the dirt, yelling for
Kieto to come out and avenge his older brother.

Oceanians flocked to the walls to see what the noises
were about and were appalled by what they saw. This was
worse than eating your enemy. To treat a corpse with such
disrespect was something only uncivilized people would
do, people who in their ignorance knew no better. When
the Oceanians ate their foe it was to ingest their mana,
their courage, their skill at warfare, and even then whatever
remained of the body would be placed on an ahu, a sacrificial platform, as an offering to the gods.

Kieto had at the time of Totua's death been in the temple
with Kikamana the Farseeing-virgin. He had been communing with his atua, through the high priestess, when
suddenly his ancestral spirits screamed in his head. Never
had this happened before and both the priestess and Kieto
went white with fear.

'What are they saying?' asked Kieto, putting his hands
over his ears but finding it impossible to block out the
voices in his head. 'I can't understand what they're saying.'

Kikamana, more familiar with the language of the spirit
world, answered him.

'They say that a great offence has occurred. They say
they have been humiliated. They say that at this moment
someone is causing them great insult outside the walls of
the pa . . .'

Kieto rushed outside the temple to hear the moans and
shouts of his people on the platforms above, as they witnessed that which was offending Kieto's ancestors.

When Kieto himself saw what Guirk was doing with his

brother's body, he was enraged beyond reason. He ran to his quarters and found three throwing spears. Running back up onto the battlements of the pa, he stood out over the walls on a projecting platform. When Guirk next came thundering past him, the corpse of Totua bouncing and jerking on the end of the rope, he threw all three spears in quick succession.

Guirk did not even bother with the shield, but held up his magic sword instead. The spears were parried by some unseen force, skimming away before they reached within a body-length of the Celtic warrior. Guirk laughed, waving his sword at Kieto.

'Come out and fight, you weakling,' he called. 'I'll give you a taste of what I gave your brother.'

Indeed, Kieto would have answered the challenge there and then, by jumping down from the platform to the ground outside the pa, but Kikamana anticipated his rashness. She ordered some priests to take him and hold him down, which they did while he kicked and struggled, crying that he had to avenge his family, his ancestors, and slay the barbarian.

'When the time is ready,' said Kikamana, 'but not now. You would be cut down out there, leaving the army leaderless. You must look to your responsibilities.'

Kieto knew what she meant and indeed did calm down. With Guirk's taunts in his ears he went back to the temple. There he fell on the floor and wept bitter tears, assuring his atua that he would one day even the score.

'Justice will be mine,' he whispered hoarsely. 'I will have it. I will have the head of Guirk. But I will not consume his eyes and liver, nor devour his heart, for he is not fit even to be eaten. He is a man without honour.'

Kieto's ancestors had to be satisfied with promises.

A steady drizzle fell on Hupa and Craig as they made their way through the mountains. Mist swirled in the passes around the peaks through which they travelled. They were cold and hungry, following in the wake of the strange force that Craig had released from the chalk room in the high tower. He wondered now if it had been an accident that he had passed the tower. Surely some force had taken him there, for why else would he have been encouraged in his act by the voice of Dorcha?

When they finally came down out of the mountains they were in a lush green valley, with orchards all around. Here there were natural hedgerows bursting with flowers. Birds flitted from bush to bush, singing beautiful songs. Animals with red fur and bushy tails leaped from branch to branch. There were pools with clear water. The air was pleasantly warm, with seeds floating on it like small canoes.

They found a type of tree with a small dark green leaf, a sapling of which seemed suitable for a bow. The sapling bent without snapping and sprang back into its former straightness when released. Craig cut one of these flexible rods with his sword and gave it to Hupa. She still had the cord from her old bow and set about fitting it to the rod. Then Craig went off to look for some suitable hafts, while Hupa rested on a mossy bank beneath a great oak, enjoying the smell of wild herbs.

A brief spell of sunshine came out and she fell asleep on the damp ground.

She was woken, not by Craig, but by the hand of a beautiful youth. She smiled sweetly at him. He was dressed in a flimsy garment which was blown against his body by the breeze, emphasizing his delightful shape. Around his head he wore a halo of blossoms. Similarly around his ankles and wrists were delicate alpine flowers. His smile was enchanting, revealing strong white teeth. Flaxen hair flowed behind him like a swept-back veil. His eyes were of a purple hue, speckled with golden flecks. His step was so light he seemed almost to float like a white tropic bird.

Hupa had never seen anything like him. Perhaps some local person might have suspected he was not all he seemed, but she was an Oceanian. There were many strange people in this country of Land-of-Mists. She looked up, startled, as he bent down and kissed her cheek. Then he stroked her neck with a slim soft hand. He seemed to be carrying something down by his side and on looking hard she saw it was an earthenware jar.

He offered her a drink.

'Would you partake of some refreshment with me, beauteous lady?' he asked. 'I have been so lonely these past days . . .'

His voice was like the ringing of delicate wooden bells. He sat down beside her and she could feel the warmth of his thigh against hers. She wanted to enfold him within her arms, caress him, kiss those sweet lips. Instead she just stared at him dumbfounded. Finally, she took the jar from his strong hands.

'What kind of drink is it?' she asked.

Her voice sounded peculiar to her own ears, sort of thick and husky, but she was too interested in the young man to worry about the oncomings of a sore throat.

'Mead, made from the honey of bees, mixed with fermented elderberry juice,' he said, flashing her a wonderful smile. 'Summer wine we call it. It is so cool and tasteful. Try it.'

He held it up to her lips and she took a sip, finding it lighter than she thought it would be, considering the rich fruity aroma. It slipped away on the palate leaving but a tingle behind. It was difficult not to gulp it down, it was so refreshing. There was an underlying hint of alcohol, but nothing more than that. Certainly it was sweeter and more delicious than kava, with the same effect.

She was embarrassed to find she was dribbling out of the sides of her mouth, like an old woman.

'What are you doing here?' she asked the youth, as she

wiped away the wine with the back of her hand. 'Do you live in these parts?'

He pouted divinely. 'I have been abandoned. It is good that you came along. Perhaps you will give me some of your interesting company, just for a short while? I am so starved of mortal affection . . .'

He placed a hand upon her arm and looked into her eyes entreatingly.

Mortal affection? That was a funny way of putting it.

'Well, I'm not sure I can stay *too* long. My friend is out looking for arrows for my bow. Once he returns we must be on our way. But while I'm here I'm willing to talk.'

He smiled. 'Have some more summer wine.' He held the jar up to her lips again.

She found herself drinking, talking, laughing with the youth, until things became less lighthearted. They lay in the grasses together, the wind-blown seeds tangled in their hair, the soft breeze stroking their naked bodies. Why she was naked she did not know. She did not remember removing her clothes, but it felt natural enough.

The youth told her he had been waiting for her all his life, that she was the answer to his dreams. Words came from his mouth more intoxicating than the summer wine.

'You were sent to be my ash tree,' he told her, stroking her brow. 'You will be my tall and stately support. Do you think you could love me?' he asked her coquettishly. 'Could you stay with me?'

Hupa looked into those purple eyes with the golden flecks. A sensation of drowning overcame her. She fought for air, speaking thickly, her head spinning. 'I think I love you already – I've – I've never known anyone like you. I want to stay here in this valley with you for the rest of my life.'

More summer wine went down her throat.

Her mind began to spin in a dizzy fashion and her limbs grew lethargic. She felt as if she were slipping away, down a long black shaft. He filled her head with nonsense, chattering like a thousand sparrows. At the same time a lightness of spirit entered her, making it all feel quite unreal to her. Hupa would not have been surprised had he vanished before her eyes and she discovered it was all some trick of the light and shadow.

His face was like a small white delicate shell, a *precious wentletrap*, drifting in and out of her vision. Finally, he took her hand and began to lead her away. Hupa found him impossible to resist. She was walking very awkwardly, stumbling along like a two-year-old child, and she put it down to the drink. In fact she felt peculiar all over, as if there was something wrong with her arms and legs, though she was not given any time to decide what that might be, for the youth trilled away in a voice like a flute. She would have fallen over, several times, had he not prevented it with his strong arm.

They entered a copse, a ring of trees in the middle of which was a circle of fawn-coloured toadstools. Somehow they both found themselves standing inside this circle and when they stepped out of it the scene had changed. The trees were much smaller, the flowers quite tiny and the grass spread like a closely woven blanket over the gentle hills and pastures between.

'What's that perfume?' she asked, thickly.

The youth said, 'Flowers and tree blossoms. It is always spring here. We don't have winter or high summer . . .'

We don't have winter. Hupa was vaguely aware that this was a strange thing to say, but she could not put her finger on why that was so. *Here.* Where were they then, that he should say they were *here*? Perhaps she had missed something with the passing of time? Did it matter? She thought not, so long as she could have some more of that summer wine.

Small, delicate-looking people began to gather round them. Hupa was not sure where they had come from: they seemed to appear out of the ground, or from behind trees, some of them perhaps even from the sky. They clustered around her like children with sticky fingers, touching her face and hands, everywhere. Where they touched they left a residue which stained her clothes and skin peat brown. It was as if their fingers were horse chestnut buds, oozing brown sap. She noticed many of them had stormflies stuck to the tips of their fingers, which they licked absentmind-edly every so often.

'Who are these creatures?' she asked, mildly alarmed. 'Are these your people?'

The youth nodded. He seemed to have lost a lot of his stature now and was smaller than before. When Hupa stared into his face she decided it was not so startlingly handsome as she had first imagined. Now his features seemed sharper and more shrewish, like the faces of the other little people around them. Though they were smooth and without lines there were centuries of experience in those countenances.

They appeared to have lived a long time, without gath-ering the signs of age. They had an unnatural smoothness of complexion, which was like mother-of-pearl. Their bones were angular and showed through their waxy skin. The depth of their magenta eyes when Hupa stared into them seemed fathomless. These were ancients, beings who had been alive when one of Hupa's great-great-grand-mothers had been a young girl walking the hills of Raiatea, picking fruits and wild mushrooms.

'Have I been here before?' she asked, finding a feeling of familiarity creeping into her sobering mind. 'Do I know you – do you know me?'

'Dance!' cried one of the creatures, ignoring her ques-tion. 'Let us dance!'

Immediately reed flutes appeared from within folds of clothing. Logs were found to use as percussion instruments. A musical instrument like Hupa's bow was drawn across the strings of a heart-shaped hollow implement to produce a high sweet sound which thrilled her from her hair to her toes.

A lively tune was struck and the creatures began leaping up and down, twirling, flying through the air in graceful arcs to land neatly on one pointed toe. Soon Hupa found herself dancing too, without restraint, though her movements were the clumping steps of a disorientated giant. She kept falling over, much to the amusement of the little people. Normally quite supple and quick on her feet, she found this lack of co-ordination and balance irritating. Yet the harder she tried, the more she made mistakes and ended up on her back.

When she had grown weary of dancing however, she began to feel concern about Craig. He would be waiting for her at the spot where she had left him. There was something about this whole episode which was uncomfortably familiar. In the back of her mind was the thought that these creatures would not let her go, unless she did something to please them, something to put them in a compliant frame of mind.

'Shall I sing for you?' she asked. 'Shall I sing some old songs to aid your dancing?'

Her lilting voice floated out over the glade in which they were dancing.

The little people stopped dancing immediately and put their small hands over their ears.

'Stop that noise,' they yelled impolitely. 'Stop her making that awful racket.'

Clearly they did not appreciate her gift for sweet music, her genius as a songster, in this part of the world. They scowled at her and kicked oak mast in her face. One of them grabbed her ankle and tried to topple her over. Hupa stood there helplessly, wondering how she had managed to upset these creatures.

'Play for us!' they ordered. 'Let us have one of your best tunes.'

Someone put a flute into her hands. Now Hupa had a fairly mediocre talent for playing an instrument. Like most Oceanians she enjoyed the flute, but had given up lessons halfway through childhood. Her rendering of a seafaring tune was not exceptional, though it might have nestled quite happily in the full sound of a orchestra. She was not used to playing solo and was shy to start. However, once she did she was astounded to find her notes high and sweet, not at all like her normal playing tone, and she delighted the little people with her rendering of a traditional Oceanian song.

They certainly seemed to prefer her playing to her singing.

They flocked around her, looking at her rather disconcertingly straight in the eyes as she played.

'*My* mortal,' cried the youth who had brought her to this place, with admiration and possessiveness in his tones. 'She belongs to me. She's mine, mine, mine. She shall remain with me for ever . . .'

'Dusky maiden!' chanted others. 'Dusky maiden. Dusky maiden. She can play like an angel.'

Hupa's flute drew other creatures, of a different aspect, from out of the foliage and woodlands around them. They came with pointed ears and sharp noses. They came with long fingers and knobbed joints. They came with dewdrop eyes and skins encrusted with algae. Of human shape, but not of human mind, they emerged from recesses in the landscape, to watch and wonder at this person who had brought such music to their region.

Animals and birds came too: deer stood alongside wolves, ducks by foxes, to listen to her flute.

When she had finished, the little people asked her questions, some of which she could not answer.

'Have you been taken from your village by any dragons?'

'Are there giants where you live?'

'Where is your kingdom?'

She answered those she could and said she did not understand the others.

The dancing began again, and the quaffing of the wine, and night seemed never to come. They fed her and gave her wine, since she could not seem to get her hands in the right position to do it herself. When they were tired, when she was tired, they lay on the grass and slept.

During one dancing session, Craig suddenly appeared at her side, looking angry. He confronted her, saying, 'Why did you come here? I followed your tracks. Don't you recognize where you are?'

'No,' she replied, helplessly. 'Where am I?'

'It doesn't matter now,' he said, looking down at his feet with a puzzled expression on his face, 'we have to get away. I can't think properly at the moment. Not with this damned music playing. I have to think of a way to get them to let you go.'

She was not given the opportunity of speaking with Craig again for a while because the youth who had brought her there became jealous and drew her away from him. Even when they stopped dancing, the creature stayed with her, resting by her side, his eyes on Craig.

Whenever she lay her head on the grass it felt heavy and swollen – a big-domed thing – but since she had not stopped drinking wine from the moment she had set eyes on the youth it did not seem at all surprising to her. She was drunk. She knew she was drunk. She was so drunk that most of what was happening was a blur. That was why she could not stay on her feet, or sing properly, and why her head felt twice its normal size.

On waking they began cavorting again, sometimes pausing to eat mushrooms, or nuts, or small berries from the bushes, but the cycle of merry dancing and rest seemed never to end. Hupa, continually asked to play the flute and dance, grew weary of spirit.

She began to feel hollow and spent, and wished it would

all end. When she looked at Craig, lying on a grassy hillock not far away, he seemed to have changed. He did not look himself. During one rest period someone went up to Craig, who lay not far away. He was a square, chunky creature. They were whispering, but loud enough for Hupa to hear them both. Hupa looked quickly into the face of her possessive youth and saw that he was mercifully fast asleep. She listened intently to what passed between the chunky creature and Craig.

'What are you doing in fairyland?'

'Who are you?' asked Craig. 'Your face is familiar, but I can't recall where . . .'

'King Laurin,' whispered the other quickly. 'You remember me? I am King of the Dwarves. You found my mantle for me. I owe you a favour. I ask you again, what are you doing in fairyland? Do you not know if you remain here much longer, you will never be able to depart?

'Your lady has been taken,' said the dwarf-king, 'no doubt by that fairy youth who sleeps beside her – they who are without mercy have her in thrall. You two mortals will be danced to death, if you stay. They will make you play until your heart bursts in your breast. You must depart from here as quickly as possible. Don't look back. Simply walk away, towards that light that shimmers in the east.'

'How will I get away?' asked Craig, distressed. 'My feet won't do what I want them to without support.'

'Your head is on back to front, that's why, you idiot.'

Craig's hands went up to his face. Hupa looked down at her own body. It was true. Her vision was slightly fogged but she could now see that her feet were facing the wrong way. She could see her buttocks and the small of her back when she pressed her chin against her shoulder blades.

'Oh, what fiendish creatures these little people are,' Craig croaked. 'And what's wrong with my head it feels swollen and bruised – and,' he ran his hands over his face and chin, 'and my nose feels thick and bristly!'

'Someone has given you the head of a pig. Probably that youth.'

It took a few seconds for these words to sink in, but when they did Craig was appalled. He felt over his head with his hands again, finding that Laurin had spoken the truth. Despair filled his heart.

'Hoghead? Pigface? Me? Oh, you cruel gods . . .' wailed Craig, though it came out more of squeal than a howl.

'Quiet, you fool,' hissed the dwarf-king, looking round, 'do you want to wake everyone? We must get you away from them.' He became rather severe, staring at Craig as if he were very disappointed with him. 'If they find out you're the one who set the beast free, then they'll kill you anyway.'

'Set the beast free?' repeated Craig, weakly.

'You let the beast out of the tower, didn't you? One of my mountain dwarves saw you. Don't you know what you've done? I'm not at all pleased with you myself, though I know it had to happen *sometime*. The world must change over the course of time and you are one of its instruments of progress. If not you, then some other chosen man or woman.'

'What is the beast?'

'No time for that now. Get going now, take your lady with you, while they're all fast asleep. You'll have to look over your shoulder as you walk.'

'What if they wake and see us,' Craig asked, fearfully.

'You must borrow Hel Keplein, my mantle,' replied Laurin. 'While it is about your shoulders, you will be invisible. I'll follow your trail out of here later, when the furore has died down.'

'Can you do that?'

King Laurin snorted in humour. 'A wild pig running away from the hunters leaves a trail like the wake of a hurricane.'

'That's not funny.'

'Leave it hanging from some young oak tree. Leave a marker to show me which tree.'

'I shall snap one of the branches to show you which tree to look under.'

Laurin looked horrified. 'You will do no such thing. To cause such agony to the tree is not necessary. Would you have it weeping in pain? You will leave a white stone as large as your fist an arm's length from the tree. We'll find it easily if you leave such a marker. Now quickly, put this on . . .'

The dwarf-king waved his arms around Craig's shoulders and sudddenly Hupa's friend disappeared. A few moments later she felt herself being lifted up and enfolded in something soft. Craig was carrying her, the cloak about them both.

They turned their back on the dozing fairies and walked eastward, towards a brightness in the sky. Craig found if he glanced over his shoulder, every so often, he could remain going in the right direction. He walked for a very long time, until finally they discovered themselves back in the place where Hupa had met the devious youth.

'We've made it,' she groaned, as he placed her on the grass, noticing their bodies were now normal.

'What a stupid thing to do,' remonstrated Craig, as he draped the cloak on a young sapling he obviously believed to be an oak. 'To go off with a man like that.'

'You can talk,' she protested, vehemently, as he took a large white stone from a stream and placed it at the base of the sapling. 'I seem to remember you did the same with a maiden once. Have you forgotten King Uetonga's people?'

That shut him up, though he still looked annoyed.

The pair of them then fell into a proper sleep, one from which they knew they would awaken refreshed. While they were dozing Hupa dreamed that a strange dark cloud in the shape of a beast came floating through their camp. It drifted over them like smoke and wound through the trees, over the stones and grass, touching everything with its paws.

When the couple woke they saw that King Laurin's mantle, Hel Keplein, was now completely visible. It was a voluminous silver cloak which flashed in the sun. Now anyone could see it, steal it if they wished. Hupa wondered if they should hide it, but Craig was of the opinion that Laurin would be by soon to collect it and Craig felt he had to obey the king's instructions to the letter.

'We'll just leave it there,' he said.

They vacated the place, quickly, with troubled minds. On the way, Craig collected his sword, which he had hidden in a cave not far away from their camp.

He had not wanted to be robbed of the weapon by Hupa's abductors, and there had been too many of them for it to be of any use in a fight, so he had taken the wise precaution of secreting it in a crevice before following her tracks.

It felt good to have it back in his possession.

3

The rain came down as a drifting mizzle, finding its way into every crease of the body, irritating in its persistence, impossible to ignore.

'Call this rain?' Craig said, obviously irked by the weather. 'Can't the skies do better than this? When it rains in Oceania, at least it does so *thoroughly*. This is just a fine seaspray, only we're not out on the ocean. And it never stops. Where does it come from, this more-than-mist-but-not-quite-rain? At least when it rains out on the islands, it comes down in a recognizable flood – and then when everything is wet, it stops.'

'I wasn't talking about the rain – you changed the subject – I was speaking of your foolishness,' Hupa said.

'*My* foolishness? You're the one who went off with a pretty young boy.'

'Have you forgotten Princes Niwareka so quickly? You were beguiled by her in just the same way. You're supposed to be a sensible married man, yet it's all right for you to go off with any feminine creature who blinks and smiles at you. You are so wanton.'

'I am not wanton – I am loyal and true.'

Hupa was prepared to keep up her tirade the whole day

long, being contrarily incensed at Craig for her own fickleness. However, as they were talking Hupa heard a small sound in the trees behind them. She quietly fitted an arrow to her bow.

'Come out, whoever you are, or I'll . . .'

She was never able to finish the sentence, because a figure wearing a blue smock stepped out of the trees. It was a hideous dwarf with strange ears. Hupa gave out a gasp and took a step backwards. Craig stared hard, but was less impressed, having seen many such creatures recently.

'Who are you?' said Craig. 'Did you follow us out of fairyland?'

'I am Urgan,' the creature replied. 'You see the form of an elf, but I am actually a mortal like you. I was taken from my cradle as an infant and raised in elf-land. Now I wish to go home to my real people. I did indeed follow you out of fairyland and was grateful to be shown the way. I saw King Laurin speak to you and knew he had given you instructions on how to leave that world. I followed the tracks you left. You have enabled me to escape from that prison bounded by the power of fairy will. May I travel with you further, until I am in my own country?'

'Why are you so ugly?' asked Hupa, with a shudder.

Craig gave her a look of censure, but Urgan shook his head and gave her a sad smile.

'I'm sure I was not intended to be thus, but when one lives in elf-land one takes on the camouflage of an elf in order to survive. Too long there and the disguise becomes permanent. I fear I shall remain ugly, even though I have left the creatures who stole me from my mother's breast while she slept.'

'Oh, you poor man,' cried Hupa, her naturally sympathetic instincts rushing to the fore. 'Perhaps you will change back again one day? Don't give up hope.'

'I shall try not to.'

Craig said, 'Of course you must travel with us. We are

going to the south, to where a great battle is being fought between Oceanians and Celts.'

'Oceanians? Are they some kind of fairy folk?'

'No, they're foreigners, from islands far across the ocean. We are members of that invasion force. This young woman is an Oceanian. I am half-Celt. If you feel you still want to travel with us, after learning who we are, you're most welcome, but I shall understand if you wish to withdraw.'

Urgan shrugged his elfin shoulders. 'It matters nought to me, whether you are spotted snakes or windhovers. I am lost in this world, never having known it, and need the company of mortals who know its paths.'

'Then you'd better find somebody else,' muttered Hupa, 'because we're just as lost.'

'Ah,' replied the elf. 'Then we shall be lost together. At least you are company.'

Hupa said in a puzzled tone, 'How is it that you and I understand one another – do you speak the Oceanian language?'

Urgan smiled. 'I am fairy. How did you understand the youth who beguiled you? Fairy people learn things from nature. I can imbibe your thoughts. I am told your innermost desires, simply by listening to what the wind has to say about them. Your secrets, the secrets of the wind, flow into me. The wind has been everywhere, knows everything.'

After they had eaten a hare shot by Hupa and roasted over a small fire, she said to Craig, 'By the way, I lost an arrow when I was hunting.'

Craig raised his eyebrows. 'So?'

'So the pedlar Hookey Walker told us the arrowheads were magic and I *couldn't* lose them.'

Craig nodded, thoughtfully. 'That's true he even proved it to us.'

'Perhaps it was a trick?' said Urgan. 'These pedlars, you cannot trust them. They have all sorts of tricks up their sleeves. They wish to sell their wares and will do anything to get you to buy them. Some of them claim to sell such things as love potions, elixirs, drinks which will render the user invincible in battle, drinks which will make a man or woman immortal – all these are the province of fairies and witches, not travelling salesmen.'

'You think he lied?' asked Hupa.

'I have no doubt about it. If they were magic when he sold them to you, they would be magic now. Magic is not a thing which fades or wears off.'

'That's true,' said Hupa. 'If I ever see Hookey Walker again I'll pin his ears to a tree with my last two arrows.'

'You have *three* arrows,' Urgan pointed out.

'Perhaps the final arrow will be for his nose.'

The three companions then set out, walking through the foothills. As the evening came on they came to a great loch of shining water. Craig remembered his father's wish and took the sword from his waistband. He sighed. He would be loath to lose the weapon, to which he had now become strangely attached. Yet a promise was a promise.

'I must cast the broadsword into the waters,' he told Hupa.

Urgan said nothing, but watched as Craig drew back his arm and sent the blade skimming over the surface of the loch. It did not fall in with a splash as expected, however, but went spinning in a curved sweep, to come hurtling back towards Craig. It buried itself point-first at the young man's feet.

'What an extraordinary thing,' said Craig, plucking the sword from the turf. 'It was almost as if the sword was reluctant to enter the water. Was that some of your doing, Urgan? Some magic you learned in elf-land?'

'Not I,' said the elf. 'I am as puzzled as you are.'

Craig tried throwing it again, and once more it went spinning in a wide flat arc, horizontal to the shining waters, and returned to plant itself at Craig's feet once again, this time up to the hilt. Several more throws produced the same effect, until finally Craig said he was giving up.

'It's clear I'm not going to be successful with this – perhaps the waters themselves are magic?'

With the sword continually burying itself in the earth, the broadsword had taken on a silver sheen. The earth had the effect of polishing the weapon, so that the blade was now shiny. Urgan reached over and gently took the sword from Craig's hand, to inspect it more closely. He pointed to something on the blade: some words etched into the metal.

'What's this?' he said. 'Did you know this weapon had been specially forged for someone? The weapon itself has been named, as well as bearing the name of its owner. This is only done when a sword is of great worth. The craftsmanship which goes into such a sword will have come from a great weapon-maker. Look, there is an egret etched on the crown of the hilt. This is the mark of Walberwicke, one of the divine blacksmiths.'

Craig took back the weapon and stared at the writing on the blade.

The words said: *Onsang's Stele Sweord – SUNDERER*

Urgan read the words as Craig's finger traced their course along the bloodgroove of the blade.

'Steel?' mused Urgan. 'I have heard the fairies speak of this metal with disapproval. It is said to be tougher than iron – an unnatural metal fashioned mistakenly by the alchemists, as they searched for ways of turning base metals into gold. Fairies cannot work magic on things which are not natural. This is why they would hold it in disfavour.'

'Tough, is it?' said Craig.

He walked over to a rock and swung at it. The blade struck the granite with its sharp edge, sending out a high ringing note. It split the stone in two halves. On inspecting the honed edge of the weapon, Craig found it was still sharp. The granite had not chipped or scored the metal in any way. This was truly a strong weapon: stronger than any Craig had held. He felt the power in it, as it nestled comfortably in his grip, as if it were moulding itself to the contours of his hand.

'If that had been an iron sword,' said Urgan, 'it would have shattered.'

'Magic, is it?' Hupa asked.

Urgan shook his head. 'Not magic, for I have already told you, the blade is steel. Even fairies have difficulty with steel. I would say it does not need magic. It is, in itself, a perfectly balanced weapon with an unbreakable blade – what could magic do to improve on this?'

'Why didn't it fall in the loch?'

'Perhaps your father wishes you to use the sword for some purpose, before passing it to him? I would say that a spirit sent the weapon flying back to you. Keep it for a while. You may have need of it,' said Urgan.

Craig saw the truth in this and decided the ugly elf-man was right. Besides, there was no way the loch was going to accept the sword. He could not stand on its banks for ever, throwing a sword which whirled back to him every time.

'I shall keep it until I have used it,' Craig said, 'and then send it to my father.'

Douglass Barelegs visited the witch on the mountain at great risk to his safety. He was inside Albainn, from which he had been banished by Cormac, and if discovered he would be hanged. Cormac had declared Douglass an outlaw and there were plenty who would enjoy taking advantage of such a proclamation. Once the war was over Cormac would no longer be war chief and go back to being just another clan head. Then Douglass Barelegs could return and take his revenge on those who had wronged him.

She was huddled against the stone needle, staring down into the glen beyond with a sharp expression.

'Well, hag? What news have you of the son of my father's murtherer?'

'How do I know? He is lost,' she said, tracing idly in the dust with a child's thighbone. 'Lost in Engaland or lost in Albainn. Causing all kinds of havoc and mayhem. Never should he have been let loose in our countryside. Ye muckle-headed doety-brain. Tis yer ain fault this mither o' disaster is roamin' free, interferin' wi' the natural ways of the world.'

'Don't talk to me that way, woman,' growled Douglass, 'or I'll cut out your spleen and feed it to my dogs.'

She turned on him fiercely at these words.

'Dinnae mention food to me,' she snarled. 'D'ye no ken what that furriner has done? He has let out the beast! He has set the beast upon the likes o' me and my kind. Ask yer questions, Douglass son of Douglass, for the time has gaen when I could answer them.'

'What are you talking about, woman?'

'I'm talking of magic. He has set loose the beast who will destroy us.'

'How do you know this?'

She stared at him with malice in her expression.

'Because I'm *hungry*, damn you. D'ye not ken that witches are *never* hungry. What d'ye think it means then, if I feel ravenous?'

'I don't know,' said Douglass, helplessly.

'Why, ye brainless loon – it means I'm no longer a witch – I've lost the means to work my magic.'

Douglass was not sure whether the crone was telling the truth, or whether she simply wanted more for her information. They all used tricks, pretending it was too difficult to peer into the lives of others, telling you the auguries were not right, that the portents were not good, pointing to a dark sky or a strange flock of birds. All this was to nudge the price a little higher.

'You greedy bitch,' cried Douglass. 'Tell me exactly where the bastard murtherer is, or I'll lift your head.'

'Go to hell, ye blackhearted dog,' she spat back at him.

'Here, cut it off – what have I got to live for now?'

She stuck her neck out like a viper poking its head from a hole in the ground.

What could he do? Douglass had to be a man of his word or he would get no discipline. He whipped out his sword and decapitated the hag: one swift slice through gristle and bone. She had begun shrieking before the blade had struck. The head continued to scream as it rolled down the mountainside, bouncing like a loose rock from crag to crag, until it disappeared still wailing over the edge of a precipice.

The remains of the body shrivelled before his eyes, making him start back in horror. Before very long it looked like a dried black lizard draped over the scree. Douglass booted the husk and it broke into pieces, discharging a foul khaki-coloured powder into the atmosphere. The wind took the powder, blowing it into his eyes and up his nose.

'Filthy old termagant,' he coughed. 'Had to get in the last word, eh, whut? The end of magic, is it? Will the sun go out? Will the sea swallow the land? Will the mountains roll into the glens? I think not, ye crimped pig's crinkum. I bid you an unfond farewell and hope ye end up a turd travelling through the gut of the hound of the Otherworld.'

With that he made his way back along the blustery ridge, being thankful at least that this was the last time he need make this climb through the high cold winds.

PART NINE

Briar Wood

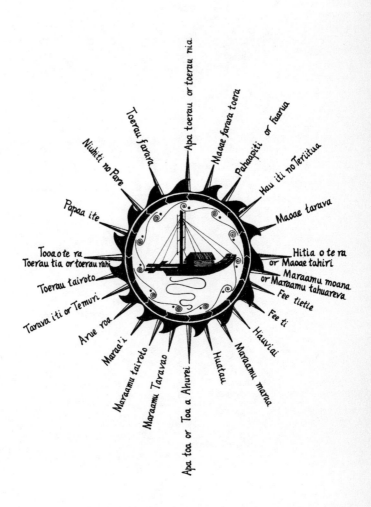

1

Once more Punga had left the battle of the giants to see to the welfare of his charge, Craig, son of Seumas. It was Punga who had pointed the elf-man in the direction of the real world, so that he could act as a guide to Craig and Hupa. Now Punga had to attend to himself again.

He looked about him at the utter devastation and destruction amongst the mighty supernaturals. Many were the fallen. Eagles picked at their entrails on the mountain-tops. Their hearts had fallen amongst wolves in high places, to be devoured like the offal of deer. Their livers were in the mouths of wildcats, hurrying home to feed their young.

Most of the more formidable gods had already gone.

Maomao was now nothing more than a wind without will: only the anguish of the Great Wind-God's dying cry was in its howl. A goddess called The Morrigan, Phantom Queen of Death, Sexuality and Conflict, was but a smudge on the face of the sky. Tawhiri-atea, Storm-God, wave-whipper, leveller of forests, had himself been levelled to the ground. Many, many more.

But Punga was just managing to survive obliteration. Because he was a minor god, he often went unnoticed by the Great Gods roaming the battlefield, looking for worthy opponents. He slipped here and there, managing to hold his own against gods of similar stature, and escaped the attention of the great.

Still, he was sorely wounded. The blood from his cuts and holes stained the clouds. It seeped into the evening heavens and dripped from the moon and stars. Blood was everywhere, draining from gods and goddesses on every side. There were red rivers flowing through the canyons of the sky. There were scarlet streams gushing between towers of cumulus. The bright hues of death and oblivion were ubiquitous . . .

'What a beautiful sunset,' said Hupa. 'How pretty the sky looks when it turns that colour.'

'Yes,' replied Urgan, 'but I am listening to Craig. The sunset can wait. There will be others.'

After Craig had described the region of the country where the Oceanians were at war with the Celts, Urgan explained that he knew where it was and how to get there.

'I thought you had never been out of fairyland,' said Hupa. 'How do you know the ways outside?'

'Fairyland is not a completely separate place – it is this country and yet it is *another* country. They exist as one, yet you cannot be in both at the same time. How can I explain it? You are people of the sea, are you not?' said the ugly elf. 'Consider this, you have a beautiful scallop shell, hinged at its foot, two perfect halves which fit exactly together. An insect cannot be on one half and on the other at the same time, yet it can be said to be crawling over *one* whole shell.

'This is somewhat like the land of the fairies and the land of the mortals – they exist together, as one, but yet inhabit two different portions of space. I have been to the region you describe, but to the exact same fairyland one, not to the one inhabited by mortals.'

The two Oceanians digested this piece of information with no real difficulty, since they came from a place where spirits and ancestors lived alongside the living, there being only one land, one sea, one earth for all.

Hupa said, 'I believe things are the way you say they are, but tell me how is it that we have been running into people of magic all the while?'

'Because this Craig is special, being kinsman to many in this land, yet coming from another . . .'

Craig listened intently as Urgan explained his origins to Hupa, who stood amazed at what she heard.

'. . . and his father Seumas-from-the-Blackwater did not spring from earth without relatives – he too had a father, a mother, brothers, sisters, cousins, ancestors. One of those forebears was a fairy, way back in the mists of time, when mortals and supernatural folk commonly met and loved one another in the morning mists of a spring day, amongst the primroses and forget-me-nots, protected oft-times by the dog-rose briar.

'Also his mission here is empowered with Goodness, which gives him special privilege. You pair have been drifting in and out of fairyland the whole time you have been on your travels.'

'Did my father really have brothers and sisters?'

'His clan is a small one,' explained the elf, 'but yet there are those who carry his blood. No true brother or sister exists, for Seumas was the only one to survive the cliffs until he was past his manhood. All his siblings fell to their deaths before they reached their fifteenth year. The Picts from the Blackwater are in the main poor estuary and coastal dwellers, who live by that which the shoreline has to offer. They exist on a diet of crabs, seabirds' eggs, shellfish and the like.'

'It's true, my father gathered the oil from the stomachs of fulmar birds. He climbed cliffs to snatch the fulmars from their nest and strangled them before the birds could disgorge their precious load.'

'A hard way to earn a living,' said Urgan, 'but if one has

nimble feet and does not fall easily, then the rewards are better than if one spends one's time collecting cockles and mussels from the estuary mud.'

Craig said, 'How do you know all this?'

'An elf from elf-land knows more than he needs to know, if he or she holds an interest in human affairs.'

Craig nodded. 'And what of my father's name? How did he come to be called "Seumas". It's not a name I have heard amongst the other Celts. What does it mean?'

'Your father was named after a monk-errant, a holy-man who came over the seas, from a distant kingdom out of which has sprung a belief new to this part of the world. This "monk" also touched your adopted mother, Dorcha, on the brow with his hallowed fingertips when she was but an infant.

'Seumas-the-monk drifted to this land by coracle and tried to preach against the local gods in favour of a One-God, tried to change the ways of the people, and was burned to death inside a straw dog for his trouble. This monk-errant was before his time – many people were not ready for change. The druids especially, for it was they who ordered his live cremation.'

Hupa shivered. 'A dog made of straw? Like a wicker shark, I suppose – but we do not burn people in wicker sharks – they are merely signs of tapu. But have the people been changed at all by what the errant-monk Seumas told them? I know Dorcha believed that such change was coming. And Seumas-the-Black's mother must have thought so too, or she would not have called her child after the monk.'

'Why yes, many have, and this One-God religion is spreading throughout the land, though very slowly. Even now there are monks on the outer Farne Islands, who plan to come here despite the dangers. The time of the many-gods is ending. The time of magic is passing. The One-God and a practice called "science" to which several wizards and sorcerers are now turning, will eventually replace these two beliefs.'

Craig said, 'We understand about the One-God, for we have a Supreme Being, the Old One called Io, who is so superior to the other gods that he lives alone above the Twelfth Level, neither seen, nor touched, nor heard, even by other gods. He communicates by means of his Mareikura – spirits of light who are his messengers and servants.'

'That sounds like him. That sounds like the One-God.'

'Has Io grown so powerful then, that he has no need of the other gods at all?' asked Hupa.

'If he is the One-God.'

Craig nodded, thoughtfully, then asked, 'This thing called "science" – do you believe it is good?'

'Inherently evil,' replied Urgan without hesitation. 'I would not trust it a thumbnail's length.'

While this discussion had been interesting and threw a great deal of light on the confused and confusing world, Craig felt it was time to move on.

'You said you knew a short-cut to the battlefields?'

'Yes, but it is through Briar Wood.'

Hupa commented, 'You make it sound a dangerous place.'

'Not so much dangerous in that it threatens life, although many have lost theirs in it through stupidity, but it can delay travellers for years. On the other hand, if you pass through unhampered, it might save you days on your journey.'

'The chance of years against days does not sound much like a bargain to me,' Craig said. 'And why have people lost their lives if it is not dangerous?'

'They panicked and lost themselves.'

'But we have you to guide us,' said Hupa, 'so we shall not lose ourselves.'

Urgan nodded, smiling. 'This maiden with the bow, a

huntress of the dawn if ever I saw one, has brains as well as skill with a weapon. Can she shoot true?'

'She could hit a sparrow on the wing,' replied Craig with a grin, 'if she wanted to, which she doesn't, because she kills only to preserve life.'

'A maiden after my own heart,' said Urgan, 'and is she spoken for?'

'In marriage? No. There isn't a warrior who would dare ask her. None can match her skill and our warriors are notoriously concerned about their manhood. They would hate being put to shame by their own wife. Also, she has a reputation for being bad-tempered.'

'I have not,' replied Hupa, hotly.

'Would it bother you?' asked Urgan. 'To have a wife who could beat you at a man's game?'

'Not at all, but I'm already married, otherwise . . .' Craig paused, then finished what he was going to say ' . . . otherwise I would ask her to be my wife this very moment.'

Hupa gave a little gasp and stared at him, misty-eyed. Craig had known that his words were unwise, but he wanted to say it once – just once – to have the truth out in the open. However, he had no intention of carrying any of it further. He had his wife, whom he loved, and his children whom he adored. To put those at risk was madness. He could not hurt those he loved in order to indulge an immediate passion.

'Well, if you don't want her,' cried the hideous dwarf, 'then I don't mind having her.'

'I am not a bundle of sticks!' cried Hupa. 'I wouldn't have either of you if you came to me as gods with flowers growing out of your orifices. I hate men.'

'Then you love women?' said Urgan, his ugly face dropping in disappointment.

'Not in the sense you mean, though I prefer their company to that of crass males,' replied the spirited maiden. 'I just think men are boors. They love themselves too much.

They have this air of superiority which is not matched by their wits or their talents. Men live a myth. Give me women every time.'

'Except when they chatter like roosting starlings,' said the elf.

'Even then,' muttered Hupa. 'Even then. Better than the grunting of men. Better than that.'

'I *like* this maiden,' said Urgan. 'I will marry her if the chance ever comes. She has such a way with her. I love her to distraction already. I could bide awhile with her.'

'Could you now?' said the young woman. 'Well, I doubt a creature as ugly as a toad gets many chances . . .'

Craig made a noise of disapproval, but Urgan laughed. 'No, no, Craig – that's her spirit – that's what I love about her – she puts such *feeling* into her words. Cruel words, but true. I *am* as ugly as a toad. Uglier, even. Now, let us get down to making decisions – do you wish to go through Briar Wood, despite all that I have told you about it?'

Craig said, 'I must get back to the pa as quickly as possible – we must take the chance.'

'Then let us to it.'

They followed a winding dusty path through granite foothills, between forests, over burns, around chalk pits, until finally they were faced by a massive tangle of rose briars as tall as a forest of oaks and elms. On entering they found the brambles were as thick as a man's leg and went sweeping from the ground in huge barbed vaults whose apexes were high above their heads. The monstrous stems, some green and succulent, some brown and brittle, were covered with thorns the size of women's thumbs. A person might stumble and be stabbed to death before he or she was able to rise.

The floor of Briar Wood was covered in petals from the huge dog roses which grew on the vines. Their colours ranged from white to purple-black. Those that had lain on the ground for a long time, forming a soft mattress beneath the travellers' feet, were brown with age. They were so thick that sometimes the three sank down to their knees in dying blossoms. Any daylight which managed to penetrate the tangle of dense briars, drifting down through great shooting arches of wicked thorns from above, turned to a russet hue before falling on the still floor.

'This is a magic place,' whispered Hupa, as she picked her way beneath the arcing vines with their talons ready to pierce her unblemished skin. 'Is this a magic place, Urgan?'

'Of course,' replied the elf. 'Briar Wood holds many secrets and any place with secrets is magic.'

Carefully and cautiously, they threaded their way through the sepia forest, tinged with green on its canopy above, until they came to a place where the briars were even more numerous and impossible to get through without cutting them.

Craig took out *Sunderer* and began to slice a path through the twists of barbed vines. On the way they passed a place where pale-skinned figures in iron apparel – *armour* Urgan called it – had been trapped by the monstrous snaking, hooked brambles, caught there like birds, perhaps to flutter and die. The tangle of burnt sienna vines formed a cage so secure that it would have taken the three companions over a day to release the men.

There were five together, their metal exoskeletons rusting to a reddish-brown which melted into the ochre hues of the forest around them. One or two still had on their helmets, their faces half hidden from view. Yet one, a youth of great beauty, still had his sword in hand and was standing upright, the sturdy rose briars holding him fast in his position. They wound around his limbs and torso like giant serpents, locking him.

The youth's blue eyes stared out in blindness at Hupa. Though his skin was wan, his lips were cherry red in the raw umber light. Slim fingers fashioned for more delicate work than wielding a weapon, were wrapped around the hilt of his sword, as if he had but grasped it just a moment ago. It almost seemed as if he breathed shallow breaths beneath his metal breast.

'Are they really dead?' asked Hupa in a quiet voice. 'Or just asleep?'

'Perhaps between the two,' replied Urgan. 'This is a magic woodland after all. Best not to try to wake them though, for then they would surely die. If they are at rest, then there is a purpose for them being so. See, their garments are torn, but there is not one spot of blood, though the thorns prick their pale flesh with sharp points. Look how their shields are trapped high above the brambles, as if they were taken from their hands and carried upwards by the growth of decades.'

'Their swords look better than the one I have,' said Craig.

Urgan replied, 'Do not even consider exchanging yours for one of theirs. Would you rob these poor trapped creatures of their weapons? If they are not dead and eventually wake, then think how they would feel. And do not imagine you found your own blade by chance young man – *Sunderer* found its way into your hand – not the other way around. Onsang was a warrior saved from the sea by your great-grandfather. He sent his weapon from Ifurin to help you through troubled times ahead.'

'What troubled times?' asked Craig, staring at the sword in his hand. 'When will I have need of such a weapon?'

'Sooner than you think,' grunted the elf, but would go no further with his explanation. Urgan hesitated before adding, 'Also it is the sword your father killed Douglass for – it is, in a sense, responsible for your existence and your presence here now. Without the sword Dorcha would never have fallen from the cliff, your father would not therefore have attempted to save her, thus landing both of them in Kupe's hands. The Oceanians would not have learned of the whereabouts of Albainn and Engaland, and you would never have been born.'

'How do you know all this?' asked Craig, looking wonderingly at the instrument responsible for a whole history. 'Do you know all things?'

'Not *all* things,' replied Urgan, 'but the more I am near you the more secrets I am told by the wind.'

They left the men in armour to their fate.

Urgan knew that if the three companions were to survive Briar Wood, nothing must be touched, everything must be left the way it was. It was unfortunate that they had to cut their way through the brambles, slicing through the succulent vines, but this was necessary. To attempt to wake the waxen men who lingered under the flying briars, caught in the tresses of climbing roses, soft petals for their sheets – or, if they were lifeless, for their shrouds – would surely bring misfortune on the small group struggling to reach the other side.

Later they came to a place where above their heads were hundreds of dead birds, pierced through the heart by thorns. They were magpies, cuckoos, and all those birds which perpetrated evil acts on their own kind – nest-robbers, chick-killers and the like. The living briars dispensed rough justice to such creatures for its own dark reasons. It was judge and executioner in one and afterwards became the gibbet, displaying the robber-killer birds to others, perhaps as some kind of warning, or perhaps simply to promote its own power.

Further on still, deeper in Briar Wood, they passed under a hundred or so human corpses, skeletons with the flesh still dripping from the bones. Weapons too, caught in the briars, had been borne up. Some kind of battle had taken place before the brambles had grown in this area and the bodies and their trappings had been carried aloft as on the crest of sea waves, and were now like flotsam and jetsam on the heaving swell of brambles above.

As they struggled through Briar Wood there were many animals and birds, running, flying through the brambles as if it were not dangerous in the least. These creatures seemed to have an unerring sense of judgement which made Craig feel like an awkward lumbering creature trespassing on the earth, in a place quite unfitted for his size and cumbersome nature.

'We're lost,' said Urgan, looking upwards. 'I knew this would happen. I can't see the sun any longer.'

It was true, the canopy above had folded over to obscure the light. It was almost dark inside the brambles now. A chill went through Craig. If they got lost in this place they were dead. There was nothing to eat, nothing to drink. They would soon wilt and fall on that springy mat of petals, perhaps to sink down to the roots and become food for the briars.

'How can you be lost? You were brought up by the fairies, weren't you? Aren't you supposed to be a part of all this, a part of the natural world? How can you become lost in something of which you are a part?'

It was a hot-tempered and frustrated Hupa that spoke these words.

'My kind of elf, which is closer to a gnome or a goblin than a pixie, doesn't have all those attributes you mortals consider fairies ought to have. I couldn't find my way out of a badger sett, if I didn't know the way. I was all right when I could see the direction of the sun through the briars – I knew which way to go then. I'm lost now.'

Hupa said, 'What about you, Craig?'

'How would I know where we are?'

'Then it's up to me,' growled Hupa, sniffing the air. 'Fortunately I still have enough of the dog in me to follow an animal trail . . .'

'You were a dog?' said Urgan.

'A bitch. Craig and I met some kind of sorcerer in a hut who changed us into dogs – we think. I still retain some of the canine instincts.' She sniffed again. 'See that track,' she said, pointing. 'That's an animal path. Follow it. I'm sure it'll lead us to the edge of Briar Wood. After all, what beast could live in here? This wood is a dead place.'

During their journey Craig also noticed that something was happening to Urgan. By degrees he seemed to be growing taller, losing his squatness. At the same time the lumps and wrinkles on the elf's face were smoothing themselves out. The change was almost imperceptible and at times Craig wondered whether it was merely a trick of the light, rather than an actual occurrence, so he said nothing to either Urgan or Hupa. Now, as Urgan was caught in a shaft of light, he saw that he had indeed been transformed into a handsome young man.

Craig was unable to comment on this, however, for a new emergency arose.

Suddenly he was trapped in something which required his whole attention. The briars were no longer static, but had begun to quicken in their growth, springing from the earth around the companions, as if trying to separate them, trying to trap them like the armoured thanes they had seen earlier. Thorns sprang out like claws from a cat's paw. The three companions had to continually jerk their heads from side to side, to avoid a spike in the eye or throat.

'What's happening?' cried Craig, hacking like mad at the snaking vines which twisted and curled in their flight from the earth to the sky. 'It's growing too fast!'

'Cut! Cut!' yelled Urgan.

Craig did as he was bid, his sword arm working like mad, chopping, slicing, slashing at the undergrowth and overgrowth which vomited from the earth. Very soon his arm became tired and he had to change hands. Finally, exhausted with having to keep up with the growth, he threw the sword to Hupa and told her to carry on the fight.

Two-handed, the slim young maiden did her best to keep the foliage at bay, but soon her arms began to tire too. She passed the weapon to Urgan. Urgan set to with a fury, hewing a path for them all through the briars, until eventually there was light on the other side of the russet woodland. Verdant hills could be seen and a blue sky. Urgan continued to hack away, until at last the three companions emerged from the thorny cage.

'Out,' breathed Hupa. 'We're safe.'

Urgan lay on his back on the grass, exhausted. Craig fell down beside him. All three felt as if they had narrowly escaped a living death.

'You said it wasn't dangerous,' Craig grumbled. 'I think we were lucky to get out.'

'I lied,' said Urgan. 'You don't expect elves to tell the truth, do you?' He laughed. 'It was highly dangerous. It was the most dangerous thing I've ever done. I feel lightheaded. We got away with it. And we saved three days of walking.'

'You mean we could have ended up like those poor men in iron cloaks?' Hupa said.

'Highly probable,' Urgan replied. 'We could be stuck in there – at least until the soft-nosed beast Craig released from the tower came by.'

'Why? What would that do?' asked Craig.

'You'll find out.'

Suddenly, Hupa let out a cry. 'You've changed,' she said, almost accusingly. 'You're different.'

Craig rolled over and looked at Urgan. There he was, now a youthful man, tall and quite handsome – for a pallid-skinned native of the Land-of-Mists. His shoulders were broad, his chest deep. Urgan's complexion was turning a healthy, ruddy colour. His clothes, which had burst at the seams, hung from him in tatters, revealing everything he owned in the way of manhood.

Hupa turned away, blushing furiously.

'Why have you changed?' she asked. 'What happened to you?'

'I told you. I was taken from my cradle as a baby . . .'

'You said you were torn from your mother's breast as an infant,' she corrected.

'Poetic licence. The fairies took me, leaving a changeling, which died shortly afterwards – a sickly elf that would not have lived anyway. My mother saw only me in the cot, the fairies having left an aura on the elf.'

'How did you manage to change back again, after being an elf for so long?' asked Hupa. 'Is it because you are now out of elf-land and amongst mortals?'

Urgan winked at Craig, before replying, 'It was love that did it. If you hadn't fallen in love with me, Hupa, I should still be a hideous dwarf, not the handsome young man who stands behind you now . . .'

She turned, crying, 'I don't love . . .' then spun round again. 'Will you cover yourself?' she demanded.

'With what?' he asked, reasonably.

She took off her tapa bark skirt, her shift being long enough to fall down past her hips and thighs.

'Put this on,' she said, holding it behind her. 'And don't stare at my legs.'

Urgan wrapped the skirt around his waist.

'I'm not used to wearing women's clothing,' he said, 'but I think this suits me, don't you?'

She turned now and stared at him, a grimace on her face.

'You look like Boy-girl on a bad-taste day.'

The three companions continued their journey through a wilderness consisting of marshy bogs and dreary flatlands. The sky was black with dark clouds, through which only a little light filtered, making the scenery around them even more sombre. To make matters worse there were gallows on every rise from which hanged men and women dangled in various stages of decomposition. Grim faces stared down at the travellers as they passed beneath: cracked skulls with eye-sockets picked clean by crows.

'We are coming to the country which harbours your enemy, Douglass Barelegs,' Urgan told Craig. 'You must soon confront the son of the man your father killed.'

'The lord of this region must be a cruel ruler,' replied Craig, 'to want to display death in this manner.'

'He is indeed a man whose spirit is in need of some cleansing,' said Urgan, generously. 'His name is Skaan and he gives sanctuary to murderers and cut-throats, fleeing from justice. Those people who hang there on those gallows are men and women who made the mistake of refusing to bend to the will of Skaan, or who tried to organize a rebellion against him.'

After the fields of the hanged people they followed a dark river to a windswept moor upon which stood great slabs of stone, like doorways from around which the dwellings had collapsed and rotted into the earth. These structures were decorated with twigs, feathers, red-clay shapes and figures and, grotesquely, human heads along the lintel and human hands at the ends. There were feet at the base of the uprights. There were also symbols and motifs painted on the stone uprights in blue woad.

The fleshly appendages were in most cases rotting, though some were fresh. Again the birds were at work, gorging on the soft parts, pecking between fingers and toes.

'Scarefolks,' said Urgan.

'What?'

'Those caricatures, they're meant to frighten people away. Like scarecrows frighten birds. These are scarefolks. We're getting near Skaan's castle now. It's called Eagal Keep.'

Craig knew that 'eagal' meant 'fear' in Gaelic.

'Well, they certainly frighten me,' said Hupa, shuddering. 'What are they meant to be?'

Urgan shrugged. 'Stone men with human heads? Some people say they walk the moors at night and eat those who are lost abroad. You can believe it if you wish. Soon there will be no more of such things, when Craig's beast gets to work.'

'You keep calling it *my* beast,' said Craig with some irritation. 'It does not belong to me.'

'You set it free – therefore it is your beast.'

It was coming on evening as they approached Eagal Keep. Craig had never seen anything like this fortified dwelling. It consisted of unhewn blocks of granite built in the fashion of drystone walls. Each stone fitted in with those around it and formed an uneven structure held together by its own weight. There was little symmetry about the design: it was as if the building had formed during a terrible gale in which blocks were blown together in no ordered fashion. It sprawled over the undulating ground like some overweight crustacean, not more than twice the height of an ordinary man.

Yet it looked formidable, with uneven slits through which arrows could be fired. It had ramparts and standing stones behind which the keep's occupants could hide while throwing spears. Whole trees sprouted from one or two places, obviously used to support the weak areas. Rooks still roosted at the top of these trees and were even now quarrelling noisily, as those birds always seemed to do. Some of them were pecking at animal hides, which had been draped over the walls to dry in the sun. Smoke rose from several fires in various places inside the structure. There were no sentries visible.

Neither was there a strong door. A deerskin had been draped over a hole in the side of the keep. This pelt hanging from a beam served as an entrance. It was so small, however, that only a single man could pass through while crouched low, so that the defenders could immediately chop any intruders down one by one and stomp them into the dust.

Urgan gestured towards the castle.

'There you are, my friend – inside you will find Skaan

and his guest, Douglass, feasting or fornicating – their two main pleasures in life apart from chopping pieces from live human beings for use as decoration.'

'Why don't they ever kill each other, these evil men?' asked Hupa.

'Everyone needs allies,' replied Urgan, 'but you can be sure if there was any profit in it, these two would not hesitate for a moment before destroying one another.'

'Look,' said Craig, 'the curtain's moving – someone's coming out to meet us.'

2

It was a tall thin man who came out of the keep and confronted the three companions. The sun had now gone down behind the horizon and night's shadow was moving across the land. The man stood before them as someone with obvious authority might stand before peasants, looking them up and down with distaste in his expression. Finally he spoke to them.

'You will get no food or shelter here. This is Eagal Keep, the castle of Lord Skaan. If you don't want to be hanging from a gibbet by the morning you'd best show us your backs.'

'Who are you?' asked Craig. 'Are you a priest?'

The man leaned forward, peering at this stranger with keen eyes that tried to penetrate the darkness. Suddenly, seeing something he did not like, he jumped backwards. He went from arrogance to pitiful terror in a moment. His features were twisted in fear and his arms and legs shook violently.

'You have the mark of the devil on your face!' he cried. 'Help, ho! Here are demons!'

Despite the man's shouts no one came to his assistance. Whether men came to the rugged arrowloops in the walls to see what was the matter, Craig did not know. They were merely slits of darkness to his eyes. He only knew he had to get his message across and leave this place. 'I am no demon. I am Craig, son of Seumas-the-Black. Half-Pict, half-Hivan. Tell Douglass Barelegs that I will meet him out on the moor at daybreak. I wish to speak to him alone. If he is accompanied, he will find me gone.'

'Help, help! My master's enemy! Come quickly.'

Urgan stepped forward and slapped the man around the face, to bring him to his senses.

'Did you get the message – on the moor at dawn.'

With that the elf-man who had come out of fairyland gripped Craig by the arm and urged him to get away. Hupa followed quickly behind, seeing flaming torches appear on the battlements of the crude castle behind them, flickering as figures passed behind narrow windows. There were shouts then, the sound of a drum beating, followed by that of a gong. Shouts of 'Where foe? Where foe?' pierced the night's shielding cloak.

Once safe in the darkness of the moor, the three rested under one of the stone scarefolks. Hupa was too exhausted to be frightened by the massive figures around them. A lapwing's feather once dipped in blood, now dangling from a cord, actually caressed her brow as she drifted off into sleep.

Craig was too agitated to sleep soundly and kept waking, the sound of foxes barking coldly on the moor making him start up from time to time, thinking his father was calling him again from the depths of freezing Ifurin. Urgan kept the watch.

At daybreak the blare of horns and the baying of hounds could be heard from the south. All across the moor from the direction of the castle clumps of birds flew up as if startled by an approach. Someone was racing along the edge of the dawn. Urgan went to a rise and watched from there.

Black shapes of tors emerged from the darkness to float on the morning mists of the undulating moor, some flattish and long like boats, others tall and peaked with thrusting towers. Birds shot from the heather like stones from a sling, to alight on gorse and begin their songs. Wild horses galloped away to the east, manes and tails flying. Peat hags hunched against the oncoming day, as if affronted by its approach.

Finally Urgan called to Craig, 'He comes.'

'Is he alone?'

'Quite alone. The dogs you hear must be still in the keep. Douglass wants you very badly.'

Urgan retired, taking the sleepy but concerned Hupa with him, moving off to a distance.

'This is between them,' he told Hupa. 'It began before you were born.'

'And it will end before I die,' she murmured, 'but if he harms my countryman he will suffer.'

Craig heard these words but he was in no position to debate with his female companion. He waited, sword in hand, watching carefully as a big warrior approached at a quick walk. There was wrath in the man's bearing, and a certain pleasure at having his prayers fulfilled. There was revenge printed in his stride as surely as if it were written in blood on his forehead. On his head was a wooden helmet, a mask of oakwood, which he pulled down over his face as he drew nigh. In his fists was a double-handed, double-edged sword of great weight.

He stopped in front of Craig and regarded him for a moment.

'At *last*!' he said. 'Now ye will feel the cleansing touch of my sword. I will cut out your heart, ye damned whelp, and in so doing expunge this dishonour from my own. Your fether killed mine – now the sons stand one against the other. I will avenge the wrong or die in the attempt.'

'Let me see your face,' ordered Craig.

Douglass took a step back. 'What?'

'I cannot fight a man who hides his face from me. Are

you a coward that you dare not let me see whether there is truth or whether there are lies in your features? What is it that you have to keep secret from my eyes?'

Douglass whipped off the helmet, his eyes blazing.

'There – damn ye, damn all your kinsmen, damn the earth ye stand on, damn your mother and most especially, damn your fether – may the whole pack of ye be driven from the face of the earth and herded up some loathsome god's arsehole, to rot there amongst the shite for all eternity . . .'

'We must speak,' said Craig, now that he had the man face to face. 'My father . . .'

'Damn his polluted soul!'

'My father told me to make my peace with you. He bitterly regrets the killing of your father and is willing to acknowledge the injury he has caused you as that man's son. I cannot fight you, even if I wanted to – I made a deathbed promise to Seumas-the-Black that I would make my peace with you. Nothing on this earth would make me kill you, so I am asking . . .'

Craig got no further. The blade of the great battle sword flashed in the early morning sun. It whistled through the air and would have taken off his head if he had not been agile enough to dance out of its way. Douglass seemed to be expecting to miss with the first blow, for he instantly twisted the blade and brought it up from under, skimming Craig's right shoulder. Craig felt a sting as the honed edge of the great sword took a small slice from his upper arm.

'I don't want to do this,' Craig yelled at his adversary. 'I have no wish to kill you – I can't go back on my promise to my father.'

'More fool you,' snapped Douglass, preparing for another blow. 'Whatever barbarian gods ye pray to, do it now.'

The sun was above the horizon now: a great blinding disc of light. Craig parried the next two blows with

Sunderer. He worked his way round so that he had the sun behind him. Douglass was then staring directly into the glare. The Scot had to squint to see his opponent. Craig kept himself in this position, dancing agilely out of reach of the unwieldy weapon that Douglass swung at him with wild, terrible blows.

If it had not been for *Sunderer*, Craig would have been struck down within the first few moments. The steel broadsword had five times the strength of the iron sword of Douglass. It swallowed blows from the heavier weapon, taking bites out of the great iron blade. Soon the once-honed bright edge of Douglass's weapon was blunted and chipped in many places. The big Scot could not understand why his sword was so ineffective. He renewed his attacks with vigour and strength, his great swinging strokes hissing past Craig's head, while the Oceanian skipped and leapt, his own strokes a flurry of quick slices, the flashes from the blade serving to further confuse his foe.

It was heavy work for the Scot. His weapon was weighty. Finally Douglass stopped for breath, leaning on his sword for support. Craig stepped forward quickly. He chopped at Douglass's iron sword with his own much tougher steel blade. There was a *crack* and the double-bladed weapon snapped off about a third of a length from its point. Douglass fell on the turf looking stunned. Then his arms went up around his head, to ward off any blow at his skull.

Craig reached down and offered the Scot his hand.

'Come on, man – we can talk about this. It wasn't me who killed your father after all. Surely the sons need not make the same mistake as their elders?'

Douglass spat on the hand and jumped to his feet. He snatched up his broken blade and thrust with it. The jagged end pierced Craig's side, leaving a gaping uneven wound. Craig heard a cry from Hupa as he sank to his knees clutching his side. He could feel the warm blood oozing through his fingers. Standing above him, Douglass was wielding his broken but still effective weapon two-handed. A blow was directed at Craig's skull, intended to split it.

Craig rolled sideways. Douglass's sword struck a flint in the turf, giving out a ringing note, sending up sparks. The Scot shouted in frustration, swinging sideways. The side-swipe missed Craig's head by the thickness of a fingernail. Craig had had enough. He was never going to convince Douglass to lay down his arms and talk peace. Craig swung up and down, one stroke, and chopped the left foot of Douglass in half.

Douglass crashed to the ground. He gave out a grunt of disbelief. He sat up quickly and looked down at his foot, staring at the appendage, sliced as cleanly as bacon. The other sandalled half with its toes lay a yard away.

'Ye bastard!' cried the Scot. 'Can ye no fight fair?'

Craig staggered to his feet, clutching his wounded side, to stand over his adversary.

'I told you I didn't want to fight at all.'

'Go shag a wasps' nest, ye tattooed bastard.'

Craig raised *Sunderer* over the man's head. Douglass sneered up into his face. Craig brought the blade down with a swish. At the last moment he turned it from the Scotsman's neck. Instead the sharp steel snicked through the wrist of Douglass Barelegs, severing his right hand. Douglass stared in horror at the stump, just inches from his eyes.

'Ye bluddy bastard,' he yelled. 'Ma hand!'

He picked up his own hand by the fingers and stared at it, knowing it could not be reunited with his wrist. Then he flung it from himself like a piece of useless meat. He stared up into the face of his enemy.

'Kill me!' he roared.

'No,' said Craig, as the other two came to stand by the pair. 'I promised my father I would not.'

Urgan said, 'You're finished as a warrior, Douglass. You brought this on yourself. Take up sheep-rearing, some gentle occupation. You'll never fight again . . .'

Douglass stared with visible hatred into the faces around him, then keeled over as the weakness caused by loss of blood overcame him.

Urgan first tended to Craig's wounds, finding some yarrow and binding it into his cut side with strips of cloth. 'What is the herb?' asked Hupa.

'We call it "staunch grass" or sometimes "thousand leaf",' replied Urgan. 'It will help the blood to clot.'

Hupa insisted on tidying up the binding herself, though there was really nothing wrong with it. She helped Craig to his feet, telling him to lean on her. Giddy from blood-loss he was willing to use her as a crutch.

In the meantime Urgan bound up Douglass's wounds, as he lay unconscious on the grass. Even if he lived – for men often died of such wounds if they went black and rotten – the big Scot's fighting days were indeed over. With only half a foot and no right hand he would not even be a match for a six-year-old with a sharpened stick.

The sound of a horn came from not far away. Warriors in wolfskins pinned with bird-bones at the collar came running across the moor with hounds at their heels. They reached the place where the three were standing. One fellow with a great black beard and wild staring eyes stepped forward. He glanced at Douglass lying motionless in the grass.

'I am Skaan. Is this man dead?'

'Crippled,' replied Urgan.

Skaan looked hard at him. 'I know who these two are, but who are you?'

'I am Urgan of Umberland, taken from my mother's breast at birth and raised by the fairies.'

At these words the group of warriors backed away from Urgan quickly, pulling on the leashes of their hounds.

Skaan stared, looking Urgan up and down. He too looked nervous and uncomfortable.

'Did you do this?' he said, eventually, pointing to Douglass's wounds.

'No,' replied Urgan, 'this was between the stranger and Douglass – I had no part in it. I am merely their guide. But,' he smiled, 'you know the ways of the fairies. I have things at my fingertips which would make you borderers sweat in your bed at night just to think of them.'

'Such as?'

'Would you like to see your dead mother, wizened and dwarfish, popping up and down from the reeds as you hurry across the moors at night?'

'That I would not.'

'Or your headless father – whom you decapitated yourself – roll his talking skull into the room where you sleep?'

'Nor that either.'

'Then you will know we must part as friends.'

Skaan stared at Urgan for a very long time, his black beard glistening with dried spittle, then he nodded.

'Be on your way before I turn you into tripe, the three of you. And be warned, brown-skins,' he told Hupa and Craig, 'there's an army of Angles coming down from the north. They have heard of your landing. They'll destroy every last one of you. You had better get in your little boats and go home.'

'You know this for certain?' asked Craig.

Skaan grinned a mouthful of blackened teeth. 'I know this because I shall be joining with them.'

Craig nodded. They left the warriors to carry Douglass back to Eagal Keep. Urgan went on the other side of Craig and helped to take his weight. Together the three of them left the border country and went down into Albainn.

On coming to a loch which they had to cross, Urgan fashioned a coracle from reeds caulked with clay. It was not the most lake-worthy of craft, but it would do for a single journey over the shining water.

'Are you sure this will carry us?' asked Craig, dubiously, staring at the flimsy-looking vessel. 'It doesn't seem as if it'll take much to sink it.'

'It'll be fine so long as we keep it balanced. Don't stand up suddenly. In fact, don't stand up at all. Just sit upright, back to the wall, with your legs pointing to the middle of the coracle. Let me do the work.'

The three companions settled into the boat, which was a cramped craft to the two Oceanians: even fishing canoes used in local island waters had more room than this tiny coracle. Urgan paddled them out onto the glistening waters of the loch, purple in the evening light as it reflected heather on the surrounding mountains. It was a calm and tranquil end to the day, with nothing but the plash of the oar to break the silence. Not even the sound of birds, out on the still waters.

Only the midges caused any annoyance and these were not as bad as they had been earlier in the season. Overhead a fish eagle wheeled about above the surface, but it abruptly glided away quickly on the edge of a breeze as if it had seen something it did not like in the deeps.

When they were halfway across a monstrous scaly head, dripping mud and weed, suddenly broke the surface not far from the coracle. Parts of a body also appeared behind the head: a body ridged with spikes and spines. Water streamed from the creature's back, as the head rose ever higher out of the loch. Hupa gave a shout of alarm as the monster's mouth opened to reveal rows of savage-looking teeth. Two fleshy horns protruded from the monster's head, giving it the look of a sea dragon.

'A taniwha!' cried Craig.

Instantly and instinctively Hupa fitted an arrow to her bow. Before Urgan could stop her she stood up and fired at the beast. The arrow struck the creature behind the ear. Its huge mouth opened to cavernous proportions and the wounded beast let out a bellow of pain and anger which echoed around the mountains and glens with a deafening sound. Its eyes turned hot and red as it regarded the puny little being which had wounded it.

Hupa stared in alarm at the beast as she fought to keep her balance in the unstable coracle.

A quick flick of some previously hidden fin or tail removed the offending dart from behind the monster's ear. Then the great green creature dived below the waters causing a shock wave to wash towards the coracle. Hupa overbalanced even before the wave hit the craft, toppling into the water. The two men clung to the coracle, trying to keep it steady. If it overturned they would have a long hard swim to the far shore.

'Wait until the waves have settled before we pull her back in,' said Urgan.

'Don't tell me how to manage a boat,' grumbled Craig. 'Our people are raised with them.'

Finally the waters calmed, while Hupa trod water, anxiously peering around her for signs of the taniwha.

'What was that?' she asked, as they dragged her back into the coracle. 'Did I kill it?'

'You gave it a mosquito sting,' snorted Urgan. 'What a foolish thing to do. Did you believe you could destroy the loch monster with a little arrow?'

'We have rid the world of monsters in our time,' replied Hupa, haughtily.

'Monsters as large as that?'

'Well, no,' she admitted, 'but I'm sure I gave it more than a sting.'

'We'd better get out of here,' Urgan said, paddling in earnest. 'If the monster decides to come back, we'll end up as fish meal.'

They took turns to paddle now, as Urgan grew weary, and gradually made their way to the far darkening shore. Luckily the monster did not return to take its revenge on Hupa. She was inclined to think she had taught it a lesson, but Urgan shook his head and said the monster had been in the loch since the beginning of time and would be there at the end of time, and no maiden from far isles was going to change that.

Before they reached the bank, Craig threw his father's sword into the deep loch. This time the water took the blade, swallowing it. Craig watched its silver shape as it slipped down to the seemingly fathomless bottom like a diving fish.

'Now my father will be able to defend himself against the monsters of Ifurin,' he said. 'If he has not been devoured already.'

'Seumas will still be whole,' Hupa persuaded him. 'He was a resourceful man in life – and so in death. He will have found some way to survive while you used the sword. Otherwise he would not have rejected it the first time, giving you the opportunity to use it in your fight with Douglass Barelegs.'

'I hope you are right,' said Craig.

Craig's wound was healing quite rapidly, but whether that was due to the herb or to fairy magic was a matter for speculation amongst the two Oceanians. By the time they finally came to the country where the Celts and Oceanians were still executing the war, there were but hard white scars on his shoulder and side to show where Douglass's sword had struck.

Urgan told the other two that they were still many days walk from where they wanted to be and that they would have to do something to speed up their journey time.

'What can we do, grow wings?' asked Craig. 'I can't believe how far we are away from the pa.'

'When you travelled with the two Jutes, and as dogs, you were always heading north. You went deep into fairy country. Of course you ended up a long way from home. What did you expect? But I have a solution.'

Both Hupa and Craig looked at Urgan expectantly.

'What are we to do?' asked Hupa.

Urgan pointed to some mystical shapes out on the moor ahead of them. They were largish creatures with tails like flails and necks with soft, floating manes. They moved like gods across the landscape, incredibly fleet of foot. Magnificent in form and movement, they were muscled beasts of beauty, whose very presence on the earth seemed to have been conjured by supernature. If the strength was flowing out of the gods, it was surely flowing into these splendid animals of which Seumas had been proud.

'Horses,' said Craig. 'What of them?'

'We catch three of them and ride them to your pa.'

Hupa laughed, a little hysterically. 'You must be crazy – we can't ride *those*. They'd kill us.'

'Nonsense,' replied Urgan. 'Horses and humans are made for each other. You wait and see . . .'

Urgan had them build a corral of staves with reed-leaf lashings, with a gate through which they could herd the horses. Then the elf-man went and stood on a crag at the back of the corral and whinnied just as those creatures out on the moor whinnied, causing several horses to stop in mid-canter and stare at the corral. Urgan continued calling, until a small herd of mares headed his way, answering his call with their own. Urgan was the stallion whose females were coming to their master, while the hidden Oceanians prepared to rush out and shut the gate behind the unsuspecting creatures of the wind.

They were of course wary of the open gateway, but Urgan kept up his pretence of being a stallion and eventually the mares entered the corral.

Hupa and Craig ran out and slammed the gate shut on the creatures, who immediately went absolutely berserk, kicking and screaming, lashing out with their hind hooves, biting the air savagely with their teeth, whipping their heads back and forth, and trying to jump the fence which surrounded them. Only when night fell did they give up in exhaustion.

'I will break three of the horses,' said Urgan, the next early morning, 'but once I've broken them in, you two will have to ride one each. I want no faint hearts.'

The Oceanians said nothing, but watched in rising panic as Urgan lassoed the first mare and climbed on top of this kicking, bucking creature. He was thrown almost immediately, somersaulting several times through the air before hitting the soft peaty ground. To the amazement of the other two he immediately scrambled back on the horse, wrapped his legs around its girth, clung on hard to the mane hair, and continued in his attempts to break the spirit of the animal under him.

Although Urgan was thrown off the horse's back several times, he always climbed back on again immediately. Gradually he wore the beast down, until finally it gave in. It stood there allowing him to mount and dismount. Urgan rode it around the corral, growing in confidence all the time. When he got off the beast the last time, he tied a rope around its neck and handed the other end of the rope to Hupa.

'This little brown horse – a chestnut we call it – is yours, Hupa.'

'Do I want it?' she asked, trembling.

'Don't be such a baby. It's tame now. Take the rein.'

She did as she was told, not taking her eyes from the horse's face, wondering when it was going to try to bite her.

'ARRRGGHHH!' Craig yelled suddenly, his face suffused with pain.

'What is it?' cried Hupa.

Craig sat down and held his foot. He pointed dramatically at the mare.

'That sneaky – mare – stood on my foot,' he complained. 'Urgan – do you call that tame?'

'A horse is never *completely* tame. You always have to

be the master of it and they'll always have a go at those they feel are inferior to them. You have to look them in the eye and not flinch. They can smell fear. I never saw such a pair of cowards as you two. Hupa, get on the mare's back, now. If you hesitate any longer you'll never be able to ride.'

Urgan cupped his hands like a stirrup and told her to use it for her foot. Once her toe was in his hands he tossed her up on to the horse before she could complain or back away again. She sat there looking tense and terrified. She felt she was sitting on a treetop, high off the ground in a strong wind, on something completely unstable. Between her slim thighs was this monstrous living, breathing volcano which might erupt at any moment – and without any decent warning.

She waited for it to bolt, her heart racing ahead of her. She could feel the sweaty back on her bottom – could *smell* the sweat – and this did nothing to calm her fears. Gingerly she reached out to pat its neck, the way she had seen Urgan do.

The horse snorted and shook its head impatiently.

'That's right. Hold on – yes, even that tightly – to the mane,' said Urgan, 'I'll trot you round.'

He took the woven-grass rein and led her round the corral, first at a walk, then at a trot, finally at a mild canter. Initially she was rigid with fear and complained that it was hurting her bottom. Then she began to relax when nothing untoward happened. She began to get the rhythm of the trot and canter, using her knees to rise and fall with the movement of the mare. Gradually a smile appeared on Hupa's face. She clung on to the horse like a little girl, delighted with her first ride.

'I shall call her Brownie,' said Hupa. 'My little Brownie.'

'How original,' muttered Urgan, drily. 'But I suppose there are other meanings of the word – especially to one who came out of fairyland. Brownie it is.'

When he felt she had been on the horse for a good while, Urgan gave Craig a turn. Craig, on seeing that Hupa had done so well, was less apprehensive. He too was soon enjoying a slow trot around the ring, his arms wrapped around the horse's neck. Once he had been on her for a while Hupa became a little jealous and reminded everyone that Brownie was her horse and she thought Craig had been on *her* horse long enough.

Urgan did not bother to break in two more horses. Instead he selected the mares he wanted, then took some shiny dust out of his pocket for them to sniff. Once they had inhaled the fairyland snuff, they became docile enough to ride. In effect he had tamed them by using magic. Craig and Hupa were perplexed by this. They confronted him with the subject.

'Why did you physically break in that first horse, if you could do it using magic?' asked Hupa.

'I wanted to see if I could,' replied Urgan, simply. 'Why do things the easy way, when you can do them just as well the hard way?'

'Now I know he's mad,' Hupa said to Craig. 'And this is the man I'm supposed to be in love with?'

But there was a light in her eyes when she said it, as she watched the elf-man moving amongst the horses he had tamed.

The time came for them to mount up.

Craig got on his mare, a big roan one with a white flash on her forehead. He gripped the grass rein and gave the horse a little nudge in the ribs with his heels. The roan trotted out through the gateway obediently. Craig was exhilarated. Hupa rode up beside him. They glanced at each other and then laughed, both full of the spirit of riding. Here they were, high on a horse's back, feeling like royalty. There was nothing like it. And so far they had only trotted or cantered.

'Time to gallop,' cried Urgan, nudging his mare through the pair of them. 'We must ride like the wind!'

Urgan set the pace, flying out in front. Once Craig's mare saw the other pair building up to the gallop, she too took off. The wind rushed past Craig's face and for a moment the colour drained from his complexion. He had never moved so fast in his life before. No matter what Urgan had said, this was a terrifying experience.

Perhaps a canoe had skipped over the waves almost as swiftly, but that was different. The ground rushed under him like a fast-flowing river, and the drumming of the roan's hooves on the hard earth reminded Craig of his own expertise and how his hands flew with the sticks in them as they pounded a log drum.

'This is wonderful!' he cried, breathlessly, as he caught up to the others. 'I'm scared to death!'

'So am I,' laughed Hupa.

They thundered over moor and meadow, through brake and past stone, three riders on strong young mounts. Craig could feel the hard-packed muscled body moving beneath him. He could hear the snorts of air rushing in and out of the roan's nostrils. Flecks of foam came up from the beast's mouth and splattered his face. Clearly the creature itself, with its eyes white and wide, was enjoying this as much as the person on its back. The world flashed by them at a wonderfully alarming rate. No wonder the man on the horse was king. No wonder Seumas had warned them of such creatures. One of these creatures was worth half a man's life to own.

'What a joy there is in this,' Craig shouted above the noise of the rushing wind. 'I could ride for ever!'

'So could I,' yelled Hupa.

'Unfortunately,' answered Urgan, 'we don't have for ever.'

They knew he was right.

3

The death of Totua had wounded Kieto badly. This had come on top of other bereavements: the murder of his son whose grave had eventually been found in a wood. And the disappearance and suspected death of his daughter. Kieto was sick of death: his kin were vanishing before his eyes. He would have to go home to his wife without his children. These losses had piled themselves on his head and were weighing him down.

There were days when he paced his hut inside the pa, railing at Guirk. There were nights when he prayed quietly to his ancestors, begging their forgiveness for not answering the barbarian's call. Every noon Guirk still came up to the walls of the pa and demanded single combat with Kieto. Every evening the Celt trudged back into the hills, disappointed by the non-appearance of the Oceanian chief. Finally, the taunts and jeers, underlined by Guirk's abuse of Totua's corpse, got deep enough beneath Kieto's skin to make him respond.

Kikamana came into Kieto's hut to find him strapping on his feathered helmet.

'What are you doing?' the elderly high priestess asked him. 'Are you going out there?'

'I have to,' he sighed. 'I can stand it no longer. It's a

matter of personal and national honour. We are at a stalemate. We go out to battle with the Celts, but neither side
wins any great victory. What we have at the moment
amounts to a siege. We are hemmed inside our trenches and
stockades and the Celts cannot go to their homes, but have
to camp in the surrounding hills. Perhaps my death, if it
must be so, will break this deadlock in some way. Another
war chief will be found and he will have fresh ideas, new
thoughts.'

'You don't have to go out there and commit suicide in
order to find fresh ideas. You know Guirk has a magic
shield, made from iron bands fashioned from the teeth of
the ogress Lioumere. And a magic sword, forged from the
same enchanted metal. You will be slaughtered in the same
way as Totua – cut down without mercy. Your head will
decorate a Celt's horse. Your body will be dragged headless
in the dust. Where is the honour in that? It would be as well
to seek your revenge through other minds, rather than
waste yourself in this foolish venture.'

'I know – but I can't rely on my advisors to find an
answer – the best of them has gone missing. My son is
dead, my daughter has disappeared, most likely she is dead
too, and my brother has been killed by a thick-skulled thug.
What else is left for me but to fight this loudmouthed barbarian?'

Kikamana knew that by 'advisors' Kieto meant Craig,
who had disappeared the night of the last entertainment,
along with Hupa his daughter. There were ugly rumours
that the two had become lovers and had run away together.

Kieto did not believe this – nor did Kikamana.

It was believed by right-thinking Oceanians that Craig
and Hupa had been murdered by the Celts, their bodies dis-
posed of in some way. There was mourning amongst the
women of the Whakatane, for their leader. And many of
the other chiefs missed Craig's calming influence, his quiet
reasoning. Some were calling for a change in leadership.

The foremost of the contenders for the place of chief-of-chiefs was Prince Daggan, who was also the loudest in demanding that Kieto step down.

Perhaps, thought Kieto, we do need someone like Daggan at the head of the army? Someone without morals, someone without mercy, someone without principles?

The grating voice of Guirk penetrated the still afternoon air making Kikamana wince.

'I must go,' Kieto said. 'Help me on with my war cloak.'

Kikamana, the Farseeing-virgin, assisted Kieto with his splendid warrior-chief's mantle made of dogskin and parrot feathers. Then Kieto took down a heavy wahaika club from its hooks on the wall, its edges rimmed with shark's teeth. Kieto carried no other weapons, except for a lei-o-mano in his maro. However, Kikamana excused herself and left the hut for a short while, returning from her temple with another weapon.

'A greenstone club,' said Kieto, admiring the precious weapon his high priestess offered him. 'I shall carry this with great pride.'

He laid aside his wahaika club and took the smooth, beautiful and heavy greenstone mace.

'This is the weapon of a king,' he said.

'It once belonged to a king and has been blessed by the gods. It will increase your mana. Now I must place a tapu on you, to give you the best chance of victory. You will need all the help you can get out there.'

Kikamana performed the rituals and prepared her leader for the oncoming fight. Once he was ready he stood tall and proud, his expression arrogant. A warrior did not go out to fight looking like a bedraggled dog hiding from the rain.

'*Only war can make a real man and a real man must have the war he loves*,' said Kieto, quoting an old saying. 'The only path to glory is across the battlefield, for one man, or for a nation. There is nothing else worthwhile. A man's soul will not shine like a beacon in the afterlife without great deeds on the field of battle. To be remembered in songs, to be part of one's island history, this is all that matters.'

'Not everyone believes in such ideas,' said Kikamana. 'There are deeds greater than those performed by warriors.'

Kieto shook his head. He was too upset to argue. It was the wrong frame of mind in which to go out into battle. A warrior needed joy in his heart to beat the enemy. Weariness and despair were the worst of allies in a fight, especially one of single combat. Kieto wondered whether his time had indeed come, whether his mission to the Land-of-Mists was abortive and should never have taken place. Perhaps he should have ignored the inner calling and remained a fisherman's son?

Yet events had conspired against him throughout his life, to ensure his presence on this island. The moment that giant octopus had taken Kupe's bait and had fled with it, an enraged Kupe in pursuit, Kieto's fate had been sealed. One could not ignore a land as great as this, for such a huge island would not ignore others for very long. To explore, to seek new lands to conquer, that was in the basic nature of man. If not Kieto and his people, then some future Cormac and his Celts, or some king of the Angles, thirsting for power.

Kikamana, as if reading his thoughts, said, 'Some go out after knowledge, rather than to conquer. This is the true nature of the search for mankind.'

'Like Hiro, you mean?'

'Yes, like Hiro.'

Kieto said, petulantly, 'We can't all be Hiros.'

With that he swept from the room, his magnificent cloak lifting as he walked. Those who saw him coming from the walls cried out in excitement to others.

'Kieto! It's Kieto. He is going to fight Guirk!'

There was relief in the sound, as if at last a drought had been broken by the coming of rain.

The colours, red and green and yellow, of Kieto's tall feathered helmet sparkled in the sunlight. He held his greenstone club aloft, to salute his men, his ancestors, his gods. Then he strode towards the gates of the pa, the black mood at last lifting from his shoulders. He was going to avenge his brother. If that meant death, so be it, then let death come, the quicker the better.

Outside the pa, the word was going back into the hills, Kieto was coming out to fight Guirk.

Celts began to pour down from their encampments in their dull rough garments. Cormac came with his retinue of clan chiefs. Camp followers from the countryside swept towards the place where Guirk stood waiting, nervously, knowing that at last his wish was going to be answered. Despite the reassurance that he could not lose, that the magic in his weapons ensured his victory, the Celt was tense. This was the moment for which he had been waiting and the world was looking on.

Out of the various stockades, over the ditches and dykes, came the Oceanians, also eager to see what would be the outcome of this single combat, mano-a-mano, two warriors battling to the death, each carrying the pride of his people. There had been too many listless days, too many ragged battles neither won nor lost had been fought in the mud and grit of this strange land, and the coming duel signalled a change. Whatever happened in this contest, things were not going to be the same afterwards.

A fresh breeze was blowing in from the mountains.

Once the decision had been made, Kieto put everything into his bearing and demeanour. The figure that strode towards Guirk was tall and straight, proud, defiant, confident. Guirk shuffled in his sandals, bolstered only by the knowledge that he could not lose, that the magic of his weapons were so powerful that even men like Kieto could not defeat him.

When Kieto was not far from his adversary, he did his

dance, the haka, learned from the Maori. In the bent-knee position, he stamped forward, gesturing with his weapon, his tongue out and spread over his chin, his eyes rolling. He uttered a karakia as he did so, his voice deep and menacing. The feathers on his tall helmet and long cloak fluffed and flapped in the wind, making him seem larger than an ordinary man.

Guirk, on seeing this frightening display, called forth a bagpiper and, when the wailing began, proceeded to do a sword dance, his eyes contemptuously on his enemy. Guirk had added to his protective trappings a silver helmet and chain-mail shoulder guards. These flashed in the sun while he danced, giving rise to a great cheer from the Celts.

When both men had ceased their posturing, they stood before one another, their weapons at the ready.

Around them, on the terraces of the hills, outside the walls of the pa, stood the spectators. There was not a man or woman left in the Celtic camps, nor anyone but the sentries on the walls of the pa. This single combat was about to be witnessed by the complete armies of two great peoples.

'Come on then,' said Guirk, swishing his magic blade, 'come to meet your death, you overdressed jay.'

Kieto was not one to waste time circling, bluffing or feinting; he went straight in. He brought the greenstone club down towards the shield, only to find it rebuffed by a cushion of air. He tried again. The same thing happened. His heart sank as he proved to himself that what they said about the shield and sword of Guirk was true. They had magical powers. They must indeed have been fashioned from Lioumere's teeth.

'What's the matter?' crowed Guirk. 'Lost your strength? All that prancing and dancing, no doubt. You banana-eaters will have to do better than this. You're the second old man whose ambitions have been higher than his skills.'

Kieto had no idea what Guirk was saying to him, but he guessed it was to do with his brother.

The Oceanian stepped forward again, swiping at the
Celt's head. Guirk flicked out his sword arm. The point of
the sword nicked Kieto's brow, a slit right across from one
temple to the other. Blood trickled down into Kieto's eyes,
making it difficult for him to see. Celtic warriors let out
their breath as if they had been holding it in for such a
moment. The Oceanians were quiet, knowing that Guirk
was playing with their leader, like a cat plays with its kill.

'Finish him, Guirk,' came the voice of Cormac from the
midst of the Celts. 'Finish him *now*.'

This was spoken as an act of kindness. The Celtic leader
did not like to see a man made to look foolish, especially a
leader like Kieto whom he secretly admired.

Guirk looked sullen but he raised his sword to strike the
man before him. A sudden breeze riffled Kieto's feathers as
the Oceanian stood there ready to receive the blow. Then
someone shouted from the Celt side in such a strange voice
that both the combatants turned to look. Over the plain,
from the direction of the mountains, came a dark cloud in
the shape of a feline creature, moving rapidly, expanding
over the whole region. Soon the people were in its blackness, which wrapped around them like a soft cloak,
destroying all visibility.

Then the insubstantial giant beast had passed over, was
now bigger than before, running soft-footed towards the
north.

'What was that?' cried a Celt from the crowd, as men
shuddered and women shivered. 'Was that a *god*?'

'That?' said a stranger to their camp, making his way
through the throng on horseback. 'That was the beast-who-
eats-magic.'

Guirk blinked, then turned back to his opponent.

'Time to die, you pig's orphan,' he said, aiming a blow
with his sword. 'Now!'

Kieto instinctively held up his greenstone club.

To the astonishment of the crowds, though Guirk's

sword struck the green obsidian weapon squarely in the middle, it slid along it and glanced off, singing out a metal note.

'What?' cried Guirk in surpise.

He had expected his sword to cleft the stone in two.

Kieto was swift to reply, swinging his club at Guirk. Guirk protected his head. This time the stone struck the shield, severely denting it, causing Guirk to yell out in pain as his shield arm took the force of the blow.

No magic sword, no magic shield.

Kieto went in, battering his opponent with the greenstone club, not letting up for an instant. Guirk was caught completely on the defensive. He backed towards his own people, holding the battered shield over his head. One or two ineffective swipes with his sword told him he was not going to be successful with it. He dropped the weapon altogether and concentrated on preventing his head from being crushed.

His efforts were to no avail. Finally his arm was too tired to parry a blow. The greenstone club came crashing down on his conical silver helmet, driving it down to cut off his ears, nose and upper lip with its studded edge. There was a dent in the top which had crushed his brain inside his skull. His legs collapsed underneath him. Guirk fell to the dust as dead as a nail. Kieto stood over him, panting and heaving with the effort, realizing he was the unexpected victor.

A great yell of triumph went up from the Oceanian side, followed by a low moan of misery from the Celts. Kieto took Guirk by the legs and began to drag him face-down in the mud, towards the pa. A shout from a friend stopped him short.

'Leave the body, Kieto. Leave the remains for his kin.'

Kieto stared up at the speaker who had ridden through the ranks of warriors on a horse.

It was Craig. With him was Hupa, also on one of those

terrible animals. And the stranger who seemed to know about the dark beast. These three came towards Kieto. They dismounted and stood holding the reins of their mounts.

Kieto dropped the feet of his defeated antagonist.

The young man everyone thought was dead rubbed noses with the Oceanian leader. This exhibition brought nervous laughter from the Celtic camp. Despite the defeat of their champion the Celts seemed not unduly despondent. The two friends took no notice of this ignorance of their culture, knowing that it would be misunderstood. They stood before one another, holding each other's forearms.

'Where have you been?' asked Kieto, the sound of relief mingling with joy in his voice. Then nodding at Urgan, he cried, 'And who is this who brings my daughter back to me, with all her limbs and her heart intact?'

'I cannot speak for her heart,' said Urgan, smiling, 'but her arms and legs are all there.'

'This is Urgan,' said Craig, and not willing to go into the business of the fairies added, 'he is from the borderlands.'

Kieto clasped Urgan's forearms. 'Welcome,' said the Oceanian chief-of-chiefs. 'I take it you have been their guide and I am most grateful. I thought my daughter was dead,' his eyes misted over, 'but here she is, alive and well.'

Hupa did not go too close in case her father smothered her with too much love in front of her Whakatane.

'Very much alive and well, Father.'

Once the reunion was over, there was still a serious situation lying before Kieto. His warriors were all outside the pa. Facing them were the Celtic hordes, most of them armed. One battle here, hand-to-hand, might finish the war. Yet the risks for both sides were high. There would be a slaughter, perhaps even a massacre, and many would die in both armies. In the extreme it would be reduced to the last man standing. Cormac knew this, Kieto knew it. Even if the Oceanians tried their trick of running, they would be cut down by so near a foe.

'Well?' said Cormac, reading the situation accurately himself, 'D'we fight or no?'

The interpreters shouted out the question even before it was fully out of Cormac's mouth. Everyone was wary. Everyone was edgy. Swords were gripped tightly. Spears were balanced. Clubs were hefted through practice swings. There was a tautness to the air. Once the hacking began, it would be every man for himself. The women, all except those who were armed for a fight, began to lead their children away.

'Let us fight!' cried the voice of Prince Daggan of Raiatea, from behind Kieto. 'Rally around me, warriors! I shall lead you to victory over the barbarian hordes!'

Fortunately the tension at that time had not gathered to breaking point. Warriors shuffled and stared at each other, but none went to the side of Daggan. The prince let out a snort of disgust.

'Are you *all* cowards now? Have you fallen into the ways of this fisherman's son?' He pointed with his club at Kieto. 'It has taken him many days and nights to gather the courage to fight this thick-headed creature he has now clubbed to the ground. I would have done it at the first challenge. Let us now waste no more time, but drive into the Celts with our weapons.'

Still no one moved; all stood watching warily.

'There will be many deaths,' Kieto said, 'on both sides.'

The interpreters gave voice and once Cormac understood the words he spoke.

'Aye, that's true enough,' replied Cormac, 'but it's better than rotting in camps and stockades.'

Kieto nodded. 'That's true also.'

There was utter silence over the plain for a few moments, save for the sound of birds and insects.

A highly strung warrior let out a sharp exhalation of air

and thousands of heads turned sharply to stare at him.

Then the faces turned back to the chiefs again, watching intently for the signal to begin the slaughter.

Urgan stepped forward, no longer the wizened elf he was when he had walked out of fairyland and joined the Oceanians in their quest. Now a tall handsome man of thirty years, with broad shoulders and sturdy limbs, he stood firmly between the two armies, holding up his arms for attention.

When he felt all eyes were on him, he spoke in the most dramatic voice he could muster.

'The Angles are coming!'

There was a stunned look on the faces around him – the first to break the silence was the leader of the Celts.

'What?' cried Cormac, his eyes brightening, his attention completely captured by this news. 'When?'

'It's true,' Craig said, 'they're on their way down here now. They said they were going to join . . .'

'Join forces at the border and come down here to destroy the Celts and the brown-skin invaders, both in one breath,' Urgan interrupted quickly.

Craig had been about to say 'join forces with Celts' but now saw what Urgan was doing.

'Destroy us, is it?' cried Cormac, the interpreters working with him excitedly, three of them translating the same words at once. 'Aye, well, we'll see about that.'

'It's said they have a mighty army,' Craig said, 'but what if the Celts and Oceanians were to fight together, side by side, to defeat the invading Angles?'

Urgan gave him a look as if to say, you may have spoken too soon, my friend, for the Celts were all muttering about not needing any brown-skins to help them defeat the Angles, they could do it on their own. It was their land which was being invaded after all. The Oceanians could run away to their boats and go back to wherever they came from in the first place.

But Cormac was a wise chief-of-chiefs, being from a small clan, which needed guile and cunning to survive.

'When did we last beat an army out of Engaland?' he said. 'Once – just once the Scots and Picts have hammered those bastards from the north. And then they outnumbered us two to one. But what a shock they would get to find an army to *match* them in numbers, eh? What a bloody nose we could give the buggers this time! There'd be a clutch o' widows up there on top o' the border after such a fight.'

'We'd give them such a thrashing, they'd stay up there for more than a wee while,' cried another clan chief. 'But would these painted demons join with us?'

These words were translated by Craig.

Kieto said, 'We came here to strike a hard blow, a warning blow, to dissuade any future would-be invaders of our islands. We have shown the Celts that we are not lacking in skill at warfare. Now it is time to impress upon the Angles that if they come to our part of the world with war in mind, they can expect a fiery reception from Oceanian island warriors.'

'It's settled then,' cried Cormac, 'the war between the Celts and Oceanians is at an end. We are allies against the Angles and their Jute dogs. If ye leave this land after we thrash the bastards, then there need be no more strife between us.'

A great cheer went up when this was translated by the interpreters and the whole Oceanian army surged forward to begin hugging the reluctant Scots and Picts. The hairy Celts detached themselves as soon as possible from this unseemly show of affection. They dusted themselves off subconsciously, and nodded grim-faced, as if to say, enough's enough, no more touching of bodies if you please, for we're not that way inclined down here in the cold southern climes.

Guirk's corpse was taken away by his clan for burial,

while Kikamana and Boy-girl came to speak with Craig and Urgan.

'What was it you said?' Kikamana asked of Urgan. 'You spoke about a beast-that-eats-magic.'

'It's true,' replied the man brought up by elves, whose hybrid status made him the focus for knowledge found only in the ether, making of him a universal messenger. 'Craig let the beast out of the tower. This was his destiny, the reason for his being here in Albainn. The One-God has decided it is time to end the rule of magic in the land. At this moment all our greater and lesser gods – those of the Celts and those of the Oceanians – are in their last throes of existence. They are a spent force. They have fought a great battle in their divine domains and have destroyed each other. Nought but a handful of kitchen gods survive, without power, without any force beyond that which can be found in nature, among natural things . . .'

'How do you know all this?' asked Kikamana.

'It comes to my tongue.'

'Just like that? From nowhere?'

'From *everywhere*,' he corrected. 'It is my destiny to speak the word, as it was Craig's to release the beast. We are both creatures of two worlds, children of a third culture. We have special duties on this earth.'

'Tell us more,' said Kikamana.

'Now will begin a time of discovery, slow at first, about all the natural wonders around us.'

'No more magic,' repeated Boy-girl with sadness in her voice. 'Won't that make the world a dull place?'

'Not necessarily,' replied Urgan, 'for the earth has many secrets and we know but a handful of them yet. There will be revelations to make us gasp in amazement.'

'But everything will be boringly predictable!' she said.

At that moment it began to drizzle, the fine summer rain sweeping in from the sea. A few moments previously it had been bright sunshine. Now the light was dimming above them, as the sun was swallowed by high clouds.

'There's always the weather,' said Urgan, 'if you're looking for unpredictability. No one will ever be able to cure the weather of its spontaneous character. If you want change, look to the skies.'

A distant rumble of thunder came from some black clouds over the mountains. There was a flash of light, a brightness deep within the dark folds of the heavens. A faraway thunderstorm was in progress, muted by the miles between. Were these the last dying gasps of the now feeble gods? Were they stumbling over each other, flailing blindly with weak arms, falling to oblivion as each cancelled the other out? Or were these natural phenomena, simply a change in the weather?

And was the One-God looking down at the fading light of lesser deities as he handed over responsibility for the world to ordinary mortals?

PART TEN

In the wake of the great whale

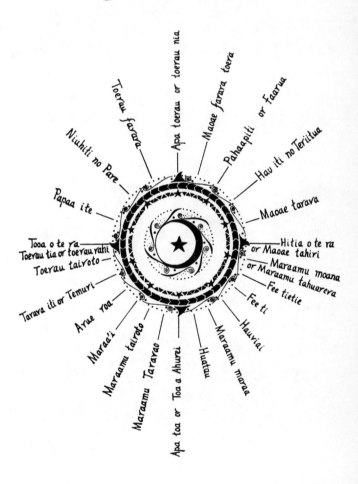

Toerau farara
Apa toerau or toerau nia
Maoae farara toera
Pahaapiti or faarua
Hau iti no Teriitua
Niuhiti no Pare
Maoae tarava
Papaa ite
Hitia o te ra
or Maoae tahiri
Tooa o te ra
Toerau tia or toerau rahi
Maraamu moana
or Maraamu tahuarera
Toerau tairoto
Fee tietie
Tarava iti or Temuri
Fee ti
Arue roa
Hauviai
Maraa'i
Maraamu maraa
Maraamu tairoto
Huatau
Maraamu Taravao
Maraamu maraa
Apa toa or Toa a Ahurei

1

The evening before the battle an Angle envoy arrived in the Celt camp asking if they would ally themselves with the northerners to fight the Oceanians.

The envoy was sent away with a flea in his ear.

Later in the night, as was the custom, the Celts sent three messengers asking for earth, fire and water. If these three were given it meant the Angles were prepared to negotiate a peace settlement on equal terms with the allies. The envoy had been returned unharmed to his people, so the Celts believed their messengers would be treated with the same courtesy. They were mistaken. Normally it would have been so, but unfortunately the present chief-of-chiefs of the Angles was a man to whom integrity and honour meant very little.

The first messenger was thrown into a pit of starving wolves and told to take his earth from there.

The second messenger was thrown down a well and was left there to drown.

The third was cast into a blazing bonfire.

When Cormac-the-Venomous heard of this violation of an unwritten code, for messengers were supposed to be ambassadors and immune, he vowed at all costs to kill the leader of the Angles, one Drathvarn from a region known as Merkia, a man known for his cruelty even amongst his own people.

The next morning a great army of the Angles came down from the north, the dawn spread behind them like a vast cloak.

On long leashes before them, six to one burly handler, ran the human dogs of war. Several hundred. These were the Jutes, naked and covered in woad symbols, running on all fours, snapping and snarling, their long blond manes hanging down over their shoulders. Every so often one of them would rise up on its back legs and let out a terrible scream of fury, only to be whipped down again into the animal position by the handlers' assistants. These human dogs with their long nails, their dirty teeth, and their insane appearance, were indeed a frightening vanguard of the huge army.

Next came the drummers and shrill-whistlers, and the men whirling bullroarers, and the horn-blowers and trumpet-blarers, marching under a variety of banners which represented the many different clans of Angles and Celts from all over the near and far north. This was a pageant, which the northerners loved. They enjoyed spectacle. Their bagpipes, smaller and different from the southern Celtic pipes, squealed and wailed along the line.

Some of the banners and streamers had seen better times, were merely flying in tatters, but it added to the colour of the second line, and the standards with their horse skulls, goat skulls and even human skulls, providing a touch of white grimness amongst the many-hued flags.

Behind the banners came the foot-warriors, on a wide front which stretched across the valley from wall to wall. Amongst them were the lesser chiefs, with their bodyguards and companions, their cloaks pinned to their shoulders with burnished bronze brooches that gleamed in the sun. These foot-warriors were armed with pikes and spears, swords and maces, bows and slingshots. The clatter of their iron weapons, and odd bits of armour, added an eerie undernote to the cries of the Jute dogs and the sound of martial music.

To the right and left were the horsemen, too undisciplined to be called even irregular cavalry. These were mainly noblemen – thanes with their sons and grandsons – the only warriors rich enough to own horses. Here and there was a wealthy crop-grower on a plough-horse, sitting several hands higher than the frisky mounts of the thanes, looking awkward and rustic. In the main the horses were protected with thick blankets and sacking, held on by leather straps, around their heads and flanks. Some wore wooden masks, with holes through which to see. Many of the horses were painted in the same way as the Jute dogs.

At the back of this enormous army of Angles came a wave of men dragging monstrous wicker and straw animals on wheeled platforms. These were the druids in their hooded habits of unbleached wool. Their faces were hidden as they pulled in their harnesses, tugging giant representations of pigs, goats, dogs, sheep, horses and men. It was the sight of these beast-shaped pyres, fashioned for burning clutches of live prisoners after the battle, which sent a chill through the waiting Celts and Oceanians. Many were the warriors who swore an oath to themselves that they would rather die on the battlefield than be taken alive and roasted in a wicker basket.

'Steady,' said Cormac to his warriors on the right of the field, 'remember we have a plan.'

It was the first time the Celts had sat down the night before a battle and actually discussed strategy and tactics. Normally they just found a piece of good ground and threw themselves into the enemy from there, hacking and chopping until it was evident which side was winning. The Angles were much the same, though they were more organized in their hierarchy and ranks: their men fought in columns, rather than as individuals, but without any set goal except to annihilate the foe.

In fact, the allies had been working all night, digging a wide shallow trench across the battleground. The trench had now been laid with a bed of grasses and kindling, on top of which was strewn a layer of charcoal. When the Angles had first been sighted, Celtic brand-carriers lit the grasses in the trench.

The enemy approached. Charcoal glowed red hot between the two armies. A swathe of blistering embers five strides in width crossed the broad valley.

The many tribes of Angles and their allies, which included two tribes of the northern Celts, stopped dead three hundred paces away. Their martial music drifted away into silence. They stood stock-still and stared at the enemy they had come to fight. For a time all that could be heard was the champing of the horses. The only movement to be seen that of the fluttering banners. The southern Celts and their Oceanian allies stood and waited, equally calm. Now was the time for a few moments of quiet reflection, for studying the ground and the foe, before the bloody battle began in earnest.

Craig tried to imagine what the Angles were thinking: what could be going through their heads at the scene before them.

They would see their old enemies, the vast majority of Celtic tribes, waiting to settle ancient scores.

But they would also see a dark-skinned multitude, hosts of brown bodies, tens of thousands of strangers from who knew where? Some of these defiant-looking strangers had tattooed faces, all had painted bodies. The brown-skinned men carried strange weapons in their hands – black iron-wood clubs of twisted and gnarled design – swords with jagged-toothed edges from sawfish – bows of another shape – tall spears and short spears with glittering mother-of-pearl points – shark-toothed daggers, stingray-backbone daggers, daggers of every description – shields of some curious matting and uncommon-looking wood – all wielded by broad and savage-looking warriors of an unknown region, some with black woolly hair, some with black straight hair.

The Angles would study the unusual clothes, would see dogskin cloaks of white and brown, tall elaborately feathered helmets of fantastic colours. Over there stood some men with bones through their noses, with grass skirts around their waists. Over here grinning warriors with teeth filed to points for eating human flesh. At the back, tall and lean men with fierce blazing eyes. At the front, short stocky men with wild expressions.

And these dark warriors, it was said, had travelled thousands of miles by canoe simply to fight! Here were peoples the like of which the Angles had never seen. A people who appeared to the pale-skinned warriors of Engaland like demons from a terrifying nightmare. All their most dreadful imaginings stood there waiting to do battle: creatures from hell.

The word ran along the lines of Angles.

'*Yfelnyss*!'

Wickedness!

The Celts had conjured up demons from the underworld to assist them in their fight.

Craig could imagine the ripple of terror which ran through the Angle army like fear through a herd of deer on seeing a pack of starving wolves for the first time.

Yet they stood their ground, unflinching. Not one man turned and ran before this awful sight. If there were demons to fight, so be it. They would fight demons. Send in the giants, the dragons and hobgoblins too, if needs must. A fight was a fight and glory waited for a warrior, whether he lived or died, so long as he did not *run*.

Yet there were more surprises in store for the Angles.

Suddenly a cry went up from one of the brown-skinned

demons. There was movement amongst the newcomers. They began to dance, but such a dance had never before been witnessed by any Angle or Jute. There was a stamping of the ground as dark warriors moved in unison, crouching, marching forward slowly, threateningly. Then they showed their tongues, flat against their chins, and their eyes rolled most horribly. They chanted loudly in ugly voices as they made their vile gestures. They jabbed with their spears, killing an invisible enemy. They enacted the defeat of the foe before the battle even began.

This time the Angles wavered, glanced at each other along the lines, found it hard to hold their places.

Fortunately at that moment the order was given to advance again and the music wailed back to life, the earth shuddered with the stamp of tens of thousands of feet, of thousands of hooves, of hundreds of wheels.

Fifty strides from the trench the dog-handlers let loose the savage, mindless Jutes. These human beasts came hurtling forward now they were off their leashes. They howled and snarled like a pack of wolves, their great manes flying in the wind, their eyes blazing. When they reached the trench they ran straight on to the coals, only to scream in agony and limp back with burned hands and feet towards their masters. The handlers, ready with their whips, urged the Jutes back over the coals. It was while they were so engaged that allied archers began to pick them off, one by one, thus ending a lifetime of misery.

The Jute dogs stood no chance; caught on the coals, or between their handlers and the trench, they were cut down swiftly by accurate fire from the allies. Both Craig and Hupa felt for the poor creatures. They recalled their own time as wild dogs and considered themselves lucky they were not among these canine Jutes now being slaughtered in a rain of arrows.

Hupa and Craig were not riding their horses in the battle, but had loaned them to some Celts. They were not proficient enough to fight on horseback yet. Once they had seen how a Celt rode the same beast, picking up a small nut on the point of a sword while hanging from the side of the horse, they realized how inexperienced they were at riding. There were Celts who could ride standing on the horse's rump, or under its belly, or sliding behind on their heels in the dust while holding its tail.

No, the two Oceanians were still rank amateurs.

At a signal from Kieto, Fijian and Samoan firewalkers then crossed the coals on their bare feet. Once on the other side they attacked the dog-handlers and the first line of Angles, engaging them with ironwood double-handed clubs. Shark-toothed weapons ripped horrible wounds into the shoulders and faces of the Angles, who fought back with pike and spear. However, no sooner had the Fijians and Samoans struck, than they had raced back over the coals again, leaving the dead behind them.

'That'll make 'em wail,' cried a delighted Cormac. 'They're not used to this kind of warfare.'

And indeed the Angle front let up a great cry of anger and disbelief on finding their enemy had wafted away like smoke to safety on the other side of the blazing trench. Some of the Angles tried running over the coals, but the rags and skins with which they bound their feet caught fire. Any that did make it across, crippled of foot, were instantly attacked by the waiting Celts. While they were in disarray the Fijians and Samoans made one or two more forays across the river of fire, reducing the numbers in the front ranks by several score.

The Angles were not used to these kind of losses so early in the battle. The chiefs in the second line called to one another for advice. Drathvarn, their war chief, who had placed himself amongst the horsemen on the left flank, screamed at his warriors to get off their fat arses and wade into the Celts and their dark allies. For a while there was some confusion in the ranks of the Angles, as men from the rear pushed those in front forward onto the hot coals, and these unfortunates turned and like wounded bulls began to bore their way back through the mass of people bringing up the rear.

Eventually men in armour and on horseback began to surge forwards, kicking the live coals out of the trench and scattering them abroad. At another signal from Kieto, Rarotongan warriors rushed forward and threw coconut shells full of vegetable and shark oil, commodities of which the Oceanians had plenty, covering the men in armour. The live coals did the rest, setting light to the oil. Soon there were thanes staggering around like burning torches, screaming as they cooked inside their metal suits. Those on horseback found their mounts bolting in blind panic. Some galloped into the Celts who pulled the riders from their saddles and gleefully cut them down.

Now that the Angles were confused, Cormac gave a signal and the ranks of the allies parted to let through horsemen dragging wet reed mats. These were raced forward and cut loose over the trench of hot charcoal. Once in place Celts and Oceanians began to stream over the mats to engage the dazed Angles. The Celts went for the mass of men to fight iron with iron, while the Oceanians, who had been briefed by the Celt clan chiefs, went for the leaders amongst the Angles. Like the Celts in their earlier battles with the Oceanians, the Angle chiefs were incensed to find themselves the sole targets of the Oceanians, who clubbed them mercilessly to the ground.

Craig found himself in the thick of the fight, using an obsidian canoe breaker to smash wooden shields aside, allowing his men to rush in and finish off the foe. Urgan was not in the fight. He had told a disgusted Hupa that he could not fight in case he killed his own father or brother, whose names and titles he did not know. Hupa was upset, though realizing that Urgan was an Angle, albeit from just above the border. She was commanding her archers, her

Whakatane, who were on the right flank, firing arrows into the oncoming horsemen.

Once the Angles had rallied, however, some fierce fighting took place in the centre line. Spears were used to drive back the Celts and Oceanians, where they overlapped on the battlefront, and there was a threat of the allies being overrun at that point, of the Angles breaking through in a great wedge. The front centre line of the allies began to crack and crumble. Cormac's and Kieto's warriors were being rolled aside as the wedge of veteran Angles drove through the gap, forcing the allies to part like water falling either side of a canoe.

At this point Kieto himself brought forward a new wave of prepared warriors. These consisted of a mix of Tongans, Hivans and Celts. The Celts were placed so that they each had an Oceanian on their right, bearing a gata waka club. The Oceanian with the club would smash aside an Angle's shield and the Celt next to him would then make a thrust with his sword at the unguarded midriff of the Angle.

The gata waka clubs were wielded with great skill. The Tongans and Hivans had practised with such weapons all their lives. Sometimes the club stroke was so hard and accurate it would spin the enemy soldier completely round, so that his back was exposed to the sword thrust. Soon the Angles began to fall back under these tactics, not ever having experienced such fighting methods before. Finally, first one, then another broke from the pack and began running. Before long they were streaming away like a comet's tail, fleeing to the far end of the valley where it funnelled them out into open country.

The enemy horsemen then tried to outflank the allied army, but Cormac had chosen his ground well. The walls of the u-shaped valley assisted in preventing any pincer movement by these riders. This natural defence had been reinforced on both sides of the glen, where the allies had placed tree trunks horizontally, their ends supported by shoulder-high rocks. Sharpened stakes had been driven into the ground between the barriers to close any gaps.

Knots of archers fired from behind these barriers, which were effective in preventing the horsemen from sweeping round the flanks of the allies. Unwilling to risk their precious mounts over such formidable terrain, some horsemen tried to chop their way through the throng of foot-warriors, only to be dragged off their saddles and clubbed to death.

Drathvarn and his bodyguards were attacked by Celt horsemen, handpicked men who knew how to use a mace or broadsword from the saddle. Soon the best of Drathvarn's companions had been whittled away, leaving the way open to the chief himself. Many of them had fought bravely, but they were battling on a narrow front, the bulk of their army behind them. The spearpoint cavalry tactics of Cormac ensured that they only engaged two or three foe at a time and this frustrated them.

When he saw that he was being defeated, the Merkian chief, Drathvarn, turned his horse. He tried to ride at full gallop to the end of the valley, mindless of his own fallen men over whom his mount's hooves were trampling. Cormac on his own mount saw the chief-of-chiefs of the Angles defecting. Bareback on his charger, he gave chase, the hair on the heads of former enemies flying as he rode after his hated adversary. Cormac's sturdy little steed caught the fleeing chief. There was the quick flash of a broadsword and Drathvarn's head bounced in the dust. Another trophy to decorate the mane of a Celt's horse.

Drathvarn's steed went riding on, a headless corpse at the reins, blood founts spurting from the open neck.

Now the advancing allied warriors, the front ranks at a run, had reached the wicker figures at the end of the valley. The druids had gone, fled when they saw the first of the deserters pass them in a panic. Their wicker cages, built to hold dozens of prisoners, were dragged back down the valley, towards the allied encampment. Later they were used to burn the bodies of the Angle dead, including the remains of Drathvarn, which were found slammed against a tree at the head of the valley. His horse had gone. Either it had run off or had been taken by one of Drathvarn's own men as transport to the north.

At the end of the day the Angles had been routed. They drifted up to their homeland in knots. In truth, many of them had not wanted to fight at all, but being serfs had had little choice in the matter. Now that it was all over they were anxious to get back to their families, to the little plots of land they worked, to their hunting and fishing. For once the Celts had won the day. It smarted, but it could be borne.

Cormac was ecstatic. 'By the Mossy Stone of Drummock Moor, we gave them a whupping today, eh, lads? They won't forget that one in a hurry.' Then he turned to Kieto and added bluntly, 'When are ye leaving?'

Kieto, when he heard this, laughed gravely. 'These Celts are curt people, aren't they?' he said to Craig. 'No standing on ceremony. Just out with it.'

Kieto affirmed that they would be gone very soon. They had one more duty to perform. Once that was done, then the Oceanians would sail away from the Land-of-Mists and hopefully never have to return.

'What duty?' asked Cormac, suspiciously.

'A funeral,' replied the one-handed Kieto, enigmatically. 'A funeral for a friend.'

This sounded rather strange, since there were many funerals to perform – or rather one great funeral for those who had fallen on the field of battle. However, Kieto told the Celt that the funeral he had in mind was one which would take place after the burial of the war dead.

'This is for the death of a great hero.'

There was much feasting and dancing in the camps of the Celts. The Oceanians had their own celebrations. The

Hivans and Fijians, and some from other islands, had roasted a few of the Angle chiefs. Somehow they did not think the Celts would approve of cannibalism, even if it was ritualized and done for a very good reason. Only chieftains who had fought hard and courageously were cooked and eaten. No one was interested in weaklings and cowards. The idea was to increase one's manna, not dilute it. Brave men only were worth eating.

Once the battle was over of course, the Oceanians had to have their tapu removed by the priests, otherwise they might damage themselves and others by carrying an unnecessary burden. This having been done, some Oceanians went off to the camps of the Celts, to seek out men they had fought with that day, and give them thanks for timely interventions on their behalf. Celts were drifting into the pa, also on the same errand. Lives had been saved on both sides, often at great risk.

Even though they had been allies in a great battle, one which would be retold as part of both their histories, the Celts and the Oceanians still did not fully trust each other. Kieto had sent for the ocean-going canoes, which had spent the summer moored in the harbour of a small island some way off from the mainland. It was time to return to the islands in the sun. Most Oceanians were by now very homesick.

The joy of battle was one thing: the feeling of bliss on being told they were going home was quite another.

The day following the battle, when all was quiet and people in the pa were recovering from the effects of last night's kava, Urgan went looking for Craig. He found him sitting with Hupa outside a hut. Instead of approaching the pair, he caught Craig's eye and motioned with his head. Craig raised his eyebrows in surprise, but then got up and went to where Urgan was standing, in order to listen to him.

Urgan seemed a little embarrassed, especially with Hupa's eyes on him. But he spoke up bravely.

'Is – is Hupa married, or betrothed at all? We haven't spoken about such things a great deal. I mean, if you yourself have some interest in her . . .'

Craig shook his head in bewilderment. 'I've told you she's a maiden. I myself am married with children. Why are you going over all this again?'

'Well, we were travelling companions before,' replied the nervous man. 'Things are different when you are wandering together. Sometimes things are said to impress, rather than to reveal truths. So – so she is free, is she?'

'Why would you think otherwise, if you've been told so?'

'In fairyland no one tells the truth. The whole place is buzzing with lies. Fairies are like that. They love to boast, they like to make things up – creativity they call it – and they love embellishing things. A fairy will never tell the truth when the lie is more colourful. It's difficult for me to get out of that frame of mind. I have been an elf for most of my life, after all. It's difficult to change.'

'You're a man now. A man has his honour to think of. You should throw off these fairy ways.'

Urgan looked shame-faced. 'I know.'

Craig did not take his eyes off the tall, handsome young man before him, but called to Hupa.

'Come over here a minute,' he said. 'Someone has something to say to you.'

Hupa, scrubbed and shining, her bow over her shoulder and her quiver of arrows at her hip, looked every part the huntress, the fleet-of-foot maiden who runs through the forest, her boyish beauty enchanting any watchers.

'What?' she said, coming up to the men. 'Yes, Urgan?'

'I – er – I wondered – that is – what is it like in Oceania – the thing is see . . .'

'He wants to marry you,' said Craig, bluntly.

'He does?' cried Hupa, her eyebrows shooting up. She went bright scarlet, then added a soft, 'Oh.'

Urgan was also as red as an island sunset. 'Well?'

Hupa smiled and looked bashful. 'All right then.'

'You will marry me?' yelled Urgan, triumphantly.

'If my father allows it.'

'Ah,' said the young man, 'I knew there would be a catch – of course, you're Kieto's daughter. Only the most important man amongst the Oceanians at this time. Only the warlord, the leader of the expedition . . .'

'I think I can speak to him for you,' said Craig, 'and I'm sure he'll give his consent. In the meantime, I congratulate both of you.' Craig looked at Hupa – a long lingering look – then gravely kissed her cheek. 'You're getting a prize here, Urgan. One of the most coveted maidens on this earth. Treat her well. And you, Hupa, do the same with him. The time for your tantrums is over. Time to become a woman.'

'I'm not giving up my Whakatane,' she said, firmly.

'Wouldn't expect you to,' replied Urgan. 'I don't want a wife who does nothing but cook and raise children.'

'Good,' she said, 'because you wouldn't be getting one of those. And I couldn't live here.' She shivered. 'The summers are bad enough – the winters would kill me.'

'Have no concern. I want to come with you. I wish to be the first Angle to live amongst the Oceanians. I want to be the Seumas of the northern tribes.'

She smiled, taking his hand. 'It's settled then.'

Craig went off to find Kieto and persuade him that his new prospective son-in-law was a good man to have in the family. On the way he collected Boy-girl to assist him, and the pair of them shared Kieto's basket late that afternoon.

Kieto was resistant to the idea at first. Urgan was not even a Celt. He was an Angle. Kieto felt he knew the Celts, through his long association with Seumas and Dorcha, but he knew nothing of the Angles. Perhaps they had certain practices which were not savoury? What did they do with their dead? How did they treat their relatives? How did they raise their babies? All these questions needed answering.

'People are much the same everywhere,' said Craig. 'They have cultural differences, but love can overcome such things. So long as they are basically good people in their heart – and I believe Urgan would pass in that respect. He's a brave man, and sound of limb and mind, and what's more he was not raised amongst the Angles, but amongst fairies.'

'I think you should trust your daughter to choose,' said Boy-girl. 'Let's face it, Kieto, she is not a typical young woman. Whoever she chooses will be out of the ordinary. This Urgan has proved himself a sensible man and was a good friend to Craig and Hupa when they were lost in this Land-of-Mists. I think you could do much worse. Some wild Hawaiian, or a Rapanuian who lives far from Rarotonga.'

In the end, Kieto gave his consent and Boy-girl went off to tell the lovers the good news, while Craig went to seek out Kikamana, to make the wedding arrangements.

Hupa was after all an ariki.

The young maiden later expressed only one sadness – that her brother Kapu was not there to see her married to this lovely young man.

Once the arrangements were settled with the high priestess, Craig asked the Farseeing-virgin, 'Is magic really gone? Are the gods really dead?'

'Yes.'

'Did I do that?' he said, feeling guilty. 'Did I rob the world of magic?'

'You had no choice in the matter – you were merely Io's instrument,' said Kikamana. 'We'll learn to do without magic – besides, there will always be little pockets, small secret places which the beast has missed – and we can certainly do without the petty squabblings of the old gods.'

'Do you know any more about this land? Do they have an Io who has survived?'

'I am told so, by a Celt woman who knows. She says the One-God religion is spreading rapidly. There have been people called monks who travelled through, but now one of them has come to settle in the land of the Celts. His name is Columba. Another, by the name of Cedd, has landed in Engaland. He has built a meeting house out of stones from an ancient wall on the mouth of the Blackwater River. The name of this house escapes me, but be assured the Angles and Celts are well served.'

Craig said he hoped so, but it was going to take some getting used to, living without gods of thunder, lightning, sea, earth and sky.

'They are still there, only now absorbed into one form, into the single creator we call Io.'

'And what of our ancestors, our atua?' asked Craig.

'They have accepted the change, just as we must.'

That evening a group of painted Picts arrived at the pa and asked for Craig. They said they were his cousins. Craig went out to meet them, men and women from the Blackwater clan. He grasped their shoulders as he greeted them, one by one, and placed his cheek next to theirs. They were as shy with him as he was with them. These were his father's relations – *his* relations – and though the meeting was awkward it was rewarding for both him and the people he met. Common blood flowed in their veins and obviously this created a bond between them. They saw Blackwater clan likenesses in him and he was amazed how familiar they appeared to him.

When they left he gave them gifts – scrimshaws carved by Seumas – and they handed him presents in return. One bright-eyed young woman who had Seumas's eyes, nose and chin, gave him a special hug and was reprimanded by her father for showing too much affection. The girl made a face behind her father's back and then smiled at Craig as if to say, 'These old people and their conventions, they don't understand, do they?'

The whole episode was a marvellous experience for Craig, who had known but one member of his family until now.

2

Before the Oceanians left the mountain country of Land-of-Mists, that place where water drops in veils from high places and no matter where a person stands he can hear water running, they had one more duty to perform. The burial of the heart of Seumas was the funeral about which Kieto had spoken to Cormac. It was a ceremony Kieto was determined to carry out with all the rites due to a great hero: one such as Kupe himself had been given.

A spot was chosen on top of the cliffs where Seumas had first been seen climbing by a seven-year-old Kieto those many years ago. It was a grassy knoll with a natural quartz headstone upon which the first rays of the morning sun fell with a sparkling lustre. This rock would be the only marker to the grave. It overlooked the wild grey-green seas into which Seumas and Dorcha had fallen, to be plucked from the tall waves by Kupe and carried off to Oceania. It was a place where the mist hung continually around the crags and the smell of salt-spray, the sound of seabirds, were ever present.

'Will he not want his marker to be next to Dorcha's, on Rarotonga?' asked a worried Craig. 'Should they not be together?'

'This is merely the home of the heart, which is an earthly relic,' said Kieto. 'You can be sure that wherever the essence of Seumas finally rests, it will be with Dorcha's. If he is not already with her, you can be sure his spirit is planning the journey which will bring them together.'

Next, Kikamana, Boy-girl, Polahiki, Craig and Kieto blackened their faces, cut off their hair and gashed their bodies with sharks' teeth. These five were the chief mourners. They donned a tapa-bark garment known as a pakoko, made of cloth which had been dyed red with the sap of candle-nut trees, then dipped in the black mud of taro-growing soil. The pakoko gave off an obnoxious smell, symbolic of the decaying state of the dead person. Finally they wore crowns made of fern, which had been singed by fire at the edges to produce a reddish look.

On the first day of the funeral the mourning dances began and traditionally no cloth-beating took place during such a time. The goddess Mueu, who gave cloth-beating to the world, had a cloth-flail the strokes of which normally dispensed death to mortals at the end of their natural lifespan. Mueu was present at the funeral of every great person and to beat ordinary cloth in her presence would have caused offence. Old habits died hard.

The Celts in the surrounding countryside watched these funeral games with great interest, wondering who it was that was to be buried, for it seemed that all the peoples of Oceania, to a man, woman and child, were taking part. There was sadness and grief in the air, like a tangible thing, pervading every corner of the land of the Albannachs.

When the Celts learned it was one of themselves, a man of little significance being a bird-strangler and an egg-collector, nothing more, they were astonished. Why, the Blackwater clan to which the man had belonged, was a small inferior cliff-top tribe, pinched and worn by poverty. They had few notable deeds to their credit, nor heroes to the clan's name. Traditionally they lived by plundering the tidal reaches, the shoreline with its meagre offerings. It was a mystery to the Celts that such a man would be given so great an honour. Why, it amounted to raising up a beach-comber or a crab-fisher and making him a god!

On the fifth day the embalmed heart wrapped in pan-danus leaves was carried on a litter and placed for a time on a stone ahu built specially for the purpose, while the Oceanians crowded round in their thousands, passing the ahu and touching its stone uprights, wailing and tearing on their hair in a show of terrible grief. The Blackwater clan, who came to see this extraordinary interment of one of their number, got so caught up in the general hysteria that they too began sorrowing and lamenting for a man they had actually forgotten a few days after he had disappeared.

The other Celtic tribes gathered on the surrounding hills, absolutely astounded by the spectacle. That a scruffy cliff-climber whom no one had heard of before now should warrant such a ceremony of mourning was incredible. What had this man done to gain such adoration from the brown-skinned nations of Oceania?

'He was brought to us by a hero,' they were told, 'and he became such himself.'

But how? What did he do? What were his deeds?

'Manifold heroic deeds were his – battles against Hivans – the slaying of the Poukai bird – the slaying of a terrible taniwha – the tricking of Matuku the demi-god – voyages of renown – many, many deeds.'

An *egg-collector* did all this?

'This and much more. He was beloved. He is missed.'

Well, it just showed you, you could be born a nothing-man in a nothing-clan and still get to the top.

The heart was then carried with great ceremony, accom-panied by songs and dances specially composed for this occasion alone, over the landscape to the grave. Once the heart of Seumas had been interred, the chief mourners remained behind, exhausted by their grief, to sleep in a rugged cave overlooking the sea. There Kieto, Kikamana and Craig sang the final song to Seumas-the-Black, to the sound of flutes played by Boy-girl and Polahiki.

Solo	This is a day for mourning, he has gone out, never to return to his house again.
Chorus	A new house will be built for him on Rarotonga, a house of fine stone, small, a house for spirits, where he may live with Dorcha for ever.
Solo	Whence came this great man?
Chorus	He came from the Land-of-Mists, found by sailing just left of the setting sun. He fell from his cliff into the arms of Kupe, who bore him to our islands, skimming the seas on voyager barks, over Tangaroa's wide ocean.
Solo	Where has he gone?
Chorus	He has gone to the place of dazzling light.
Solo	Where is his netherland?
Chorus	No man or woman knows, for it is in the land of ghosts, but he is well and happy.

When the dawn rays struck the cave from the south-east, the mourners prepared to leave the last burial place of Seumas-the-Black's heart. Just as they began to drift away a mad horseman came galloping out of the mist. He had a wounded foot and his right hand was missing. In his left he wielded a broadsword. With a terrible scream of fury he bore down on Craig, who stood not far from his father's resting stone.

'It's Douglass Barelegs,' cried a voice from the crowd.

Others took up the cry of the Scotsman's name as he swept through an aisle of mourners and Celt spectators, bearing down on Craig. Divots flew from his mount's unshod hooves, as the pair drummed over the peaty ground, weaving occasionally to avoid standing rocks. The wicked edge of the warrior's honed sword flashed blindingly in the sunlight. On Douglass's face was a look of determination. He was going to destroy his father's enemy, come what may.

'Kill him!' came the voice of Cormac, out of the crowds. 'A whole sheep for the man who kills Barelegs.'

Archers from amongst both the Celts and Oceanians began firing arrows at the fierce horseman who charged down through the avenue of watchers. Arrows began to skim past the grim rider, but none hit him. Closer and closer he came to his target, who stood helpless and unarmed by the quartz stone.

'Die, Blackwater bastard!' came the cry from Douglass Barelegs' lips. Triumph was in his eyes as he swished the iron blade, making ready to decapitate his foe. Mist swirled around him like a white cloak billowing in the wind. 'Flee, ye craven son of a sow's runt – flee!'

But Craig stood his ground, having nowhere to run.

Punga, on seeing the certain death of his charge, Craig, struggled to remain in the light for just one last act. He was fading to darkness quickly, but he managed with one last great effort to rouse the spirit of the father, Seumas, from his grave.

'*Help your son!*' cried the God of Ugly Creatures. '*Leap up, destroy the enemy!*'

Once the call had been made, Punga became as fine mist on the moorland, as night darkness on a hill, as spume on the great ocean. Like the other gods, great and small, he was now only a part of this world in natural form. Supernature was lost.

Seumas, on hearing Punga's call, woke and thrust himself into the world of the living. Fierce and terrible now that his strength had been restored to him in death, he rose from his grave sword in hand, with a mighty roar. The old warrior was three times the size he had been as a mortal man and his fury three times that which it had been on earth. There he stood before Douglass Barelegs, his visage awesome to behold, his fearsome anger unquenchable.

Douglass Barelegs saw and recognized his immortal foe and knew great terror as his own death rushed into his face.

Something happened which was unaccountable to the watchers. Some said a dark shape rose up swiftly out of the turf in front of the gravestone to loom menacingly over horse and rider. Others maintained they saw nothing but a thickening of the mist around the craggy rock. Something strange did happen to be sure but whether it was supernatural or commonplace was a matter for argument amongst the watchers. It was certain that Craig saw nothing at all, because his eyes were on the rider and horse and not on the headstone beside him.

Whatever the cause, the result was that the horse checked abruptly and swerved. Douglass Barelegs went hurtling from the beast's back. Had both his legs been sound he might have been able to grip the flanks of his steed and remain on the horse's back. But Craig had robbed him of a foot.

His neck then somehow became entangled in the reins. When the weight of his flying body had stretched the leathers to their full length, he was curtly strangled. A sound came from his throat not unlike that made by a fulmar bird being throttled by the hands of a Pict. It was a harsh guttural noise which was stemmed abruptly when the body reached full stretch.

As the body was whipped back – jerked violently on the end of the reins – all heard the snapping of a neckbone.

The sound was loud in the morning's silence.

Then the frightened horse thundered off into the mist, weaving amongst the crags. The corpse of Douglass Barelegs was dragged, bouncing, over the uneven ground. Finally, all was still again. The silence was broken aptly by a Pict.

'Good bloody riddance,' cried the voice of Cormac-the-Venomous. 'May the bastard freeze his balls off on the bleak wastes of Ifurin.'

The show over, the mourners and spectators continued on their journeys homewards, reflecting on the supernatural laws of justice which reached out from beyond the grave. Douglass had not been well liked and his loss meant little to the Celts who had seen him die. It had simply been an exciting performance which had ended reasonably satisfactorily.

The Oceanians, Craig included, left the scene and went back to the pa, walking through the mist-covered heather, seeing the deer start from coverts, watching the eagles soar overhead, hearing the foxes go to ground. Some things they would miss about this land: the huge variety of wildlife, the differentness of the vegetation, the strange vastness of the rugged landscape. Other things they would be pleased to leave behind: the chill air, the coming winter, the greyness and the misty regions.

It had been a great adventure.

Exactly one week later the ocean-going canoes put out to sea, bearing the Oceanians, a man who used to be an elf, and three horses. One craft remained beached until the others were well out on the waves. This was the canoe of Kieto, who along with others – Craig, Boy-girl, Kikamana, Hupa, Urgan, Prince Daggan and his wife Siko – were the last to leave the foreign shore. When the canoe was ready to go, Kieto turned to Cormac, who had come with a band of warriors to watch the Oceanians leave.

'Come to make sure we go?' asked Kieto, through Craig.

'Something like that,' grunted Cormac. 'One can never be certain of a thing unless one sees it happen.'

Kieto nodded and went to rub noses with the Celt chieftain, who backed away in horror.

'None o' that,' cried Cormac. 'Would ye make a woman of me?'

Kieto smiled in understanding.

Boy-girl said privately to her companions, 'It would take more than a nose-rub to turn that heap of dung and hair into a divine creature like myself.'

Kikamana laughed for the first time in years.

The Oceanians then boarded their vessel. At the last minute, Kieto went into the deck-hut and brought out the greenstone club with which he had slain Guirk. He handed it to Prince Daggan.

'You and your wife take this to Cormac, as a parting gift for joining with us in battle against the Angles.'

Daggan looked surprised. 'Why us?'

'It is appropriate,' said Kieto. 'A royal family, a man and his wife, together. Bear it between you. Give it a sense of occasion. You know how to do these things. There is no one else on board of real noble lineage. I myself am not an ariki born, not like the two of you. I lack the breeding.'

'Quite so,' said Prince Daggan. 'My dear?'

'As Kieto says, it was a fishwife who gave him birth,' she replied, with a smile on her lips. 'Beautiful gifts should be given by those who appreciate such things.'

The pair then stepped into the shallows and were solemnly handed the greenstone club. They bore it with an air of ceremonious pomp towards the Celts. Cormac stepped forward as if he had been expecting this present and waited for them to reach him. He took the club and then turned to hold it aloft, while his men cheered. Then he turned to face the sea again and raised his fist in a salute to the departing canoe. Daggan and Siko, on turning around, gave out a yell of despair.

The tipairua was now well out on the waves, sailing around the headland.

'They've left us behind!' he shrieked. 'Siko, they're abandoning us.'

The unfortunate Oceanian couple left the grinning Celts and raced to the top of the cliff, hoping to catch the canoe on the other side of the headland, but when they reached the heights, they stood there breathless, watching in helpless frustrated agony as the tipairua headed out to sea.

'Why?' screamed Siko, into the wind, her voice sounding little different from the gulls which swooped over the waves. 'Why?'

'Treachery!' came back the answer. 'Murder!'

Daggan sank to the floor, staring in disbelief as the twin crab-claw sailed craft dipped and rose on its way to meet the rest of the fleet out on the ocean. Siko stood there, however, with the wind whipping through her tangled locks. There was a defiant look on her face. As always, she was the strong one.

'They found out, somehow,' she said. 'Cormac probably told them. And having found out we were traitors, they guessed we were responsible for Kapu's death. Well, we've been banished, for life it seems. Unless you want to make a canoe and do the journey on our own . . .'

She looked down at her pitiful partner, who was weeping tears into the Albainn turf.

'No, I don't think so. You're no Kupe, my husband. I guess we're stuck here for the rest of our natural lives.'

'Where will we live?' he wailed. 'How will we survive the winter? I hear it's cold enough to make water go hard.'

'We'll fashion a croft, like these damn natives,' she replied, 'and you'll dig peat to make our fires to keep us warm. You'll learn to hunt deer, fight marauders, and make wolfskin coats for the both of us. We'll survive.'

'I don't think I want to survive – not in a place like this – it'll be utter misery.'

She stared at this pathetic man of hers and then made a decision.

'Let's die then,' she said, shrugging. 'I'll go first.'

With that she stepped over the edge of the cliff and fell head-first onto the rugged rocks below. Her body lay there for a while, as the waves lashed it, and was then dragged out into the maw of the sea. There it floated, carried by the currents and tides, perhaps bound for the distant islands of Oceania.

Daggan was left on top of the cliff, afraid to live, yet afraid to die. He was still there, a hunched motionless figure, when the Celts walked back to their crofts from the beach. They stared but made no move to aid him. He was not one they would wish to assist. No one likes a traitor – even those on whose behalf the man has carried out his treachery.

Kieto's tipairua caught up with the rest of the fleet. They were island bound. Their hearts were light, but they travelled homeward with a sense of loss in their hearts. The news from the priests was that the old gods were no more – that they were going home accompanied by only one god – the Great One, Io, who dwelt above the Twelfth Level of the roof of voyaging.

Craig especially felt the death of the god Punga deeply. Would Io have time for them all: every individual whose problems and troubles sometimes seemed infinite? Each god had been responsible for one or at most a few aspects of life. Now Io was responsible for *everything*.

Punga himself had watched personally over all ugly creatures: had had time for a little girl, a middle child, who had been not been born as pretty as her brother and sister. Would Io be as assiduous in his attentions to a small child with great worries? Who would love the stonefish, now that Punga was gone? Who would take time to shape each individual cloud, now that Ao was no more? Who would save the drowning infant now that Pere was but a cold silent star in the roof of voyaging? Who was there to blame for a capsized canoe, now that Aremata-popoa had been destroyed and his divine presence scattered and lost?

Craig feared this new world was more impersonal than the old. Like others, he felt a great sadness fall upon him, like a cold dark cloak. The deities had gone, the magic had gone, the wonderful heroes would become mere distant figures in stories of the past. Soon they would not be part of real life at all, but merely names on the tongues of story-tellers. All the great voyages were over: the oceans had been sailed and there were no new journeys to make.

All the weight of earthly cares was now on the shoulders of humankind. The responsibility was bearable, but nevertheless it was hard to bear. A new seriousness had entered their lives, which had driven out the innocence of yesterday. It might be the *right* course for the world to take, but was it the *best*? The old gods with their petty squabbles had at least made things interesting.

While Craig mused on these important thoughts, the fleet passed some landfalls. In the straits between a clutch of islands they met a great whale. They followed the crea-ture, as Kupe had followed the giant octopus in the opposite direction, which was heading towards their beloved Oceania. Thus they travelled in the wake of this huge mammal, as on a track across the open ocean.

On the way they passed a half-dozen longships manned by sea-raiders. Both sides watched each other warily. The Hawaiians, the best of the naval forces, were fortunately on the far side of the Oceanian flotilla, or they might have been tempted to have a go at these arrogant-looking long-ships. No doubt the Tahitians, who also liked a sea-battle, would have joined them. As it was, the two fleets passed each other without incident.

Craig thought he saw something in the hard light-blue eyes of the sea-raiders, as they almost brushed vessels: some hint of a future engagement.

But that was pure speculation on his part.

At the front of each canoe, Tiki sat impassive, ready to guide his people home. His place in this changed world was not dependent on the presence of the old gods. He had not been a part of their terrible struggle. After all, he

was not a god himself but the First Man, the divine ancestor of all Oceanians: as revered as the gods had been, but
not of their number.

Tiki's birth as a mortal would ensure his survival.

Glossary

Adaro: Malevolent sea-spirit in the shape of a fish-man.

Ahu: Sacrificial platform, sometimes of stone or planks, sometimes of raised bark cloth.

Airo fai: Dagger made of a stingray's back-bone.

Akiaki: Fairy tern.

Aotearoa: Land of the Long White Cloud, New Zealand.

Ariki: High-born noble.

Arioi: Magnificent dance and song company formed in ancient Tahiti which cruised between the islands and dispensed entertainment to the masses.

Atoro: Fifth rank Arioi, one small stripe on left side.

Avae Parai: Painted Leg, top rank of Arioi, equal to a king.

Balepa: Corpse still wrapped in its burial mat which flies above villages at night.

Ei: Halo of flowers.

Fanakenga star: Zenith star.

Fangu: Magic spell for various general uses.

Gata waka club: Fijian war club made from a thick curved branch with a stubby forked end.

Haka: Maori war dance.

Harotea: Third rank Arioi, both sides of the body marked with stain from armpits downwards.

Hawaiki: The mythical island birthplace of the Polynesian peoples, called the Sacred Isle.

Hivan Islands: Marquesas group.

Hoki: Group of wandering musicians, poets and dancers based in the Marquesas.

Hotu Matua: Legendary Polynesian discoverer of Easter Island and its people's first king.

Hua: Fourth rank Arioi, two or three figures tattooed on shoulders.

Hura: Erotic Tahitian dance.

Icharacha: Huge supernatural beast which roams an Otherworld of the Celts, a crustacean with a dozen horns and many legs, each leg armed with several pincers.

Ifurin: One of the Celtic Otherworlds.

I Ula: Light Fijian throwing club.

I Wau: Heavy Fijian warclub.

Kabu: Soul with a visible shape, though not necessarily human form.

Kahuna: Priest, wise person, versed in the arts of black magic. (Hawaiian word, but used here to distinguish between a 'high priest or priestess' and a tohunga, a specialist in something, e.g. funeral rites, tattooing.)

Kapuku: Art of raising the dead.

Karakia: Magic chant to use against aggressors, as protection or as a weapon. It will also drive out the demons which cause illness.

Kava: Intoxicating drink made by chewing the root of a *Piper methysticum* shrub and mixing the subsequent paste with water.

Kaveinga: Paths of stars which follow each other up from one spot on the horizon. Polynesian sailors used these natural paths as a navigational aid.

Kopu: Morning Star.

Kopuwai: Dog-headed man of savage disposition.

Kotiate club: Hand club shaped like a stunted paddle with a bite out of one side.

Kotuku: Very rare white heron.

Kukui: Candlenut tree.

Kurangai-tuku: New Zealand ogress who used her lips like a spear, shooting them out to impale the prey.

Lei-o-mano: Dagger made of hardwood rimmed with shark's teeth.

Lipsipsip: Dwarves who live in old trees and ancient rocks.

Lotophagoi: Islands of Eternal Souls, where there is no day or night, the sun always shines, and no one is unhappy.

Luch: Gaelic for 'mouse'.

Mana: Magical or supernatural powers, the grace and favour of the divinities, conferred by them. A chief has great mana naturally, but another man must build his mana (carried in the head) by doing great deeds, by becoming a famous warrior or priest.

Manu's Body: Sirius.

Marae: Courtyard in front of a temple or king's house, a sacred place where sacrifical victims are prepared.

Mareikura: Heavenly angels, servants of Io.

Maro: Waist belt.

Maru-ura: The sacred red girdle of kingship on Raiatea, made of scarlet feathers sewn into tapa cloth to form a history of the royal line.

Matatoa: 'Birdman', an Easter Island death cult which evolved during the period of the island's clan wars.

Ngaro: The food of the dead.

Niwareka: Daughter of Uetonga, King of the fair-haired fairies of Rarohenga, a land below the earth.

Nokonoko, or aito: Ironwood tree, used for making weapons.

Omemara: Sixth rank Arioi, a small circle on each ankle.

Otiore: Second rank (one from the top) member of the Arioi, tattooed from fingers to shoulders.

Pa: Fortified Maori village.

Pahi: Large, double-hulled ocean-going canoe with a flat deck between the hulls, able to carry seventy or more passengers and ten crew for a month-long voyage without touching land.

Pahi Tamai: Double-hulled paddled war canoes.

Pakoko: Mourning dress worn at the funeral of a great person.

Patu club: Hand club shaped like a stunted paddle.

Pia: Arrowroot, which when scraped is white like snow.

Ponaturi: Sea-fairies, vicious and aggressive, often staging pitched battles with heroes of Oceania.

Poo: Seventh rank Arioi, 'pleasure-making class', known as *flappers*.

Puata: Living monster conceived out of wood and clay, a boar-like creature but much larger than a real boar. A puata talks, and walks on its hind legs, but is stupid.

Puhi: High-born virgin, a maiden princess.

Putuperereko: Evil spirit with huge testicles.

Rapanui: Easter Island.

Sau: Spiritual puissance of a man or woman.

Sobesila: Fijian club.

Sokilaki: Fijian multi-barbed fighting spear.

Tai-moana: Long drum carried on board a double-hulled ocean-going canoe – 'Threnody of the Seas'.

Taniwha: Monster of some kind, perhaps a giant lizard or a fish, or a creature which assumes the shape of someone's worst fears.

Tapa: Bark-cloth made from the inner bark of the paper mulberry tree.

Tapu: Taboo, sacred or consecrated, forbidden – it applies not only to the person or thing prohibited, but also to the prohibition and any person breaking the prohibition.

Tapu-tapu atia: Most Sacred, Most Feared.

Tapua: Goblin-like creature with a white skin.

Targolo: Evil spirit which seduces people of both sexes and cuts up their genitals to kill them.

Te lapa: Underwater streaks of light from active volcanoes beneath the surface of the sea.

Te Reinga: Land of the Dead.

Tekoteko: Carving above the gate of a Maori pa, either of human, animal or demon. A tekoteko had magical properties.

Ti: Cabbage-tree.

Ti'i: Wooden images used by magicians to assist them in their spells.

Tipairu: Race of fairies who love dancing and who descend on moonlit nights to take part in celebrations, always disappearing back into the forest at dawn.

Tipairua: Double-hulled ocean-going canoe similar to the pahi but closely resembling a war canoe.

Tipua: Goblins.

Tohua: Marquesan temple.

Tohunga: Priest who specializes in tapu, funeral rites and communing with the spirits of air, sea and earth.

Tu'i Tonga: Title of Ruler of Tonga.

Turehu: Fairies from the land of Rarohenga, an Underworld.

Tutua: Low-born people, peasants.

Uetonga: King of the Turehu fairies and grandson of Ruau-Moko, God of Earthquakes.

Umu: Earth oven lined with stones to retain the heat.

Váa: Small paddled outriggerless canoe.

Váa motu: Outrigger sailing canoe.

Vis: Blood-drinking succubus.

Wahaika club: Hand club shaped like a violin.